developer
marketing
& relations

THE ESSENTIAL GUIDE

First Edition, September 2018

Third Edition, September 2020

ISBN 9798692191069

Published by

SlashData Ltd

19-21 Hatton Gardens

London, EC1N 8BA

United Kingdom

www.slashdata.co

About SlashData

SlashData is the analyst of the developer ecosystem. We help top-100 tech companies understand developer audiences and measure the RoI of their developer strategies.

With a track record of more than 10 years of data-backed developer research, we know where developers come from and where they are going. We have consistent historical data on why they get involved in development, what they are learning, in which industries and on what projects they are working, which technologies they use and how happy they are with them, and what they expect from vendors and developer communities. We track how the developer population grows, locally and globally, and how its profile changes over time.

More than 30,000 developers from more than 150 countries share their experiences with us each year through our bi-annual Developer Economics surveys. Our sample is diverse, representative and exhaustive of the developer communities out there. We translate our surveys in 9+ languages each time, and reach out to developer communities of all shapes and sizes, with the help of our network of 70+ leading community and media partners across the globe. We reach out to developers afresh in every survey, 80% of responses coming from new participants each time. Yet, our findings on technology adoption and trends are consistent, survey after survey. For further details on our methodology, please visit
https://www.slashdata.co/methodology.

Our aim is to empower the DevRel community by providing the data they need to make the right decisions and step up their DevRel game, for best developer experience. Besides "Developer Marketing and Relations: The essential guide", we produce the "Under the Hood of Developer Marketing" podcast where experts in the field share not just their successes, but also their biggest challenges with developer marketing. The Future Developer Summit is our bi-annual event for developer marketing and relations leaders. Moreover, we run the Developer Program Leaders' survey twice per year and publish the results.

You can visit devrelx.com and discover all our DevRel initiatives, as well as dig into our rich collection of developer research data.

CONTENTS

WHY HAVE WE WRITTEN THIS BOOK?

September 2020

Welcome to the third edition of "Developer Marketing and Relations: The Essential Guide". The history of this book goes back to October 2017, during the Future Developer Summit. There, Andreas Constantinou and Nicolas Sauvage fully recognized the fragmented nature of developer relations or DevRel – from the types of companies, the products they represented, and the knowledge of the practitioners. It was there we witnessed that the best practices were often locked behind the doors of the companies that mastered them. We knew we wanted to work with these leaders and develop an essential guide to share this knowledge with a broader audience of developer relations, evangelists and advocates, developer marketing practitioners and beyond.

As we have watched the practice of DevRel grow and evolve over the last three years, there is a continued need for education of what DevRel is, along with the strategy and tactics needed to run a successful program. The good news is, many of the leading practitioners from the best companies agreed to share their knowledge, stories, learnings, and best practices in this guide! We think you'll find the information insightful, whether you are a seasoned professional in developer relations or you are just getting started.

A question we often get asked at SlashData is: "Can you help us understand how Mozilla, Google, or Microsoft practice developer marketing?" (replace names with your favorite tech brands). Well that's exactly what this book aims to accomplish.

This third edition includes the original chapters from the first edition, 9 new chapters and one updated. This guide is arranged in an order that takes you from strategic issues to more tactical issues. You can read from start to finish, or jump into a particular chapter that focuses on what you need to know right now. At a strategic level, you may want to read "Using Developer Personas to Stay Customer-Obsessed" from Cliff Simpkins of Microsoft, or if you are building out a program you might try "Structuring Developer Relations", by Dirk Primbs of Google. If you are just starting out, be sure to read, "Starting from Scratch: How to Build a Developer Marketing Program", by Luke Kilpatrick of Nutanix. If you need to get many stakeholders together in a large organization, the "The Developer Relations Council: Leading and Aligning Developer Marketing within Large Companies" by Arabella David of Salesforce - a new chapter for the third edition- is a must. Then, learn how to understand numbers and KPIs in our new chapter "Measuring the success of a developer communications strategy" by our very own Rich Muir of SlashData.

We have a few chapters on events which have become a staple in the industry, such as "Growing Up By Scaling Down: How A Small Developer Event Can Make Big Impacts On Your Ecosystem", co-authored by Neil Mansilla of Atlassian, and "Behind the Scenes Of Great Developer Events", by Katherine Miller of Google. We must note that this edition is being launched during the COVID-19 pandemic, which has made the planners behind many programs re-evaluate their tactics, so you may want to read "How To Connect With Developers When You Can't Meet Them", by Pablo Fraile and Rex St. John of Arm.

As mentioned, developer programs exist in many types, as different companies are marketing different types of products to developers. Ana Schafer and Christine Jorgensen of Qualcomm describe their experiences with communities around hardware in "Hardware Is the New Software - Building A Developer Community Around A Chip Instead Of An SDK". APIs are well known as a key product in DevRel so we are pleased to bring you a new chapter by Mehdi Medjaoui, founder of GDPR.DEV and APIdays conferences, on "Developer Relations and APIs".

We can't list all of the great chapters here, but we would be remiss if we didn't point out the chapters on community, the heart and soul of any leading developer relations program. Be sure to read "The Power Of Community" by Jacob Lehrbaum of Salesforce, and the new chapter "Building an Inclusive Developer Community" by Leandro Margulis, based on his award-winning days at TomTom.

We always love to hear your comments – perhaps you read something that made a difference for your program, or you have your own story to tell. Please reach out to us at *sdata.me/dev-marketing-book* and tell us about it

All profits from this book's sales will be donated to coding organisations that encourage and assist the developers of tomorrow. Your support is much appreciated in helping out these worthy causes – more details can be found at sdata.me/dev-marketing-guide.

Andreas Constantinou, Founder & CEO, SlashData
Nicolas Sauvage, President & Managing Director, TDK Ventures
Caroline Lewko and Dana Fujikawa, Editors of the third edition, WIP

FOREWORD

Adam FitzGerald: Head of Worldwide Developer Marketing - Amazon Web Services

In 2011, Marc Andreessen published an article in the Wall Street Journal that stated, *"...software is eating the world."* (source: *sdata.me/KwFKhx*).

In that article he identified that more and more major businesses are being run on software and are offering online services to their customers and partners. I strongly believe that the trends he described in 2011 are even more evident today. You can see it in the most successful companies on the global stock exchanges, in the high demand for software developers in the job market, and in the way digital citizens are demanding more from the businesses and government organizations with whom they interact. Today, every company needs to have a software strategy or risk being outmaneuvered by more agile and adaptive competitors that deliver what the customer wants more quickly, and in the format that is easiest for them to use.

When it comes to software, the connoisseurs of technology are the developers that build and use it every day. They are the masters of the compiler, the command line, the frameworks, the test suites, the deployment pipelines and the production systems. As businesses have pushed for more nimble technical solutions, developers have created agile development practices that improve code quality, reduce project timelines, and iteratively produce new features. DevOps techniques and cloud based infrastructure have enabled those solutions to be deployed more quickly, more cheaply and at a scale that can respond to global demand. The developers and site reliability engineers are the ones on call 24/7, alerted to every system anomaly or traffic spike. When something does go wrong, they are the people called upon to rollback updates, squash bugs, and restore order.

With these critical responsibilities, developers are calling the shots when it comes to technical decision making.

C-level executives can no longer make decisions about technology use at their company as a favor to an old college buddy or because of a nice round of golf with a sales person.

Developers are selecting tools, platforms and infrastructure to get the best results for the systems they are building.

Building a tool, an API or a platform that developers love can delight your customers, disrupt your competitors and transform your business. So, if you are a business that wants to move quickly and wants to use software as a way to compete in your market, you have to understand and engage with developers.

How do you reach out to developers and convince them to use your product? This may sound like a classic marketing problem, but if you apply traditional consumer marketing techniques to this audience you will be destined to fail because developers abhor marketing. Developers are analytical, careful, loyal, data-driven and extremely busy. They have little patience for marketing hype, sales pitches or buzzword-filled promises of future capabilities. They have real, concrete problems to solve, right there in front of them, and they want help from people and sources that they trust.

Fortunately, the experts who have written this book have spent decades of their careers thinking about how to engage with these developers. Their combined wisdom provides a map for you and your company to create the kinds of things that developers care about. Chapters in this book will describe how you can grow your developer community and how running a developer program for experts in the field will encourage them to advocate for you. You will learn about the dynamics within a developer community and also learn what you can control and what you cannot. This book also provides information about where you can find developers, both online and in real life, and how to hold a real conversation with them from organizing events to managing your online community. And, if you are not yet sure who you are conversing with, there is even a chapter on the use of developer personas. This book provides some extraordinary insights from those who have worked in the developer marketing field as it comes of age.

For me, developers are the fulcrum for business innovation. Over the coming decades, some companies will embrace developers, earn their trust and help them solve their technical problems. Those companies will be the most successful businesses of the 21st century.

Introduction | Measuring the success of a developer communications strategy

Richard Muir: Data Journalist - SlashData

In the previous edition of this book, we introduced the idea of the developer as a decision-maker. The developer as an influencer. The developer as a powerful agent within an influential team, steering important technological decisions and being personally invested in the outcome.

With this in mind, successful communication is crucial, especially communicating with them in their language and through the channels they use. With developers being such a diverse (and sometimes challenging group with which to engage), the stakes have never been higher for getting your communications right. Here we'll help you to decide what to measure, and how to define the success of your team and your business.

How do you measure success and why does it matter?

Tl;dr: Measuring success lets you:

- Understand what works, so you can do more of it
- Communicate successes and failures

1

- Justify your decisions
- Allocate resources effectively
- Track your progress
- Time travel (no, seriously)

Before we get into the how, let's dip our toes into the why. Why does measuring success matter? Here at SlashData, we believe that data beats opinions. Every time. The short answer, therefore, is that you should measure success because it's the only way of understanding the truth of a situation. Measuring the success of your developer relations program is the only way to know if what you are doing is working. Not only that, measuring the results helps you to understand what works well, so you can do more of it, and what works not so well, so you can do less of it.

Another way of looking at this is that measuring the impact of your efforts is the best way to allocate resources efficiently, and for maximum effectiveness. For example, we see time after time that developers want technology companies to spend more time and effort answering questions on forums, and less on organizing conferences. Getting answers in public forums is the fourth most important feature for developers, yet it receives a satisfaction score ten points lower than conferences, the 18th most important feature. We know this because we ask developers which developer program features are most important to them, and how satisfied they are with the support that technology companies provide. At this macro level, measuring success (satisfaction, in this case) shines a light on how resources are allocated ineffectively across the industry. Now imagine taking this data-driven approach and applying it to your internal processes. What might you find? What decisions might you take? How would you justify them?

When you use data to make these decisions, the justification becomes easy. It is right there in front of you. Why should you divert resources away from organizing conferences, and towards answering developers' questions? Easy, because that is what developers want and they're currently not very happy with what they are getting. Measuring success lets you justify your decision. Seen another way, if you cannot back up your decision with data, are you sure it is the right move?

Sometimes, even the most data-driven decisions don't turn out how you expected - the ground shifts under your feet or a competitor makes an unexpected move, or maybe a global pandemic shakes things up a little. That is OK, these things happen. By using data to drive your decisions, and to measure the outcome, you can track your progress. You can communicate your successes and failures. Most importantly, you can *quantify* the impact of any changes. Not only changes that you effect, but also changes imposed upon you. Because here's the thing: data begets more data. The next time you sense trouble brewing on the horizon, you can look back in time through your data and see what happened the last time the ground moved under you. You can anticipate the scale of any impact, and take steps accordingly, influencing the outcome. Trust us, your boss will thank you.

In short, measuring success lets you decide what, exactly, you should be doing, and how you should be doing it. It also lets you make informed decisions and facilitates meaningful communication with your team and with stakeholders.

Deciding what to measure

Hopefully, I have covered the why, and hopefully, you are convinced enough to carry on reading to find out the how. You will have to wait a little longer for that. Because before knowing how to measure success, you need to know what you are going to measure. Before you even start to think about what to measure, you need to understand what you want to change.

That is what developer relations and marketing is all about. It is about creating and effecting the change that works best for you and your developer community. The world is going to change anyway, so why not get a hand on the steering wheel?

In order to know what changes you want to make, you need to understand what your business goals are. Fundamentally, any commercial developer relations program lives and dies by its ability to increase usage. To increase usage by developers already engaged with the platform, or to attract new developers to the platform. We need to be more specific; of *course* the goal is to increase usage – that is the direct (or often indirect) path to putting money in the bank. But what is it that you specifically want to achieve? Do you want to increase the frequency of usage for a specific product or API? Do you want to inform developers about an imminent major version and a potential breaking change? Preventing a decrease in usage is often easier than driving an increase, after all. Or do you simply want your developers to know that you're thinking of them?

Now, let's zoom right in on the developer. What do you want them to do? What behavior do you want them to start? To stop? To change? Fundamentally, what is the purpose of your developer relations program? Nobody cares for meaningless marketing, least of all busy software developers. So, let's get the message clear, and consistent, and make sure it's relevant.

In order to know the message, you must first understand your audience. Are you marketing to existing customers, or are you running an acquisition campaign? If you are marketing to developers that already use your product, it is likely that you already have loads of information about them. You will have usage patterns, an email address, hopefully, some geodemographics, and maybe even a company name. All of this data helps to build your picture of what that developer does, what you want them to do, how you talk to them, and how successful you can expect to be.

But what about an acquisition campaign? Maybe you are using Facebook audiences or advertising on more specialist platforms. Well, first of all, you want to know how many people you can reasonably expect to reach. This data helps you answer that all-important question, even before you begin. Is it worth it?

Is it worth it? Using data to inform and appraise strategy

With our developer population calculator (sdata.me/Calculator), you can figure out just how many developers fit your target audience and where you can find them. Looking for inexperienced professional developers? Then look no further. Of the 917K professional developers with less than a year's experience, East Asia has 276K of them.

East Asia has the largest population of inexperienced professionals

Q4 2019 (n=775)

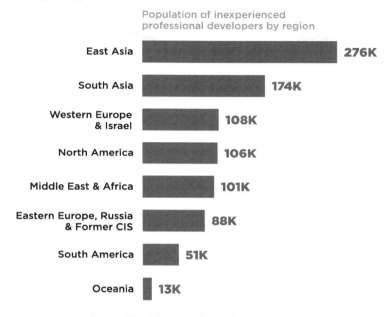

Population of inexperienced professional developers by region

East Asia	276K
South Asia	174K
Western Europe & Israel	108K
North America	106K
Middle East & Africa	101K
Eastern Europe, Russia & Former CIS	88K
South America	51K
Oceania	13K

Source: *Global Developer Population Calculator*
www.developerpopulation.com | © SlashData 2020

Developing a regional strategy is one surefire way of getting better at communicating with developers on their terms. We find that not only do the socioeconomic factors in different regions affect developers' immediate views and desires, but also that these differences echo at a macro level, shaping the way technologies, and even vendors, are adopted in different regions. For example, developers in Asian regions are consistently less-satisfied with having access to resources in their native language; unsurprisingly, given the anglocentric nature of technological change to date. This also means that developers in these regions are quicker to take up emerging technologies since they are less burdened by convention and existing structures. In this way, understanding your developer audience through a regional lens will not only help shape your short term tactical approach, say translating resources aimed at inexperienced professionals into popular languages in East Asia, but would also contribute to your longer-term strategy by adding another perspective to your expectations of your product's adoption rate.

One other important differentiating factor for developers is what language they use. Understanding language usage patterns amongst your developer audience will also help you to optimize your short-term decision making, with an eye on the longer-term strategy. Over half of our group of 910K inexperienced professional developers are using JavaScript with a third using Java or Python. This is interesting enough, but when compared with experienced professionals, of which there are 13.6 million, we see that developers collect languages as their career progresses. Two-thirds of these more experienced professionals are using JavaScript and around 40% are using Java or Python. It is not surprising that developers are learning constantly, but armed with the information that JavaScript, Python and Java are used widely amongst early-career *and* experienced developers (for now, at least!), you can safely invest in supporting these language communities, knowing that your effort is unlikely to be wasted.

Over half of inexperienced professionals use JavaScript

Q4 2019 (n=509)

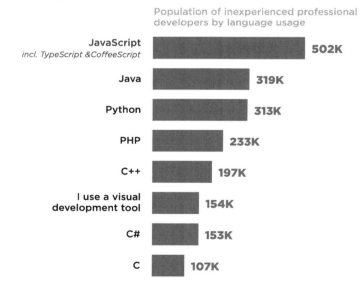

Population of inexperienced professional developers by language usage

JavaScript *incl. TypeScript &CoffeeScript*	**502K**
Java	**319K**
Python	**313K**
PHP	**233K**
C++	**197K**
I use a visual development tool	**154K**
C#	**153K**
C	**107K**

Source: *Global Developer Population Calculator www.developerpopulation.com | © SlashData 2020*

JavaScript, Python & Java are still the most popular languages for experienced professionals

Q4 2019 (n=8,348)

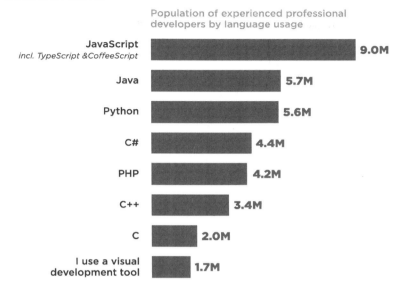

Population of experienced professional developers by language usage

JavaScript *incl. TypeScript &CoffeeScript*	9.0M
Java	5.7M
Python	5.6M
C#	4.4M
PHP	4.2M
C++	3.4M
C	2.0M
I use a visual development tool	1.7M

Source: *Global Developer Population Calculator*
www.developerpopulation.com | © SlashData 2020

If you have created a regional strategy and are segmenting developers by language, you're doing much better than most. These two data points are easy to collect, easy to interpret, and very powerful indeed. But there are as many ways of segmenting your developer community as there are developers, and you can use many different data points to create your developer personas (though please don't segment by technology! - https://sdata.me/segment). Creating developer personas is another common, and powerful, way of gaining a deeper understanding of developers' motivations and needs, and, just as importantly, of sizing your potential audience.

Knowing how many developers there are helps you to understand your penetration into a particular market. Will this developer marketing campaign be looking to get those difficult, marginal gains in a territory where you have already captured a lot of the market, or are you entering a market with lots of headroom to grow? Knowing the size of your target audience helps you to calibrate your expectations for your developer marketing efforts. This information is especially powerful when you combine it with first-hand experience of the success of your efforts, here we're referring to click-through rates, signups, downloads and page views, and moves us nicely onto the next stage of this approach; actually choosing which KPIs to track and who will be interested in them.

Knowing your audience

Developer marketing is a cross-disciplinary subject with many stakeholders. On one side, you have the marketeers, those responsible for interpreting the developer personas or segments (you do segment your audience, right?), and creating the messaging and branding that will draw these developers in. On another side, you have the developer advocate. These are the people who represent the developers' point of view, because they often are one. They understand how developers want to be talked to and they have an ear to the ground for direct, qualitative feedback from developers. Next, you have product managers. At the core of any developer relations program is a product, be it an API, a managed service, an IDE, or a framework. One of the most certain ways of ensuring that developers use your product is to listen to them and act on that feedback. Finally, you have the top-level managers and executives who take a more holistic approach, looking at success from several perspectives.

Each of these groups is going to want a slightly different view of what developers do and think. Your marketeers want to know how well developers engage with the communications, messaging and campaigns. Your developer advocates might be trying to understand the community dynamics or particular pain points that developers face. Your product managers want to know which features are being used and what developers are requesting next. In the next section, we'll talk about what KPIs we use at SlashData to give a nuanced but powerful view of the success of a developer relations program that can be applied to all these use cases and more.

Don't forget the developers, either. Although they might not see the results, they're still important stakeholders in the success of your developer relations efforts, maybe the most important. Whichever metrics you choose will impact them more than any other group. So, choose KPIs that will benefit the developer - KPIs that value them like the asset they are.

Choosing a set of KPIs

OK, so you've got an idea of the art of the possible. Now it's time to look at what you can actually do with this knowledge. Here's where you decide which KPIs you should use to track success, and this happens to be our particular area of expertise. At SlashData, we measure success in developer relations in all kinds of different ways. We measure developer satisfaction with resources or with products; we measure engagement, adoption and rejection. We understand what developers think is lacking, and what they love. Most importantly, we back up our decisions with hard science and contextualize them with experience and expertise.

We use four metrics to give a 360-degree view of the performance of a developer relations program. We selected these metrics because they cover many different aspects of measuring the success of developers relations, and do so with very little overlap. In short, they are efficient and effective:

1. Adoption rate - How many developers use a product or vendor
2. Engagement rate - How often developers use a vendor's resources
3. Satisfaction score - What developers think about a product or its features
4. Reasons for adoption or rejection - Why developers chose (or rejected) a product

These metrics work together to give a nuanced view of success that is not only relevant for people with different interests, such as marketeers or product managers, but is also flexible enough to measure the impact of many different changes to a developer relations program. Here is an example from our Developer Program Benchmarking report that shows how the top developer programs in the world compare against each other for adoption, engagement and satisfaction:

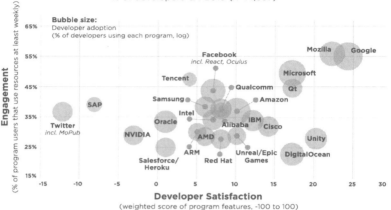

The developer program benchmark:
Google, Mozilla & Microsoft lead the pack

% of developers Q4 2019 (n=14,597)

Source: *Developer Economics | State of the Developer Nation Q4 2019 | © SlashData 2020*

You can clearly see how, when combined, these three metrics allow for very fine differentiation between otherwise similar developer programs. Take IBM and Intel, for example. When comparing these two vendors by engagement or adoption, they appear to be almost identical, however, the difference in satisfaction between them allows us to tease out this important difference. When you can understand in fine detail the differences between two developer programs (or products, or regions etc.), then you can take targeted and meaningful action to change the situation to your benefit. These KPIs, therefore, allow for developer relations practitioners with different interests to take meaningful and effective actions at a variety of levels.

Are you an executive interested in growing the developer community in South Asia?

Consider looking at the changing adoption rates there. The wide-angle view will give you an insight into the cumulative impact of the different pillars of your developer relations strategy and efforts, while a deeper dive into the data will help you to hone this strategy and focus on what works for different segments. Because our metrics are calculated from the opinions of individual developers, we can look at the data from different angles and understand who is using a product, what they think of it, and how you can reach these developers.

Are you a product manager looking to optimize your feature development budget?

Then you will be especially interested in why developers reject or adopt a product. By looking at the adoption and rejection reasons developers give for your product *and* your competitors, you will be better able to carve out your niche in the product space. You will understand why developers choose your product and be able to take steps to protect this advantage, whilst at the same time capitalizing on your competitors' weaknesses.

Are you a marketer looking to understand the success of a recent email campaign?

Developers' engagement behavior will be especially interesting for you. Understanding which of your products have the most engaged developer community will shine a light on what you can hope to achieve, and tracking changing engagement rates will help you to understand what works best for the different segments of your community.

Are you a developer advocate who wants to target improvements to a product's documentation?

Documentation satisfaction scores will help you to understand where the gaps are and point towards those vendors leading the way. You will be able to zoom in on users of a particular product or language, or developers in a particular region, and make micro-improvements to squeeze out those last marginal gains.

Our wealth of experience in measuring the success of developer relations has led us to create this framework for selecting metrics that will help you to effect positive change. The KPIs we use were born from this framework. When you are choosing a suite of KPIs to measure the success of your developer relations program – and we do recommend selecting a few – here are some things to keep in mind:

1. **Be realistic** - this is where the groundwork of understanding the market, and your performance within it, helps you to select SMART objectives, with the emphasis here on 'Achievable' - what you can actually influence.
2. **Be considerate** - and by that I mean, choose KPIs that are easy to understand. Be considerate to your

colleagues by not hiding KPIs behind definitions and acronyms.

3. **Know your data** - you want to choose KPIs that are sensitive to change, but not so sensitive that they fluctuate wildly. Choose KPIs that you can calculate with the data you have and remember that you can always get someone else to help ;-)

4. **Tell a story** – keep in mind, you are trying to change behavior. You are trying to change not only developers' behavior, but also your colleagues' behavior. Telling a story is the most compelling way to bring someone round to your way of thinking. Choose KPIs which combine to tell a story and watch your team come together to make it come true.

5. **Think about the ramifications** - we already know we are trying to change behavior, but what about any unexpected changes? Do the KPIs you have selected incentivize the right behavior amongst your team, or have you unwittingly created perverse incentives for a negative behavior change?

Let's wrap things up

Here you have it; a window into the SlashData way of selecting KPIs to measure the success of a developer relations program. You have seen why we think that data-driven measurement is so absolutely vital (and I hope you agree!). You have read a few ideas about how to decide what to measure, and how to think about your audience. Finally, you have been introduced to the KPIs that we use to measure the best performing developer programs in the world and you've also seen a framework that will help you to select your own. This is just the tip of the iceberg; you will discover more ways to boost your developer relations program in this book and you can always refer to devrelx.com for more free resources, including Under the Hood of Developer Marketing podcast, webinars, free graphs and more.

Chapter 1 | Using Developer Personas To Stay Customer-Obsessed

Cliff Simpkins: Director, Azure Developer Marketing - Microsoft Corporation

Introduction

At Microsoft, our mission is to empower every person and every organization on the planet to achieve more. Since our founding moment, our customers have always been at the core of the platforms we build, making them more productive - from Altair BASIC to Windows, from Visual Studio to Office, from Minecraft to Azure.

But as your customer base scales, particularly when you build a platform, it becomes easy to lose or splinter your team's focus. As your scale grows, your engineers may start to build for who they know (themselves, their team, or the last three customers they spoke to last month); your product managers start to lean on analysts to tell them what to build; and your marketers can start to test their messaging with the developer team building the campaign website (yes, that happens!).

To keep your team aligned, you need to define what you want to achieve, and what success looks like. Most engineering teams today use product specs to keep folks aligned on the features and capabilities that they are building, but I posit that many companies today fail to clearly define why the product is being built in the first place,

My favorite tool for keeping everyone on the same page is the persona. About a decade ago, I started using user personas built by our usability labs team in engineering, but I've increasingly spent the last six years in product management building several evolutions of developer personas for use across Windows, covering mobile app developers to PC and console game studio developers, and helping mentor other teams on how to build developer personas as well.

In this chapter, I'll introduce personas within the context of a developer-centric company (as opposed to something P&G would take to market), and discuss how personas can make a difference in the product development and developer marketing lifecycle, highlighting a number of learnings I've had along the way.

As a little about me, I've been at Microsoft for over 14 years, in roles spanning developer evangelism, .NET product planning, product management for Windows Phone and Windows, and the last three years doing developer audience marketing. As I mentioned above, personas have increasingly been a core ingredient in my work over the last ten, first appearing when I was working on Windows Communication Foundation (WCF), and increasingly becoming more and more core to my work, and my team's work, with each passing year. In my final years at Windows, our three-question persona gearbox was core to everything we did - our research, our event registrations, and our developer program. We used them to build our content, plan our marketing campaigns, and how we did (by target persona). Hopefully by the end of this chapter, you should walk away with an understanding of what a good persona looks like, and a spark of interest in helping your team become more customer-obsessed.

Why developer personas matter

As products are built and brought to market, they should also carry a means of measuring success, whether it's an API, a user interface, a website, or a paid advertising campaign. But often, this measure of success isn't shared, and a team is neither clear nor consistent on what success looks like, leaving each team member with their own perspective on who will use their offering, and how they should use it. And, as a result, the product experience feels fragmented and mis-aligned. To bring everyone into alignment, the team needs a shared definition of where they are going and how they know when they have been successful.

For me, the need for this shared definition - a need for organizational alignment - happened around 2011 as my team discussed the keynote we were building for a major developer conference. In the room were executives from the different groups involved in the event - engineering, marketing, evangelism, and PR. As we discussed the keynote structure and flow, opinions and interests both meshed and clashed (as they often do). Each person spoke from a position of authority about audience needs, with the same refrain – "…but developers want…". To support their point, each person flagged different, and sometimes conflicting, core audience needs, and the key aspects that they felt should be highlighted in flow and demos of the talk (e.g. business value, tooling advances, cool tech advances, productivity, etc.).

After the discussion, my PR guy and I talked about how fragmented our target 'developer' was for the event, and we started thinking about how we needed a common vision to anchor our narrative. We decided that the group needed some sort of shorthand that would allow us to break up the generic 'developer' into smaller, more defined communities that had defined pain points and aspirations. This, we reasoned, would allow us to discuss the keynote's scope (i.e., it's not for 'Peter', but instead for 'Paul' and 'Mary') and elevate the narrative beyond a feature-palooza.

In the year that followed, my team went on a journey to build out five developer personas, with a business focus on three of them: 'Ravi', 'Jerry', and 'Tyler'. Within two years, our developer personas became core team assets and a variable in our business planning - we structured our offers and programs based on the business and life goals of each persona, we included them in our marketing agency briefs, and we even based our competitive analysis on the personas. For example, we asked "how does an experienced independent developer ('Jerry') approach DevOps?" and compared the answer with a different persona, such as a line developer in a larger company ('Lana').

The magic of personas is that they provide a composite view of a larger audience, and they allow you to make that audience a part of your product's narrative. And while lots of industries use personas in their marketing, I personally believe they are crucial in developer marketing for one simple reason - developer personas provide an easy way for non-developers to understand this audience. Consumer and B2B marketing are both established disciplines, with defined approaches, best practices, and benchmarks. But developers behave differently: they evaluate and trial products differently, they value and consume content differently, and they prefer a different sales model.

Once we started using personas in our efforts, we found PR and developer marketing to be much easier and more effective.

What is a developer persona?

Wikipedia describes a persona as "a fictional character created to represent a user type that might use a site, brand, or product in a similar way...a representation of the goals and behavior of a hypothesized group of users. In most cases, personas are synthesized from data collected from interviews with users...They are captured in 1–2-page descriptions that include behavior patterns, goals, skills, attitudes, and the environment, with a few fictional personal details to make the persona a realistic character" (sdata.me/TodxCy).

As a simple example of a persona, I like to reference what I think of as developer persona canon, developed by Microsoft while working on Visual Studio 2005. In a 2004 blog post, Nikhil Kothari framed the essence of their three product personas:

- 'Mort', the opportunistic developer, likes to create quick-working solutions for immediate problems and focuses on productivity and learn as needed.

- 'Elvis', the pragmatic programmer, likes to create long-lasting solutions addressing the problem domain, and learn while working on the solution.

- 'Einstein', the paranoid programmer, likes to create the most efficient solution to a given problem, and typically learn in advance before working on the solution.

Back in 2004, these personas helped cleanly define what would be done for the VB programmer, the C# developer, and the C++

developer. Today, although technologies have evolved, I believe the core developer personas still exist - they just tend to use newer frameworks and models (e.g. Ruby, PHP, Go, TypeScript, etc.).

There is much more to these 2004 personas than the super simplistic statements, but they paint a crisp picture, They have even sparked much debate over the years within the developer community, with developers often complaining about the stereotyping and pigeon-holing that they can lead to, particularly for those falling into the 'Mort' label (an early incarnation of the modern malign of the 'script kiddy' by an 'elite programmer' of today).

To further clarify what a persona is, let's take a moment to also briefly examine a few other common practices that are used to describe a product's users, such as market segments and taxonomy attributes, and explore how a persona is different from each of these other approaches. It's important to note that what you use is not a binary choice - there are many folks (my group included) that use personas along with one or more of the approaches below.

Personas vs market segments

Wikipedia defines market segmentation as "the process of dividing a broad consumer or business market, normally consisting of existing and potential customers, into sub-groups of consumers (known as segments) based on some type of shared characteristics" (sdata.me/ICfoSw).

The use of market segments is most handy on the business-oriented side of the house because they're easy to build marketing programs upon. You can cleanly size an opportunity, you can build a lookalike audience pretty simply, and you can measure the ROI of your campaigns using easily observable audience attributes.

The idea of a market segment is similar to a persona; in fact, there are a number of folks that tend to use the two terms interchangeably. Both approaches break a larger market into smaller groups using shared characteristics (needs, interests, and habits). However, the two approaches and outputs are quite different. Market segmentation tends to be a quantitative, or data-driven, process using exhibited/measurable behaviors or traits. User personas tend to be a qualitative process, using internal personal drivers and motivations.

As a marketing segment example, a marketing team might look at the same population of developers used for personas, and create the following market segments, starting from easily measured attributes such as where they work:

- 'Enterprise developers' work for large corporations with 1k+ employees, with a focus on building internal applications and services; they are productivity-minded and trend towards proprietary technology stacks.

- 'Emerging developers' work at startups and tend to be younger; they are very tech-forward and prefer building upon open stacks.

- 'Partner developers' work at platform or service companies, building offerings that increase the productivity of their customers.

The team might even further divide the market segments by their purchasing patterns, or perhaps further slicing by organization (community, academic, small/medium business, enterprise) or by region (western markets, eastern markets, emerging markets) because market segments tend to start with how their campaign targets users or measures sales conversions.

Personally, I tend to believe that personas are more powerful than market segments for product and campaign creation, but market segmentation is more powerful in execution and measuring the success of what you take to market. Market segmentations often rely on observable characteristics of your audience - where they are and what they do - making it easy for your marketing team to find your target customers and execute. Personas tend to focus on the, often invisible, needs of your audience - what drives their adoption and usage of your offering. And while it's easy to build a product aimed at 'an entrepreneurial moonlighter', it's much harder to quantify and target them in a look-alike audience.

If you are using these two approaches together, I recommend finding an easy way to map how they relate, and understand that the mapping is almost never 1:1 (e.g. software companies in the 'partner' category are likely to employ a mix of 'Einstein's and

'Elvis's; enterprises are likely to employ a mix of 'Mort's and 'Elvis's).

Personas vs user taxonomy attributes

Another common practice is to anchor a target audience on one particular attribute in a user taxonomy, whether it be a role, an industry, or a programming language.

- User roles are most commonly used by engineering groups to call out what job activity is using their product (e.g. 'backend developer', 'web developer', 'mobile app developer').

- Industries (or 'verticals') tend to come into play when there are specific needs, requirements, or behaviors that play out in different types of business (e.g. manufacturing, government, education).

- Programming languages is a pretty self-explanatory grouping (e.g. C++, Java, C#, JavaScript/Node/Angular).

While I believe that user attributes are pretty important for understanding how and where your products are being used, I think that anchoring on these attributes as the way of defining or understanding your audience can put you in an overly-narrow niche. In addition, it tends to turn the focus of your storytelling on product features, rather than thinking about underlying needs that you are looking to satisfy.

Characteristics of a persona

In its simplest form, a persona is a fictional character with a backstory and their own journey to give them depth and to make them interesting to your readers, your engineering and business partners.

If you have a lot of experience, much of this story is based on your intuition and experience with your developers. If you are new to your product's developers, it's time for you to go and either run some focus groups or meet a number of them so that you can start to better understand them, In the basic portrait, I look to include the following details:

- Basic Demographics: To make this person real, give them a name and create a composite of who they are using what you already know about your target developer audience, perhaps anchoring on someone you met at a recent event that you think well represents your user base: what is their age? Where do they live? Where do they work?

- Customer Journey: Now dig in further on what you know about your developers (such as discussions, customers meetings, focus groups, or surveys): How does the developer's world interface with your product or platform? What does their journey generally look like as they move through their world, and as they make contact with yours? Depending on your audience and how established your offering is, this can be either a basic view on their journey as an individual (Past → present → future), or take the shape more of a traditional adoption funnel (Background → awareness → engagement → adoption → advocacy).

- Motivations and aspirations: What drives this individual? Why do they do what they do? What motivates them? What inspires them? Who inspires them? Where do they want to go?

- Pain points and fears: Again - go back to their drive, but from the opposite angle. What keeps them up at night? What do they dread? What do they fear? What are their blind-spots (known or unknown; professional or personal)?

With a basic portrait of our developer, I start to dig into this fictitious character and explore two additional characteristics that create the story of their journey:

Inflection points (adoption triggers): What are the major moments in their life as it relates to your offering? What moves them to the point of making a change? And what is the process for exploring that change?

Adoption facilitators: What can you do for these personas? I tend to break this out into at least three organizational 'calls to action' ('CTAs') - engineering, programs and offers, and marketing - to say "what you can do to help 'Bob'" and provide 1-3 very clear and crisp CTAs on what we can do to help this developer to minimize their pain points and attain their aspirations.

Backing it with data - general demographics, social graphs

Once you have your basic character story written out, then you're ready to flesh it out with market trend data and facts. This helps you round out your persona and refine the portrait away from anecdotal stories, and ground your character in the real world. To do this, I turn to survey data and syndicated research that summarizes larger market trends around my audience.

At this point you may be saying - hold up - why are we only now pulling in market trends and data? Where did all the other stuff come from, if not from data? Well, let's return to how we defined a persona, as a "representation of the goals and behavior" of a group - we are starting with what we know about the internal drivers of our audience, rather than their outputs or observable behaviors. If we started with the market data to define our grouping, we would be doing a market segmentation.

A sample collection of developer personas

In 2012, I set out to build my first collection of personas, the ones mentioned at the start of this chapter. I was doing developer marketing for Windows Phone at the time, and the team built out five personas as shorthand for the mobile developers in the market at the time:

- 'Ravi' worked at a large company that wanted their brand present in mobile, but weren't a mobile company. Although technical, he was business minded and always considered ROI in any mobile investment.

- 'Jerry' worked at a small, mobile-first company that was striving to be ahead of innovation on the platform. He was a developer by background, and in mobile for the excitement. He knew what he was a good at (coding) and was keenly aware of what he wasn't great at (business).

- 'Lana' was part of a team of mobile developers, either as a team member or as a team lead - but filled a number of roles in her day-to-day that would be divided across folks in larger application or web site teams. She was passionate about her role, was ambitious, and was most concerned about the productivity of her and her team.

- 'Tyler' was our mobile moonlighter, passionately building an app in the evenings and weekends. Although he wasn't doing mobile development for a living (often due to a lack of original IP or a business plan), he felt personally committed to his apps and his users.

- 'Nate' was our mobile hobbyist, dabbling in mobile development to experiment or learn, but he didn't invest any significant effort in what he's built.

It's important to note that the mobile space has changed a lot since the early years, but the above represents the state of western mobile development in the early days. The personas themselves also evolved over the years, matching both the changing times and the changing needs of the marketing group, as we targeted developer building for PCs, Xbox, web, IoT, and mixed reality devices.

The persona work in 2012 was built on a foundation of a few years of audience understanding work, both qualitative and quantitative in nature. And we invested an additional year of persona-specific research, talking to almost a hundred developers across the United States and Western Europe to understand why they did what they did. The persona research format was also my personal favorite - we interviewed developers in peer pairs (also known as 'dyads') with such questions as 'if you were a developer super-hero, what would your power be? And who would be your sidekick?' The facilitator we used for the work had a lot of fun with the discussions, and it helped to disarm an otherwise guarded group of developers and uncover some brilliant psychological gems.

For these personas, I'd like to call out a few interesting elements that add texture to the model:

- Developers can, and often will, inhabit multiple personas - I've seen lots of devs who were a 'Ravi' or 'Lana' for work, but a 'Tyler' or 'Nate' at night or on the weekend as they experimented with new technologies or platforms.

- These mobile developer personas held for both app and game developers, which was a constant topic for debate in the company. We focused on the personal drivers of individuals and we found that their personal goals and challenges were similar, even though the technology, workbacks, and team roles differed between app developers and games developers. At the time, the similarity held both within the small organisation/team level ('Jerry') and at the large company level ('Ravi') because most large game studios (e.g. Square Enix) thought of mobile games as an extensions of their console/PC offerings (much as Facebook, at the time, thought of their mobile apps as an extension of their desktop browser based experience).

- Similarly, the personas held across Eastern and Western developer shops. When we went to Asia, we had to create variants for our 'Jerry' and 'Tyler' persona to address differing personal and cultural drives, but the core of the personas held.

To help make our personas useful, we created a number of reference materials to flesh them out: we created a landing page for the content and an overview PowerPoint presentation to introduce our five developers (in full slide form and a recording of the presentation of the slides), a dedicated slide deck for each of the five personas, and some additional deliverables for our three marketing-focus personas (the platform decision makers - 'Ravi', 'Jerry', and 'Tyler').

One of the additional deliverables was a wall poster for each of our three focus personas. As you can see from the snapshot of the upper half of Jerry's persona poster, the poster tried to bring the persona to life (digression: Jerry's image is actually a lead mobile developer at the time - to get a real developer vibe, we traded professional headshots for a release form that provided photo usage rights). We blended personal information, actual quotes from actual mobile developers, and market trend data (e.g. platform adoption trends for that persona from analysts such as SlashData, relevant internal survey data, as well as other sources) to bring the persona, and their customer journey, to life.

Meet Jerry

Experienced independent

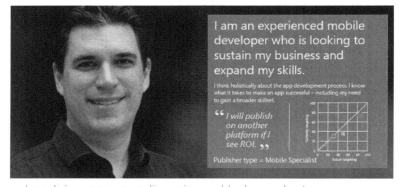

I am an experienced mobile developer who is looking to sustain my business and expand my skills.

I think holistically about the app development process. I know what it takes to make an app successful – including my need to gain a broader skillset.

" I will publish on another platform if I see ROI. "

Publisher type = Mobile Specialist

Jerry's journey as an Experienced Independent

Where I've been | Where I am | Where I want to be

Show me the money

67% Say that the business opportunity is critical to their decision to bring apps to Windows 10.

In search of ROI

2.8 Platforms on average. iOS for the money, Android for the reach.

Start-up partnership with contract work to pay bills

- 12% just me
- 60% 2-5 devs
- 23% 6-30 devs
- 5% 11+ devs

I am a self-driven performer

67% Have more than 5 years of software development experience

I want to keep growing my business. Success means users and revenue.

Windows 10 decision factors:

- 67% Business opportunity
- 43% Porting guidance
- 34% Middleware tools
- 37% Porting costs
- 30% Skill building
- 30% Windows 10 toolkits

On the lower half of the poster, we focused on 'How we can help Jerry', focusing on common concerns we heard from these developers: their motivation, platform selection, team needs, process pain points, what they wanted for their code, and what they wanted for themselves. This half was quite straightforward: the left side brought forth a quote (such as "Speed to market is critical" under 'Process'), while the right side highlighted a corresponding suggestion (such as "Show transparency during certification - get their app out there, so that they can gauge the response and iterate rapidly. Fast publishing process.").

The persona posters were hung in the company's hallways to help our [internal] customer adopt of the team's product (in this case, our research and point-of-view), and also to help the reader feel more informed about the market and our target customer, which allowed them to internalize and use the persona.

Using personas

With personas in hand, let's turn our thinking to usage, both within your group and outside of it. Where and how you use them will vary based on the type of company in which you operate; in our case, some of our engineering partners used them as the intended 'audience shorthand' within engineering scenarios and product value proposition work but primarily, our personas were used within the developer marketing organization. In fact, my team increasingly used our personas as the core of our marketing efforts over the five years following their inception. I did so many educational presentations on the topic of personas that I'm still known in some parts of Microsoft as 'the Windows persona guy', with reverence by those that bought in, and with an eye roll by those who didn't yet understand the value contained in this approach. That being said, I've also been bought many a drink (whether with alcohol or caffeine) by those who once sighed at the persona concept, but who later found the faith after changing roles or companies!

Marketing agency briefs

When our team engaged with agencies for marketing campaigns or content development, we included a simplified version of our target personas (10-12 slides of the larger deck). Initially, we did this because an agency wanted to know more about the audience, but this quickly became a best practice in our RFP process as it yielded much better campaign pitches on the first try.

Campaign and offer development

If you've done your homework and captured the motivations of your target audience, you can start to use your insights around the customer journey and adoption decisions to build a marketing plan around each audience.

For example, in Windows Phone, we targeted each of our key three personas via different developer marketing motions.

- For 'Ravi' developers, we used our business development teams as part of our larger conversations with the executive decision makers in the business, which was often the key for investments.

- For 'Tyler' developers, we built a gamified developer program with Nokia called DVLUP and engaged at the community level, building a sense of fun and fraternity.

- For 'Jerry' developers, we ran a number of programs and offers that helped both improve their business (design help, business consults, and marketing help) and helped them feel like a bigger fish in our ecosystem.

Developer messaging

Every marketer does messaging a different way. At Microsoft, we generally follow a standard positioning and messaging framework process. This comprises a top-line marketing message for the offering along with three messaging pillars that support it. How you best align your offering's messaging and positioning is well beyond the scope of this chapter, but what I'd like to hit on here is how I used personas to evolve my team's approach to something as structured as a messaging framework.

After a few iterations of the developer messaging for Windows Phone, I tried adapting my approach to create a messaging framework with four variants: a core messaging framework that follows the normal process, but also adding a messaging framework variant that is tailored to each of our key three personas. The approach used three-steps:

1. First, we would do some qualitative testing on our messaging with small groups of developers to understand what they liked, or didn't like, about our top-line developer messaging, both from a conceptual and wording point of view

2. Second, we would also inquire about some of the broader concepts in our offering and probe for areas that either delighted the room or felt like we stepped on a landmine.

3. Third, we adjusted the messaging for audience, potentially swapping messaging order or even sometimes one of the core messages with a brand new one. We would then go back and revisit our core messaging with the findings and evaluate if we needed to make any changes to the larger framework, as well.

As you go down this path, it's important to approach developer messaging with a growth mindset. For me, it was helpful to work with some professional focus group moderators early on to learn how to enter a discussion with curiosity (rather than trying to correct what may first be seen as a misguided or misinformed opinion) to gather insights on structuring my storytelling to developers.

Platform usability

It's worth noting that developer personas are also useful in evaluating the usability of the platforms we are marketing. When one thinks about how to adopt or position a platform, you most likely think about feature sets and checkboxes - what's present and what's missing. That thinking is about half of the picture - the quantitative half of the picture. Equally important is the qualitative half of the adoption picture - whether that experience was delightful or painful. A recent artifact I've seen is the idea of Friction Analysis in adoption. As we looked at messaging, and we noticed that the different personas experienced the platform differently. This brings us back to 'Mort'/'Elvis'/'Einstein' in how they approach building UI using user controls. Each persona wants something different from the development experience, and each brings their own collection of requirements and biases. For example, 'Mort' wants to quickly lay out his UI visually, and finds UI templates very productive; while 'Elvis' puts a lot of value on the ability to tweak user control properties and override the default behaviors.

By understanding each persona's perspective and assumptions, you can properly build and position a product to that audience. And by sharing a common persona set between marketing and engineering, all of the teams share a common lens for designing and building your product. Particularly when your product can prioritize the audience and be clear in what they want and need, it's much easier to build a product that meets those requirements and delights them.

Tips and tricks: persona creation

So let's turn our discussion to the process of creating personas. As we discussed early in the chapter, personas can be as simple or as complex, and as cheap or as expensive, as you want them to be. In this section, I've pulled together a collection of points that are worth considering as you embark upon the process of creating your personas.

Persona project kick-off day

As you kick off the persona creation, it's critical that you gather up and include all of your extended stakeholders. I've found it critical to include key folks attached to the product - marketing, engineering, and developer relations - to understand what is already known about your audience, and what additional information would help them better meet its needs.

Much like organizing focus groups, I recommend sitting down with stakeholders with aligned purposes and mindsets to make the most of your time. And, much like running a focus group, you may want to use a neutral third-party or facilitator (either external to your company, or just external to your group) to help allay any fears of organizational bias on the part of your stakeholders. In the conversations, you'll want to explore the following:

- How would they use developer personas in their work?
- What do they use today?
- What do they know about their target audience?
- If they had to group your audience into three groups, how would they do it?
- How do they measure success with the developer audience?
- Can they share their last business review on progress with their target audience(s)?

For efficiency, you may want to set up a unified kick-off meeting to set some context for what's coming, when it's coming, and what you want/need out of everyone. This will help you to define the work to be done, and to let everyone know that the work brings together voices and perspectives across the company.

And as you progress, you'll want to communicate across all groups on general project progress - no less frequently than monthly. You'll also want to communicate with each group on progress with any findings as it relates to their questions and/or problems. Don't underestimate the value of having the larger group communications; giving everyone visibility on the left-to-right coverage of the project helps them see the personas through a larger lens than just their own.

Understand your existing customer segmentation

Particularly if you're in product management or developer marketing, it's critical to look at your existing customer segmentation, and how your company goes to market with your company's market segments. As we discussed earlier, there are many ways that you can divide and group an audience, and everyone will have their own way of slicing and dicing the group.

For your personas to take root in the business, you'll need to speak the language of your business and be able to express how you go to market with your personas. If you can't frame your personas that way, you will spend a lot of your time fighting the existing model and trying to explain how persona 'a' maps into segment 'b', or risk all of your work becoming shelf-ware. Returning to the original goal for your personas, they need to advance your organization by aligning goals and audience across the company.

Talk to your target customers and understand their story

As you build your personas, don't spend all of your time behind one-way glass. While funded research has its place in the effort, it's critical to get to know developers by going where they are and observing them in their natural habitat:

- Visit them in their work environment. As you build out your personas, drop in and chat with your developer audience to understand what they do and why they do it where they are. And while you're there, take some pictures for the reports. To find some local developers while you're out on business travel, you can reach out via LinkedIn or just connect with a few via your engineering or developer relations team. If they're customers or partners, they would love to have you drop by.

- Talk to them at events. While you're at a relevant event, hang out at your booth, or break your chains and walk the floor, introducing yourself and getting to know those around you. It may feel odd at first, but you'll be surprised at the conversations you'll have at an event. It's a great way to get an unprompted view of your company, the market, and what's on their mind. Those attending paid to go to that event, after all, so they must be invested in the topic.

Storming and norming

After you've come to understand what your business needs and what your developer audience wants, it's time to get creative and iterate, iterate, iterate. This portion of the process is much more black art than science, but a few things that work for me:

- Sticky notes: I love writing down everything I think is interesting in the 'Characteristics of a persona' section of this chapter. Then start looking for commonalities, much like a quant-based cluster analysis…except this is all stuff in their head.

- 3 question gearbox: As you start to get to your groupings, see if you can define 3-5 characteristics that define that group. These characteristics would be the 3 survey questions that you place in a survey or event registration to understand which personas you're reaching, or the messaging you want to test. For my mobile developer personas, it was around (1) why they did it (pure hobby; moonlighting; profit), (2) size of team/company, and (3) decision making authority.

- Granularity: You generally don't want too many personas to represent your audience. You should push to simplify and collapse groups where you can, but keep it granular enough to be useful.

- Test it: Lastly, build out a composite of your persona(s) and test it out with your stakeholders and with your work deliverables. If it helps and moves things forward - awesome! If it doesn't - it's time to iterate!

Always be hustling

Once you have your personas in hand, the work doesn't stop. Much like your engineering partners, you have a minimal viable product, so ship that thing and start hustling and iterating to drive constant improvement.

Internal promotion

Don't underestimate what goes into marketing your work internally, whether you work in a small company or a big one - folks either adopt your work or it becomes shelf-ware, locked away in some file folder or abandoned on an island of misfit toys. For me, the posters and monthly presentations on the topic helped a lot. But your mileage will vary.

Cultural refinement

Once you build and ship your initial product (remember - always be shipping), check it for unconscious bias and/or sample bias. In my case, we built our personas based on US and Western European experience and data points. The following year, we tested it in Asia (in China, India, Japan, and Korea) and found interesting cultural differences anchored in such things as community interactions and career movement. As one example, we found that in China, particularly in Tier 1 cities, most developers were less interested in taking risks on new or radically different platforms, for fear of hurting their trajectory out of programming and into management.

As necessary, tweak your personas or make notes within them on how to execute your marketing campaigns according to local area or audience variations.

Always be learning

Lastly, the tech industry is always changing. You (and your personas) should be prepared to change with it. Always bring a growth mindset to your work and assume that everything you do should be reviewed annually to see if you're still in touch with the market your developers represent.

- As part of your marketing post-mortems (for events, campaigns, and releases), evaluate whether you landed your product with your target persona(s). Did you reach your target developers? And, on the flip side, did the developers you reach properly represent your personas? In our case, our 'Jerry' persona changed a lot in its first year of life, going from teams of 1-2 to 1-5, and going from an entrepreneurial focused developer to one of empowerment.

- Stay out there with your audience, attending at least 2-3 developer events per year - and remember that your own events don't count! Much like you did when you built the personas, talk to your developers and ensure that you still have the pulse of your community. And if you sense that sentiment or motivations are shifting within your audience, it's time to revisit.

- Finally, stay up on your industry trends and be sure that your team thoroughly reevaluates your personas every 2-3 years to see if your groupings still hold. Although some groupings can be evergreen (Mort/Elvis/Einstein), the mobile developer personas in this chapter are definitely dated and no longer effective...you don't want your marketing programs to feel like syndicated television reruns from ten years ago. By continually checking the industry perspective, it helps prevent you from living in a bubble if your audience is getting more and more niche.

Over time, you'll probably come to think of your personas as a set of close virtual friends, just as I did. Just remember to enjoy your time with them while you have it and be ready to let them go as the world takes you down different paths!

Chapter 2 | Successful Developer Email Marketing

Desiree Motamedi: Head of Developer Marketing - Facebook

Throughout this chapter, you'll learn about Facebook's developer marketing journey in relation to email; from our challenges and insights on how to solve them, to best practices, audience insights, and where we see email marketing headed in the future. Development is about improving technology and moving forward. It is not a one-way street - we're all building together. We apply this mindset to our marketing to tailor our messaging to the audience and give them what they want and need.

Introduction

Email has been around for decades and is used by billions of people around the world as a way to rapidly exchange electronic messages. As a fast, free tool, it seems only natural that marketing has used it since its early days to connect with people. In 1978, Gary Thuerk, a Marketing Manager at Digital Equipment Corp sent what is considered the first mass email. It was a marketing message promoting the company's machines to several hundred people over the pre-Internet network, Arpanet. The results were impressive, generating more than $13 million in sales for the company. Email marketing was born! (Source: ComputerWorld sdata.me/CljUnz)

Much has changed in the 40 years since 1978. Checking email on a computer is no longer the primary way people communicate online. In fact, according to data collected and analysed by Litmus Software, more email is read on mobile than on desktop email clients, with 47% of email opened on a mobile device (Source: "The 2017 Email Client Market Share," Jan 2018 sdata.me/DBAJQu). Furthermore, a recent study revealed that mobile email conversion rates have caught up with desktop conversions, with both at an average of 3.3 percent for the year. (Source: MarketingLand, March 2018 sdata.me/kKMYpa).

With 72 percent of consumers in Litmus' 2016 State of Email report stating that email is their first choice for brand communication, and more than 225 billion emails sent every day (a 5 percent increase from previous years), email continues to play an important role in brands' marketing strategies.

To stand out from the crowd, marketers have to blend creativity with data, tailoring their content to be relevant to their audience and reaching them at the right time, in the right place. And if you're working in developer marketing, you have a particular challenge because traditionally, developers hate marketing. They want communication to be authentic and useful. Keeping that in mind, it's essential to take an honest look at developer email marketing and ask tough questions, such as:

> *Will the reader think we're trying to sell them something?*
> *Are we using a developer-driven approach?*
> *Are we pushing our products or services rather than creating value and trust?*

It's more important than ever to get this right today, with so many companies vying for developers' attention.

No one taught me about developers

As the Head of Developer Product Marketing at Facebook, a significant portion of my job entails understanding how developers think, what makes them tick, what keeps them up at night, and how Facebook can ultimately help them do their work better. Over the course of two decades, I've gotten to know this demographic inside and out through a plethora of go-to-market strategies that my teams have helped build and execute.

Through it all, there have been no rulebooks or guidelines on how to specifically target this demographic. There was no "*How to Market Facebook's Products to Developers for Dummies.*" Through endless hard work, a ton of trial and error, and the support of fantastic marketing teams, we've begun to understand how to fine-tune our message to developers. However, the nature of this particular demographic is that it's constantly changing to keep up with such a fast-paced industry.

A little more about my work with developers prior to Facebook — I began my career in Silicon Valley with Adobe and spent over eight years as Group Product Marketing Manager, where I oversaw several product launches, including the Adobe Flash Media Server family of products and the repackaging of Creative Suite.

Understanding developers had never been more important than when I began my tenure at Google as their Product Marketing Lead for mobile apps. At Google, I was responsible for "rolling thunder" marketing strategies, which build momentum and generate buzz to get the audience wondering 'what's coming?' before a public announcement. My team worked to build a vibrant developer ecosystem around the Mobile App Ads Platform, which includes AdMob, AdWords, and Google Analytics. I've carried over the learnings from that experience to my current role at Facebook, where I head up global developer marketing efforts.

I love working with and nurturing relationships with developers. It's fascinating and fun working with this diverse audience who are having such a profound impact on our world today.

Facebook's developer platform

Most people think of Facebook as a social media site, connecting people with their family and friends, as well as businesses. It's a place to share content, send messages, and interact with the people you care about.

But Facebook is more than that. We launched our developer platform at the F8 conference in May 2007, enabling developers to build software for people on Facebook, with tools and features to help them grow. At the time, Facebook's user base was 20 million people. Today, we're at more than 2 billion users, and we present developers around the world with the opportunity to connect with even more people.

Just as our consumer audience has grown, our developer ecosystem has expanded and evolved over the years. To achieve this scale, we have seen some organic growth. However, that's just one part of the equation.

To grow the developer ecosystem, our task in the Developer Marketing Team is to connect with and drive developers to adopt our products. We do this by using engaging content that keeps them coming back to us. We craft content, messaging, and campaigns with our end-goal of product adoption in mind. We plan email campaigns, newsletters, websites like developers.facebook.com, social postings, and more to get developers' attention.

To drive success, we've tried and tested different marketing approaches, built out a robust suite of tools, and fostered community through a variety of programs and events. Recently, we've invested heavily in forming a full-funnel marketing initiative, which involves a solid email marketing strategy aimed at engaging our developer audience. Throughout the process, our North Star has been to track and measure results, collect data across platforms and use what we've learned along the way to optimize going forward.

It's all about the data

In early 2017, we decided to ramp up our email marketing to developers, creating a full-funnel approach that ties all campaigns back to building awareness, influencing consideration, driving adoption, and increasing retention for a loyal audience. To achieve this, we aimed to accurately measure every interaction, optimizing accordingly and mapping out an ideal strategy for growth. We asked ourselves "Did that article in our last email newsletter actually drive sign-ups?", "How many of our subscribers click through?", "Did that specific newsletter article drive adoption of the product?". We wanted to discover which approaches worked, which content had the most impact, and how to keep developers engaged over time. But setting ourselves up for success wasn't easy...

First, we had to decide which CRM we would use. We had to consider functionality, support, ability to integrate with Salesforce, reporting features, data collection, scalability, and more. After weighing the options, having conducted our own research and speaking with other teams using CRMs, we landed on Marketo as the best choice for us.

To get started with our CRM, Marketo, we knew we had to pipe over our developer data that existed elsewhere, because we wanted a complete view of our audience's behavior from one centralized location. It was crucial that we not lose any of the existing collected data about our developer audience. The result was a complete database of developer signals including product adoption, online behavior, and who they are. We had gathered this existing information through tracking across our website, social channels, email campaigns, paid media, events, and third-party sites. It was important to us that we didn't lose it - it's marketing gold, after all!

To move this trove of data points into our new system, we had to enlist the help of our Engineering and IT teams. We needed coordinated resources to get the data cleanly piped in and organized in a way that would make it meaningful and accessible. Overall, integrating our data and syncing up Marketo with Salesforce took us about 6 months with the help of numerous teams. It was worth the effort to capture registration details and interests in one place, but it took some serious time and cooperation! From contact information to product adoption, page views on our websites, and more, our engineers had their work cut out for them.

With this first substantial hurdle out of the way, we would be able to build a solid email marketing strategy. With vast amounts of data, we would be able to personalize our content, connecting with our audience in a more meaningful way.

Testing, testing, 1,2,3

After successfully moving all of our data to Marketo, we set out to create a variety of email campaigns. From trigger-based to batch, we tested a slew of different approaches across content, layout, design, messaging, send day and time, and more. But consistent throughout these tests was our measurement. Tracking performance is the key to success. Equally as important is having benchmarks and goals in place to see how you're improving. To get started, do a quick online search for industry standards for delivery, open rates, and click-throughs. CRMs such as HubSpot, Mailchimp, and Marketo will periodically publish current benchmarks that you can use as a guide. Use these as a starting point, then set your own goals. Remember, the numbers shouldn't change - you need a constant to measure yourself against.

For us, we set the bar high, aiming to achieve 15-22% open rate and 1.5-2.5% click-throughs. We have kept this number and now track our performance week-over-week and month-over-month. Looking at our reports over time, we keep a lookout for any trends or red flags. Did we see a high number of unsubscribes with a particular email? Was the open rate higher on a Tuesday send? Are more people engaging with videos than articles? These are the kinds of things we monitor, and we use our findings to improve for the next send.

Pulling the trigger

With email marketing, you have the opportunity for personalization and advanced targeting to help drive awareness and adoption.

Trigger-based campaigns are based on customer interactions with your content (e.g. subscription, page visits, product adoption). They help to drive people through the funnel in a very personalized way. With these campaigns, you can map out the customer journey more precisely and make decisions based on real data. What brought them to your content? Did they take action after your first email? Did your reminder emails drive them to conversion? How many times did you 'touch' them before they adopted your product?

For nurture campaigns, all email sends are automated and are based on the actions a lead takes. To prepare for this flow, we had to map out the potential journey and actions we wanted leads to take. From there, we mapped out the potential outcomes of action/inaction and created emails according to each one. Then, we piped data into our CMS and had the logic built out to correspond with the potential developer journeys - all aiming to drive product adoption. Trigger-based campaigns are definitely not simple, but they are worth it because you gain a better understanding of the unique journey each person takes on their path to conversion. These campaigns also help to showcase which points along the way are successfully driving action, and which ones are not. This is extremely valuable insight, and it can help you make decisions to optimize the path to conversion.

The welcome nurture flow

Once a developer registers on developers.facebook.com, he or she gets added to our database. From there, we look at whether or not the developer has created an app so that we can send them one of two welcome emails.

If the developer has already created an app ID with us, they receive "Welcome Email A" with next steps and a welcome to the platform. From there, we wait 24 hours to see if the developer adopts a product. If they do, then we add them to the nurture stream for authentication services and send a prompt to adopt either our Analytics offering or another one of our products. If they haven't adopted a product, then we send two more email prompts encouraging them - one is sent immediately, and the other after 48 hours. If nothing happens after 120 hours, then we mark the lead inactive in the database and filter the type of material we send them (mostly platform updates and nothing product-specific).

If the developer hasn't created an app, they'll receive "Welcome Email B" with next steps, demonstrating platform value and encouraging them to create an App ID. In the first 96 hours they'll receive three prompts from us to create an app - the first is sent after 24 hours, second at 48 hours, and the third after 96 hours. If 130 hours go by and there's still no activity from the developer, then we mark lead inactive in the database.

Newsletter

Along this journey, we've made some amazing strides and have tested and learned from a variety of experiences, good and bad. The Facebook for Developers newsletter campaigns have been full of valuable lessons.

Our newsletters enable us to actively re-engage with our developer audience on a monthly basis, providing updates on our platform and products. We experiment with different layouts, different times of day for send, subject line AB tests, different types of content, and content length, etc. - tweaking and refining the content each month for the most significant impact.

We've also added "Share With a Friend" functionality to enable those who have subscribed to send the email to others they think may be interested. This helps us to grow our database organically.

Along the way, we've hit some bumps in the road. We used trial and error to outline a clear process for approvals, learning from each month's send what worked and what didn't. We also asked "Where did we experience delays, and what can we do to make it smoother for next time?". We also had to evaluate deliverability across devices, email service providers, and more. Other questions we asked were "Is what we're seeing on our screen the same thing someone on a different screen will see?", and "How can we make sure the experience is consistent?". Through it all, learning is key - take what you've experienced and apply it to the next version so that you're constantly improving.

It's not always an easy road to success

Although we've had great success in many ways, there have been several obstacles we've had to overcome along the way.

Technology was a challenge for us at times. Integrating Marketo and Salesforce is great when they play nicely together. However, this is not always the case. From segmenting developers by product adoption, to segmenting users into buckets by developer vs. business, it can be hard to draw a line and determine the best approach. There are many different types of people with different backgrounds and interests, so it can be hard to figure out the best way to segment them. We are lucky to have a dedicated data analyst who is able to sift through all of this information and help us to glean key insights from the data we collected. Combined with email AB testing, the insights from our data analyst help us to better understand our audience. While you may not be able to have a full-time data analyst on staff, I highly recommend you have someone who can look at all of the data you're collecting and make actionable recommendations for your marketing team.

Another challenge was determining the logic for email campaigns. It is very detailed/intricate, and all potential outcomes need to be considered. We had to go through many rounds of review and feedback about timing and content in order to align on how we thought we could drive the most product adoption through the nurture email streams.

The insights you receive about your audience based on the data you collect makes all of the efforts and obstacles worthwhile. You can get the complete picture of a person's journey to conversion, and it gives you an inside look at what marketing approaches are working, as well as what could be improved. Marketing is only as good as its data. The more you know about your audience, what's working, and what's not, the higher your return on investment.

Keep these best practices in mind for your own campaigns

Team organization

It takes a strong team to build out a robust email marketing strategy. In our case, we needed technical expertise in the form of engineers with deep knowledge of Marketo and Salesforce. We also needed product and audience insights from our product marketing managers so that we could create tailored campaigns based on our findings. In addition, we needed specialists to execute and report on our email campaigns. Plus, we needed someone - or better yet, a team of people - who could understand all of it and see the bigger picture.

For each of our team members, we ask "What are their strengths?" and "What are their weaknesses?". I consider who should take on each role, and set them up for success, because when everyone gets to play to his or her strengths and work together, great things happen. A "unicorn" who understands both the developer audience and full-funnel marketing will be very hard to find! When I hired someone to handle our email marketing, I set out to find an individual who understood the full funnel marketing approach. It didn't necessarily matter whether or not they were familiar with the developer audience because we could support them to learn over time, and onboard them by interfacing with cross-functional teams, encouraging conversations with developers and product teams both in-house and out in the world.

However, it is also important to have people on your team who have a technical understanding. They don't have to be developers themselves, but they should know what they're talking about and understand what drives the developer community. They need to understand developers' challenges and know how to communicate effectively. For example, it's important not to add a lot of "fluff" text when communicating with developers. Say what you need to say succinctly, and don't add a huge lead-up with background information. No matter what news you're sharing with developers, make sure you deliver it straight and to the point.

Stakeholders

When developing your operational process you should keep your stakeholders and team members in mind. You should be asking " Who needs to sign off on this?" and "Who will your email marketing program impact within your company?

Make sure to keep stakeholders actively involved and up-to-date, so everyone is on the same page. Send them the items you need their sign-off on, and make sure you get approvals when you need them! To streamline your projects, set up a process for incoming requests and clarify who needs to receive the initial details and next steps. Outline it all in a clear process with timelines to help manage expectations. Of course there will be times when campaigns need to be rushed (last minute emergencies can always come up), but try to plan ahead whenever possible so no one gets burned out. This will help them to absorb new information as it comes, which will happen, quickly and often. The more organized and structured the plan, the better!

Test your messaging

Run a subject line AB test using different phrasing in each and see which one gets more engagement. Strong calls to action are key. Developers want information clearly and succinctly presented to them, so your call to action should be very clear and stand out from the rest of your email. For example, our recent email subject line mentioning GDPR was a big loser, since the audience was inundated with GDPR alerts that week. Even though the information was useful to developers, a subject line featuring one of the other articles would have had better open rates that month.

Another example is our standard developer newsletter subject line. In the past, we would always make the subject line "Facebook for Developers Newsletter" followed by the month. We saw that open rates weren't what we wanted them to be, so we ran a subject line AB test. We found that including a sneak peek of the content featured in the email was much more successful. Since then, we've used this subject line structure to help drive open rates.

Be conversational

Developers are generally averse to the most common marketing techniques, especially sales-y lingo and jargon. For example, avoid words like "enhance," "robust," or "special". In general, it's best not to overuse adjectives when describing something. We've found that it's best to keep information short and sweet - be straightforward and informative. Clearly present your information and highlight key benefits. It's best to showcase your information in a problem > solution fashion.

This goes for any email, but for developers especially, avoid spammy techniques. Limit your exclamation points, keep capitalization consistent, and avoid embedding forms within the body of your email. Also be sure not to send too many emails. While "too many" is subjective and depends on your audience's interests, be sure to keep an eye on your unsubscribes, which will give you an indication if you're overdoing it. In general, we try not to send more than 4 emails per month to the same people. No matter how useful the email may be, no one likes having their inbox inundated with messages from the same company.

Product update emails should be short and to-the-point. This way the email gets to the heart of the issue quickly. Have calls to action about where to learn more or whom to contact for questions. This keeps the audience engaged and informed.

Test your layout

We recently redesigned our developer website. This new design, of course, needed to carry over into all developer-facing content, which involved redesigning our newsletters and emails. We saw this as an opportunity to see what types of content layout our audience prefers - so we ran a test. We revamped our existing newsletter, simply updating the logo, colors and font, but keeping the structure the same. Then, we created a brand new layout, shortening content sections, updating logos, colors, fonts, content types, and more. We used both, sending half of our mailing list one layout, while the other half received the all-new design. This is an excellent way to determine how to connect with your audience. Do they prefer short, bite-sized blurbs, or do they want meaty articles within their email? Do they like clickable images, or would they rather have text links? Try it out! See what sticks.

Test date/time of send

What day of the week results in the best open rates and engagement? What time of day performs better? Are you sending to different regions in different time zones? These are all things to keep in mind when considering effective timing of an email campaign.

Additionally, see what your competitors are doing, and try and find something that sets your offering apart. Don't get lost in the noise.

Track online and offline interactions

For events, send invites to your target audience via your CRM. Target your audience based on region, product interest/adoption, activity, etc. Once someone signs up, have an automatic confirmation email lined up to send to them upon form completion. Collect info on who attends and doesn't attend your event and send them follow-ups accordingly (thank you notes to attendees, sorry we missed you to no-shows). You can then use all of this data in campaigns in the future - using data about who attended an event as part of target criteria.

Think globally

Offer content in other languages/tailored to different regions. Don't just rely on direct translations, though. There are nuances between regions that will need to be taken into account for your audience to hear your authentic voice. For example, we only send our newsletter in English because the content we link to is generally only in English. We plan to localize our nurture campaigns into other languages, however, since that is static content that can be tailored to region more easily. Work with people in-region to localize your content. For Facebook, the majority of our developers are outside of the US so this is a major ongoing effort for us.

Build deeper relationships with your audience

To make email content relevant and helpful to our developer audience, we listened to our active developer database. Did they have feedback about our tools or messaging? Were the resources we sent them valuable? Through surveys, we were able to get their feedback and plan accordingly to make our emails more useful.

Showing that you are listening is important. Give your audience the mic and absorb their feedback so you can give them what they want. Hear their concerns, their questions, their preferences and use it to provide them with valuable content they're going to enjoy or find useful.

At Facebook, many of our development tools are open source, and we are a company built by developers for developers. So prioritizing feedback from the developer community across channels is key for us. By hearing what they have to say in groups, forums, social media, at events, and more, we're able to discover key takeaways that we can turn into actionable items for our marketing.

Understand the full path to conversion

To understand the journey, it's more than just measuring opens, click-through rates, and link engagement. We also need to understand how developers came into our database. Did they fill out a form for an event? Did they visit our website and sign up? Were they on a social channel and came to us that way? It's crucial to measure the full journey and compile this attribution data, overlaid with our findings about messaging/content, formats, subject lines, image style, different calls to action, and more. The more data you can pull together the better you can ultimately serve that developer's needs.

So what's next for us?

We've seen 1.8M developers download our SDKs and APIs - so it looks like something we're doing is working. Our database has grown to 3M developers, and we're going to be expanding into new regions, and marketing to developers in other parts of the world even more effectively.

For us, localization is our next white whale. We have an established global audience, and we want to do more to better connect with our developers around the world by offering email content in their language of choice. Localization is more than translations though - we also want content that is suited to each region/locale so that it's more relevant.

Lead scoring is also on the horizon for our team. Some leads are more valuable than others - engaging more, converting, demonstrating higher open/clicks. We want to have an at-a-glance view at who these people are so we can weed out those who aren't actively involved and focus more on these "higher scoring" leads. But for this, we need a system and built out criteria. It will take some planning! I'll update you about our progress in the next Essential Guide.

Chapter 3 | The Power Of Community

Jacob Lehrbaum: Vice President of Developer and Admin Relations - Salesforce

In today's connected world it seems like everything has a developer service, such as an API, an SDK, or a platform. This is because the apps and devices that brands and software developers are creating become significantly more valuable when they can share data or services with each other, or can be extended by a developer with a great idea. For example, in my digital home, I can control my Nest thermostat, my Hue lights, and even my Wemo-powered Christmas tree with my Amazon Alexa. By harnessing the creativity of the world-wide developer population, vendors are seeing their products extended and adopted in ways they never thought possible.

But simply creating a developer service is not enough to declare victory. Unless you have an incredibly differentiated.offering, you are often one of multiple options out there that developers can choose from. This is where community can become such a powerful factor in your success. Developers, by their very nature, are builders who create things that are entirely new. And in the process of creating things that are new, they often use your services in ways that you didn't anticipate and this is where community comes in. With a vibrant community, you will have developers sharing best practices with each other, helping solve challenging problems, and even sharing code to help everyone go faster. When developers see a service with a rich community around it, they are also more confident in adopting it! But community does not happen overnight - it requires focus, investment, nurturing, and patience.

Introduction

While communities can form organically, planning can turn your community into a rocket-ship. Communities exist because people grow to be passionate about your product or technology, and if you have a thoughtful program for sharing guidelines, tools and templates with developers, you will amplify their efforts in a way that will make the entire community stronger. And championing their success creates a positive feedback loop that inspires others to follow in their footsteps.

When thinking about your community, it's important to remember that they do not work for you - they are free to participate and contribute as much or as little as they wish. They may disengage if you don't meet their needs or if they feel like the community is not welcoming or inclusive. For this reason, it's critical for your community program to be helpful and to focus on their success instead of your own, internal objectives. Know how building a community supports your goals, but focus on being helpful and let the rest follow. Because it will, and your community will be stronger for it.

I've had the privilege of working with four communities over nearly 20 years in the developer tools and platforms industry: Linux, Java, Ruby-on-Rails and most recently, and currently, the Salesforce community. These communities have been incredibly varied ranging from open source with Linux and Ruby-on-Rails to industry-standard with Java, and finally company-specific with Salesforce. But in each and every community, I've been struck by the passion of the members and their genuine care for helping their fellow developers succeed.

In this chapter on the power of community, we'll explore how you can bring people together to promote organic connections and collaboration, pave a path for your community members that aligns to your goals, make your community members feel and act like insiders, discover and champion community leaders to empower your most engaged advocates, and measure your success within your company to ensure that your community efforts get the funding and recognition they deserve.

Bringing people together

Community culture

Community is fundamentally about people coming together to help each other, and the first step is to create a community that people want to belong to. A big part of that is your product itself, but there are things you can do above and beyond your product to make your community be a place that people want to spend time. One of the ways you can do that is through culture.

At Salesforce, a fundamental part of our culture is giving back. As Marc Benioff has said, "the business of business is improving the state of the world." In fact, Salesforce was founded on the 1:1:1 model which dedicated 1% of Salesforce's equity, 1% of Salesforce's product and 1% of Salesforce employees' time back to communities around the world. For this reason, we've made giving back a big part of our events and messaging, and we see the community adopting this as well! A great example of this is Surf Force, a Salesforce community-led conference in the UK that, in addition to learning about Salesforce, features surfing and a beach clean-up. It might sound a little weird, but the attendees absolutely rave about it, and it gets an incredible, international audience.

Another part of our culture is to have fun and be inspirational, which results in stronger bonds across our community as well as an approachable feel. We do this through playful copywriting, highlighting the success of people and groups across our community, incorporating fun programs into our events and campaigns like our #OhanaFriday hashtag on Twitter, as well as a family of mascots that includes Astro who believes that anyone can be anything they want to be, as well as Codey the Bear, Cloudy the Goat, Metamoose, Appy Camper, and our original mascot, SaaSy.

By combining our core values, we've seen a culture develop across our community of developers that has strengthened our community.

Once you have created a community that people want to belong to, there are a number of ways that you can help your community come together, including but not limited to developer group meetups for getting together in real life and online channels such as social media, Slack/IRC, Online Q&A and hosted discussion groups.

Developer groups

From my perspective, developer groups are one of the most fundamental components of a successful developer community. This is because having an in-person support network is invaluable whether you are just getting started, or looking to skill-up. Nothing beats being able to talk to a real human being. The people that choose to lead these groups are some of your most important allies and you need to treat them like an extended part of your team (more on this later) and give them what they need to be successful. Every company has access to different resources, but consider whether you can help with refreshments, physical space, marketing, content, or access to your experts. For example, at Salesforce we'll reimburse community group leaders up to a fixed amount per meeting. We also have an unofficial policy to ensure that our developer evangelists and product managers visit local groups whenever they are nearby, and we provide access to sessions, including slide decks and videos, from our major events so they can deliver them at their local groups.

Whether you create your own developer group program or identify and support existing developer groups will depend on the size of your community. For example, Sun, as the creator and steward of the Java Platform, was able to build and grow a substantial developer group program called Java User Groups (JUGs) and while the torch has passed to Oracle, there are still over 200 JUGs in existence today. At Salesforce, we have over 236 developer groups in 56 countries.

On the other hand, during my time at Engine Yard, we instead chose to support existing open source communities such as Ruby on Rails and PHP. Given the open-source nature of Engine Yard's platform-as-a-service, their users identified more as members of these existing open source communities. We used Engine Yard's offices in San Francisco, Portland, and Dublin to host meetup groups for those communities and others free of charge, and even paid for pizza and beer! By supporting adjacent communities, Engine Yard was seen as a sponsor and leader.

As you think about your developer group strategy, think about how your users identify and where they spend their time. If your product is part of their identity, think about creating your own groups. If your users identify as part of multiple communities, perhaps start by supporting those existing community groups and defer the decision on whether to create your own groups.

Online channels

Even if you have hundreds of developer groups arranging meetups, few companies, if any, have groups everywhere they are needed, and most meetup groups meet monthly at best. We live in an increasingly global world, and bringing people together via online channels like Twitter, Facebook, Reddit, StackExchange or Slack is an excellent way to keep the community humming 24 hours a day and 365 days a year. Why so many channels you may ask? We've found that developers want to learn in many different ways, so we like to meet them where they are and support organic efforts that spring naturally out of the community.

At Salesforce, we manage our Twitter and Facebook accounts directly, with active community participation. For example, on Twitter, we have a hashtag called #askforce that is monitored by community leaders around the globe, where you can ask for help with issues you may encounter.

The Salesforce StackExchange was created by community members and continues to be managed by the community. In addition to the Salesforce StackExchange, we also have developer forums that we host on developer.salesforce.com, moderated by 2-3 full-time Salesforce employees, a number of Salesforce product managers and a handful of carefully selected community volunteers. Each month, the StackExchange and the forums receive participation from thousands in the community, which is split in terms of its preference. Why do we continue to support both? We've found that our first-party developer forums tend to be more forgiving for new entrants to our community and a good complement to the Salesforce StackExchange.

Closing the circle with the meetup groups, we also provide online discussion groups powered by Salesforce Community Cloud, so that individual communities can engage together, with both private and public settings depending on the sensitivity of the discussion topic. In addition to online homes for each of our developer groups, community members have created groups for big Salesforce events like Dreamforce and TrailheaDX for our products, specific industries, women in tech, diversity and much more. What is special about these groups is that while we provide the infrastructure, it is our community members that create (and sustain) so many of these groups.

Pave the path

Communities are made up of people. People who have a wide range of skills, goals, and perspectives, and who are participating in the community of their own free will, not for a paycheck. Many of the best contributions I've seen from the community are organic in nature, and are nothing we could have planned, anticipated or even suggested!

Community members will see opportunities in their own local communities and come up with amazing solutions that couldn't have been anticipated. Within the Salesforce community, we have countless examples, such as members who have created their own podcasts and blogs. There are over two-dozen community-led conferences such as Midwest Dreamin' and Snowforce. The community have launched a Speaker Academy to help first-time speakers get talks accepted at conferences such as Dreamforce. We have also seen the community rally in a big way around a grassroots organization called PepUpTech, which is striving to address the disproportionate numbers of underrepresented groups in tech by helping people get jobs in the Salesforce ecosystem.

You don't need to be entirely hands-off. Guidelines, best practices, resources, and templates can help you pave a path towards the outcome you want. Let's say a member of your community wants to create a developer group. They could certainly do this on their own without any help. They could create social media handles or a blog to get the word out, spin up a group on meetup.com, find sponsors, create a talk to present and then invite their friends to come. This requires a lot of personal investment, and while some people will be successful in doing this all on their own, others will not.

You can be supportive without being prescriptive by setting up a program that includes a directory where they can list their group, a small budget so they can get reimbursed for refreshments and snacks, a guide that helps them plan their meetings, sample content that they can present, and access to speakers from your company and the community. They can still choose their own content and run their meetings how they want, but you have significantly reduced the effort it takes to run a successful meetup, and this will result in more groups, meeting more frequently, and with better agendas.

Another benefit from not controlling the process is that the community members inspire each other. Nowhere has this been more apparent than in the rise of dozens of Salesforce community-led conferences around the world. The very first Salesforce community-led event was in 2011 when Midwest Dreamin' was held in Louisville, Kentucky with 100 people. By 2018, Midwest Dreamin' had 750+ attendees, but even more importantly it has inspired over two dozen community-led events around the world, from Down Under Dreaming in Melbourne Australia, to Punta Dreamin' in Punta Del Este Uruguay to London's Calling in London England, to Jaipur Dev Fest in Jaipur India.

Jaipur Dev Fest itself inspired a wave of events in India including Hyderabad Dreamin and India Dreamin'. While we've had a hands-off approach to these events to allow them to grow on their own, we've built a web directory to help promote the events and created a standardized way to offer Salesforce speakers and sponsorships so that we can contribute in an equitable fashion across all the events. But the events are theirs, and they have the freedom to find any other speakers and sponsors they wish - and to follow any format.

So what are some of the ways that we pave this path for our community?

- Carefully craft messaging that outlines the values we hope our community will uphold

- Make resources freely available including documentation, code, presentations - we've even created a free "workshop in a box" called BAM (Be A Multiplier) so community members can run their own workshops

- Create online directories to help promote meetup groups and community-led events

- Give access to Salesforce speakers - while ensuring that we don't dominate their events

- Shine a light on developers in our community who have created impactful programs or resources, to inspire others to follow their path

- Give feedback and advice around content, activities, and experts without being prescriptive to avoid diminishing creativity

Once you've paved a path and raised awareness of the amazing things people are doing in your community, you will be amazed at how inspiring this is not just internally but externally as well.

Grow champions

When you give people room to follow their passions, they can find amazing solutions to problems you didn't even know you had. When it comes to helping your community feel empowered, you need to do three things:

- Make them feel like insiders & part of your family

- Give them the resources they need to succeed

- Highlight & amplify their success.

At Salesforce, we use the Hawaiian word *'ohana* to describe both our employees and our community. In Hawaiian culture, 'ohana represents the idea that your family members are tightly connected with each other and responsible for one another, whether related by blood or by choice. There are many ways to make your community leaders, and aspiring leaders, feel like part of your family, from hosting regular calls where you can interact, inviting them to meet your product managers and engineers and including them in focus groups or getting their feedback on your programs. To be insiders, your community leaders need to understand your products, your roadmap (as much as you can share) and even understand why you are making the choices you are making. Show that you genuinely care about their success in all your interactions with them.

Some of these champions will do amazing things completely unprompted, while others may strive for recognition as leaders in the community. Either way, creating a formal way to recognize these champions helps to celebrate their accomplishments and inspire others to follow in their footsteps.

Identifying and inspiring your champions

How do you identify your potential insiders? They are the people that stand out, for example, they can be your developer group leaders, bloggers in your community, people that have taken the initiative to create tools or other open source projects in support of your products, active participants in your developer forums or social channels, vocal advocates at your big accounts or consulting partners, or frequent speakers at your events.

You may consider putting together a special program for your insiders. At Sun we had the Java Champions program, at Salesforce we call them MVPs - a term that originated in the world of sports and originally stood for "most valuable player." By creating this program, it makes it easier to work with these insiders on a more formal basis. From regular calls to private email lists or discussion groups, to doing special summits at events or even dedicated events, by recognizing these insiders in a special way, you can inspire others to follow their footsteps or even come up with their own ways to contribute to the community. To make sure it's a fair process, we share examples of how community members have become MVPs in the past, guiding principles that determine eligibility, as well as details on the nomination process - which is entirely community driven. We also have an index with all 200+ MVPs so it's easy to see who they are, visit their community profile pages, and get in touch with them via social channels.

And these MVPs (or future MVPs) can do amazing things for your community. One of the coolest community-driven initiatives that has developed in the last couple of years is #SalesforceSaturdays. Started by Stephanie Herrera, a Salesforce MVP based in Austin, Texas, #SalesforceSaturdays bring people together on Saturdays to learn together. Whether your workday is too busy to prioritize learning, or you are looking to switch careers, sometimes the only time you can find to learn is your own personal time. And doing it together can help you progress further and faster than on your own. The

#SalesforceSaturday initiative was initially an in-person gathering, but it quickly became a global phenomenon with people connecting with each other through

the hashtag - and interestingly has taken off in India more strongly than anywhere else in the world, perhaps because developer groups typically meet on the weekends there.

Last year, there was even a global competition to see which Salesforce developer groups could earn the most badges on Trailhead. Reflecting the strong culture of learning and self-improvement in India, two groups ended up in a list of the top 5 community groups (New Delhi, Atlanta, Pune, Austin and Tokyo). As with many community-led initiatives, we didn't create it. We didn't approve it. But we did our best to amplify all efforts and shine a spotlight on the originators for their achievements. Shining a light on initiatives like these, and the community members who created them, is a great way to inspire future leaders in your community.

Sharing with your champions

Once you have identified your insiders, whether it's through a formal or informal program, you can start to do a lot more with them. We regularly get their feedback on our products, our developer program, and on our messaging for events like Dreamforce and TrailheaDX - and we truly listen to what they have to say.

Live discussions are always best to create discussion and a real-time feedback loop. As a product manager at Sun, I would regularly brief our Java Champions through conference calls in advance of any product launch and get feedback on messaging as well as roadmap input. When I was leading a redesign of the Salesforce Developer Forums in 2013, I worked with a handful of members of our community to get early feedback from them on wireframes and designs - a process which resulted in very insightful feedback that shaped our development process for the better!

It's generally a best practice to make as many of your resources publicly available as possible - ideally without gating them. This not only makes it easier for your customers to freely access your resources, but it also aids the growth of your community. Developers evaluating your technology don't have to go through an account team to learn about your products, consulting firms can skill up to help your clients with custom implementations, and students or job-switchers can consider making your technology part of their career path.

When it comes to making developers feel like insiders, you may want to go even further and expose information that you might think of as confidential, for example, early access to your new releases, roadmap plans, and even the opportunity to participate in roadmap development. At this point, you need to decide for yourself what you are comfortable sharing but it is perfectly reasonable to ask a subset of your community, those you think of as insiders, to sign the same non-disclosure agreement you might put in place with your customers so that you can feel comfortable sharing non-public information with them. This can serve to make them feel even more like they are part of your team - because they are!

Measure your success

The value of community can be hard to put a finger on. Implicitly, some companies understand that a strong community of developers helps drive customer success and adoption of your products. Other companies may be looking for a more direct connection to the bottom line. Certainly tying it to traditional business metrics can be a challenge, depending on the nature of your business.

I tend to think about the contribution of community in two fundamental ways: awareness & adoption and there are ways to look at the contribution of your community for both of these.

When it comes to awareness, I've put together marketing operation systems that have looked at how different resources and channels have contributed to deals, whether it's new signups that originated from StackExchange, Reddit, Twitter, or Facebook or even referrals where developers tell their friends to check out our product(s).

Adoption can be trickier; how do you know if a blog post that one of your MVPs wrote helped your developers figure out how to use your latest feature? Sometimes, the best way is to simply ask your community what is helping them. To get this data, we do focus groups AND surveys on a quarterly basis, since this can be an excellent way to understand the value of different community resources. While asking people directly can have flaws (people don't always remember how they first discovered you or what was most helpful throughout their journey) looking at this data in aggregate across your community can give you a pretty solid indicator of what is working.

Once you figure out which tactics have value, align on these with your executive stakeholders so everyone is on the same page and then measure them, fanatically. Do it daily if you can automate it, or at least weekly if not. And then communicate your success. At Salesforce, we use our Chatter product to share our progress with our stakeholders on a monthly basis - we track the numbers more frequently for our own team, but do readouts every month to avoid information fatigue.

Some of the community metrics we look at:

- Total number of community members & monthly growth
- Total developer groups, new groups added, and meetings per month
- Visits to our developer center & number of Trailhead badges earned
- Number of community events per year
- Number of social media followers & monthly engagement (likes, retweets, etc)
- NPS Score from quarterly surveys.

But sometimes success is less of a metric and more of an emotional story. At Salesforce, we are fortunate that our products have genuinely changed the lives of many of our developers. From being able to get a career as a developer without having the benefit of a formal technical education to switching to Salesforce from a technology that is less fun to work with or has fewer job opportunities, to using the Salesforce product to change the course of their company. By telling these stories about developers in our community, we are also able to highlight the human successes that come out of our community each and every day.

In conclusion

While this may read like a plan you can follow to build your community, the reality is that the community builds itself. Your role is to help it grow and shape its path with the programs you put in place to bring people together and champion your leaders, the successes you choose to spotlight, and the way you treat the developers that make up your community.

At Salesforce, we are fortunate to have an incredible community that has grown around our platform. Our community truly feels like part of our family, they give back to others in an incredible way, and in many cases have even built their careers around our products.

While every community is different, one thing that is common across every community that I've been privileged enough to work with, whether it was the Linux community, Java, Ruby on Rails, PHP, or Salesforce, is that the people that make up your developer community are your greatest assets.

Chapter 4 | Building an Inclusive Developer Community

Leandro Margulis: VP & GM, Developer Relations - TomTom

In this chapter I will share some of my experiences from when I led the Developer Relations organization at TomTom, where I was tasked with building the Developer Community around TomTom's Maps APIs on their Developer Portal. But before I dig deeper, I want to take a step back and review some concepts about what constitutes a "community".

What is a Community?

All of us in Developer Relations are community builders in one way or another. We want to build an ecosystem of people using our tools and solutions. But how do we define a community? I like Charles Vogel's definition from his book "The Art of Community": "*a group of people that care about each other's welfare*".

A key element of the overall developer community, albeit only one small part of it, is the "Developer Portal". This is a place where many of the interactions amongst your community members may happen. So how do we see the definition of a "community" manifested in a developer portal? We see it through the connections and communication that happen in a portal between its members.

Three types of Communication in a Community

I would say that there are three types of communication that occur within a developer community:

1. One-to-Many
2. Many-to-Many
3. One-to-One

If you're a developer, you'll likely recognize these types as they are prevalent when talking about the relationships between entities, most notably in databases, but they're just as relevant in Developer Relations.

There are different tools that enable each one of these communication types. Let's start with One-to-Many. This is the first and typical way a website communicates with its readers and users. This communication mode could also be called "broadcasting". This is similar to the way a TV show broadcasts content in a one-to-many mode to the rest of the world. Your API documentation is an example of broadcasting / one-to-many communication. A pretty basic way of broadcasting content, but a broadcast to the world nonetheless. If we want to have a more intimate, genuine way of broadcasting content to the world, where we can add our tone and points of view, we need additional tools. A blog for example, allows you to communicate with the audience of readers and users in a much more intimate way than just documentation. That said, a blog is still a One-to-Many communication method.

Now, if we allow people to comment on the blog, we are allowing Many-to-Many communication, similar to how a forum enables communications between many people.

And last but not least, if you allow people in a forum to connect with one another, then you are allowing One-to-One communication between the members of your community.

Not all communities need the three modes of communication, sometimes "One-to-One" communications can happen in a public forum and others can benefit from the conversation and/or join in. Hence, Many-to-Many communication tools may be enough for the type of community you are building, and since everyone can see the conversations everyone else is having, it encourages good behavior, etiquette, and inclusiveness. In addition, different communication modes may work better with different developers, as the definition of a "typical developer" continues to evolve.

The "Typical Developer" is Evolving

As leaders in Developer Relations and developer-oriented marketing, we are challenged with the evolving identity of developers today. Let's take a closer look at the changing developer demographic and its impact on Developer Relations and marketing to developers.

While we still have developers coming from a four-year degree computer science program, there is such a large demand for developers in the workplace now, that organizations can no longer source talent from just the traditional pool of four-year degree students and alumni. Nowadays, there are a lot of different ways that people become developers; from bootcamps to online courses to experimenting and self-learning. SlashData did a study on this specific topic and has found that developers learn to code in at least two ways on average. You will find the popularity of different methods in the chart below:

Where did you learn to code?
% of developers (n=16,702)

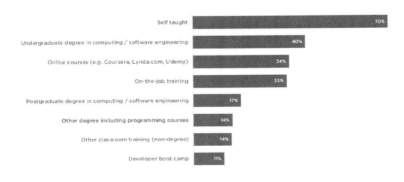

Source: SlashData | Developer Learning Patterns Q42019

There are also people at different stages of their lives becoming developers; sometimes as a second or third career. It has been amazing for me to see this change and evolution first hand, based on the type of developers attending our workshops at events such as DeveloperWeek, API World, and WeAreDevelopers World Congress. For example, I once spoke to former industrial manufacturing professionals without college diplomas, who are now getting into industrial IoT applications design after finishing their classes at Galvanize.

In addition, there is a plethora of programming languages that developers may know, and new languages are being introduced all the time. Your community needs to be flexible and inclusive enough to account for this evolution and the ever-increasing diversity of programming languages and frameworks.

There is also growing diversity in the socioeconomic background of today's developers which may affect the way each developer learns. From connectivity differences to differences in learning styles, it's best to have content in different formats (e.g., written content, video, etc.), to allow each developer to learn at their own pace and in the format they learn best.

On one hand, this evolution of the developer profile has created a very heterogeneous group of developers with different experiences that could make it challenging to provide a "one-size-fits-all" developer toolbox. On the other hand, the variety of profiles and backgrounds creates an environment for innovation and avoids groupthink. The diversity of today's developers can help build the next generation of solutions, bringing ideas from other fields and life experiences that can have a very large impact in improving people's lives.

With this in mind, we need to build communities and toolsets that can cater to a wide range of developers with different sets of skills, backgrounds, and different levels of comfort with certain computer languages and interfaces. We want each and every developer to find something helpful for them in our community and to feel included. We need to consider this when we are making design decisions for our developer portal, events, training, staffing, and so on. We'll further illustrate this, through an example later in this chapter, in which you'll see how a small change in the registration process to get an API key in the developer portal, can have a huge impact on inclusion.

How we Built Inclusiveness in our Developer Personas

In the chapter, "Using Developer Personas To Stay Customer-Obsessed", Cliff Simpkins talks about building developer personas to help you advocate for developers within your own organization. The goal is to make sure you can rally people around ideas that are easy to understand and communicate, so that you can be consistent in your messaging and targeting.

As you see your audience evolve, make sure you take that into consideration when building and/or updating your developer personas so all that work you did over time aligning everyone within your organization, stays relevant, consistent, and resonates with the evolving developer audience. This was a big learning for us when we realized we were making some implicit assumptions about who a developer is and what would resonate with them, as the results from some of our campaigns showed.

Through interviewing developers at trade shows and conducting online surveys, we would verify if the actual developers we had interviewed matched any of the personas we had created. In our first trial for the personas this was not the case, so we figured that we either got our personas wrong, or the developers that were actually using our product were the "wrong" developers because they did not match our personas. In reality it was our personas that were wrong, and thanks to the input from these interviews and surveys as well as the demographic information from paid digital campaigns, we were able to update our personas to actually match our evolving audience.

It's also important that your own developers within your organization feel that the personas you are building resonate with them, and that your own developers could potentially identify with at least one of the personas you are putting together. Hence, you may want to involve your own developers in the persona definition exercises relatively early to get their input. Remember that eventually you want these personas to be a communication tool and a common language across departments within your organization, so getting your internal developers' buy-in into the persona profiles early, can only help to make them effective communication tools.

The Developer is Taking a Larger Role in the Decision-Making Process

Due to my experience with different types of tech companies at different stages of growth ranging from startups like Quixey in Silicon Valley and my own startups, to Fortune 500 clients while working as a management consultant at Deloitte, I like using frameworks. Hence, I tend to see tech companies through a "three-legged stool" framework: Business, Product, and Engineering. There is usually a healthy tension between each leg, but there is also a dominating leg that determines the culture of the company, as well as the types of features, products, and technologies the company develops.

I would also add that an early-stage startup usually starts by being engineering-driven, but eventually needs to evolve into a more product-driven or business-driven organization to get to the next stage of growth.

I tend to look at business with a strong product-bias: I look at the end use-case that our business partners are trying to fulfill, then look at how our products can fulfill that use case either by themselves, or by combining our products with other offerings in the market to fulfill our partner or customer's end use case.

This view is important in the context of developers because the role of the developer has also evolved to have a lot more influence in the decision-making process for companies to adopt new products, technologies, and solutions.

In the past, a developer at a large enterprise company would have been instructed to use a product or technology that the product managers and business leaders have decided to use or partner with. These days, those kinds of conversations tend to either involve the developer in the decision and evaluation stages for potentially adopting a technology, or the conversation may be happening the other way around; where the developer is testing a technology and recommending it's adoption to management.

As the developer gains more influence in the decision process and becomes the subject matter expert (SME) in terms of the latest tools and trends, it's important to build awareness of your products and services amongst developers. When the opportunity arises to leverage some of your tools and services, you want them to be top of developers' minds. Thus the technology adoption process has been turned on its head. It used to be top down as discussed earlier. However, there is a whole new "bottom-up" tech adoption path, and this is where the ability for developers to try products for free (e.g., a trial period) and to combine some products with open source tools, plays a huge role.

Moreover, as the pace of technology evolution is ever-increasing, there is no way for one person or one team to be up to speed with the latest on everything that is going on. This is where being part of different communities, actively trying and building different tools, can help us stay current and relevant with the latest and greatest developments. You need to be aware of these different "developer journeys" in the adoption of a new product or tech, so that you can enable those journeys to happen within your platform, websites, conversations, hackathons, trade shows, and so on. If not, you could be missing a lot of opportunities to interact with developers at the right time when they are either making recommendations, decisions, or influencing those decisions within their organizations.

For example, while a DIY (Do-it-Yourself) developer (either a hobbyist, student, or startup developer) may be going to your developer portal to explore the products, documentation, register, and start using your APIs or SDKs; the journey for an enterprise developer may have started with a business or product conversation with someone within your company. Then, one of their engineers or developers registers within your developer portal to make some tests with your API endpoints to then continue the business or product conversation with some specific questions about your technology. There is a need to understand how different developers interact with your portal and tools and why, so you can support these different modes of interaction. If you are interested in learning more about this, check out "The Developer in Context" section coming up below.

Since developers are part of different communities, we decided to be active in different communities where developers usually congregate as well, such as Stack Overflow. We also enabled some technical conversations to happen by building a forum within our own developer portal for current active developers using our tools to share notes with each other. We also had workshops and Q&A sessions for aspiring and current developers using our technologies at Developer trade shows such as DeveloperWeek. These opportunities were also available at our hackathons so we could interact with our developers in person and learn first hand how they are enjoying our products. It allowed us to see where they might be getting stuck, so we could improve the products and make their lives easier.

The Developer in Context

From my experience, we can identify the developer in three different contexts. Depending on which context the developer is in, they will be looking for different kinds of content and tools to interact with your technology and solutions. You may need to design different journeys and information flows to cater to the developer in these three different contexts or situations:

Enterprise Developer: The Enterprise Developer is the one working in the Engineering department of a large organization. They usually get involved in the conversation to check the "tech stack" after some prior conversations between Business and Product have happened. When this type of developer is checking someone else's technology for potential adoption, they see a thriving, active, and engaged developer community as an asset, which builds trust and credibility. Remember that they will be the ones implementing your tech within their stack at some point, and if there is a healthy and thriving community to help them out if they get stuck, it helps them trust your tech more. They may also need to contact sales and support staff within your organization to answer questions about specific integrations within the enterprise technologies they are using and your tech stack. From the commercial side they may need a custom licensing agreement depending on the unique use of the technology, integrations with their stack, and data treatment.

Startup Developer: This developer could be the CTO of an early-stage startup, the head of Engineering or a software developer who wants to try the solution self-serve and will probably stay within the freemium tier of your tools and services for a while before moving to a paid tier. This developer usually prefers a "pay-as-you-grow" business model for technology use, in which they would only pay for how much they use your product or service. The more they use it, the more they would pay per month for example. They will probably use their credit card within their approval limits to pay for packages or subscriptions online and will resort to the community and/or customer support when needed.

Hobbyist and Student Developer: This could be the enterprise developer or startup developer "at night" or after regular work hours working on their own projects. They are usually active community contributors that lower the company's customer support costs. They are the lifeblood of your community. When they are ready to adopt your technology in the future, they will be aware of what you offer. If you stay top of mind with these developers, they will be your advocate internally within their organizations and influence the decision-making process in favor of your technology and solutions. Another important sub-category of hobbyist developers are students, which will soon become startup or enterprise developers. Some companies like Qualtrics, have built great businesses investing in students by giving them all their tools and services for free because they know that once those students graduate and go into industry they will need those tools in their jobs. So, who will they call and which tools do you think they will use when they are working in industry, if they already know how to use certain tools from their time in school?

Make all Developers Feel Welcome

In addition to building the right tool sets that all developers can use, we need to ensure developers feel welcomed into the community regardless of their level of experience. In the community there should be something for everyone, with opportunities to both contribute and learn from the rest of the community members.

At TomTom, we slightly gamified the community to reward the kind of behavior we wanted to see more of within the community, with the goal of encouraging productive and constructive collaboration. For example, when we first launched the forum within the TomTom developer portal and wanted more people to contribute, we had an "early adopter" badge that developers could display, and it gave us a way to thank them for helping us launch the community in the early stages.

We also took note of important qualities from other communities like Stack Overflow. Qualities such as being kind, incentivizing kind behavior, warmly welcoming community members that were contributing with either a question or an answer for the first time regardless of the complexity of the question, all contribute to a welcoming community.

Make Content, Documentation and Solutions Available in Different Languages

Not all developers are native English speakers. While programming languages are generally composed of high-level English language commands, the rest of the content in the documentation needed to understand the different functions, input, and output, can be translated into different languages to improve the developers' understanding and adoption of your solutions.

I have to give a shout out to Frank Palinkas for this recommendation. As our Senior Technical Writer in more than one company I have worked at, Frank always suggested adding an automatic translation function embedded within the documentation pages. While the literal automated translation from this kind of feature may not be perfect, it may be good enough to help a developer understand a concept or the inputs needed to make a function work and obtain the desired output.

While the languages and content to localize first may depend on the products you are offering and the specific geographical focus of your solutions, I would suggest that the text explaining the concepts around your functions and variables be translated (either manually or through automated translators) to the local language(s) where the majority of the developers using your tools and services are located, as well as the markets they are serving. For example, we have seen a lot of developers in Europe serving the US market, so the documentation has been made available in the local language where the applications are being developed, but also in English to serve the target market.

The more you can localize your offerings in the developer's local language, the more you will be able to connect with them and influence their adoption of your products, services, or solutions.

Not all Developers Learn the Same Way

Developers learn in different ways. While some developers would prefer to just read the documentation and start coding away, others may prefer to go through tutorials, demos, sample code, and videos before starting their own projects. This is similar to our days in school. You may remember that some students would never show up to class, just read the books from the class and then show up for exams and do well, while others learned best from attending classes and/or completing homework assignments in teams.

If you want to cater to a wider range of developers, you need to provide more than "documentation" and make your tools accessible to different people. Hence, some experimenters will prefer to take a sample app or code from a tutorial and start customizing it from there, versus starting from scratch and reading the documentation. Prepare your materials in a way that you have something that allows everyone to get started with your solutions. This is not only important for first-time developers but also for developers that prefer to learn in different ways. As these developers gain more and more experience, you want to make sure they keep your tools and solutions top of mind for when they are working on their next project or building the next solution.

One of the features on our developer portal that received really good reviews and positive feedback has been our "API Explorer". Within the API Explorer, developers can immediately try out the functions without having to register or obtain an API key. They can play with the parameters of a function and see very quickly how those changes apply in the rendered map next to it. From toggling the visibility of traffic to customizing how the map is shown, developers can play with and understand our technology right away.

The feedback from these true builders and experimenters has been overwhelmingly in favor of this. So based on these learnings, I recommend that you always try to create an experience for developers on your portal, so they can play and interact with your product as soon as possible in the developer journey. If an API explorer is not feasible, a link to a demo app or even an explanatory video may work.

Content Beyond your Developer Portal

In addition to all the different kinds of content you can put on your own developer portal, do not underestimate the power of e-learning and online courses. There are now more tools than ever to create "mini-degrees", both certified and not-certified, using online platforms like Udemy, Coursera, and others, for developers to take. The advantage of offering certifications is that you can create a badge for developers in your community to showcase their technology certifications and training. These not only provide developers with recognition for their efforts, but also provide a signal for others on specific topics that they can ask those trained developers for advice on.

Another important point to take into consideration with regards to e-learning is not to forget about the largest e-learning platform in the world: YouTube! Make sure you have a channel with relevant content and resources for developers to engage with on your YouTube channel. We found YouTube to be not only the largest e-learning platform in the world, but also one of the largest search engines, so it has been important for us to create relevant content on YouTube to stay top of mind when people search for our type of tools and solutions.

From an inclusion perspective, similar advice for the content in your portal applies to the content in external channels inviting developers to engage with your portal. If you can localize the examples you are using to specific geographies, as well as talk to developers in their native language through the blog posts, videos, tutorials you create, the message can resonate even more.

In a similar vein, it can be beneficial to leverage examples that are "local" to developers. One example from Maps APIs that has worked for us, is to showcase a map in product demos from the city or the country where a developer is located, rather than just some well-known "pre-set" location like San Francisco, New York, or Amsterdam. This advice also applies for your outbound marketing content for email blasts and invitations to trade events, hackathons, and meetups.

Meet your Developers Where They are

As humans, we are social beings by nature. We need to connect with other people, and we want to connect with other people based on common interests. This is particularly resonating with me right now as I am writing this while "sheltered in place" in San Francisco during the Coronavirus pandemic in 2020. While we will get past the coronavirus pandemic, a lot of the communication systems being put in place, will remain, and will have made humanity stronger and better connected for any future pandemics or extraordinary events that may happen.

During this pandemic we are seeing an increased use of not only video conferencing tools like Zoom and Skype, but also group collaboration tools like Slack and Microsoft teams, as well as forums, LinkedIn and Facebook Groups. As developers we have been using these tools for a while.

Both in analog and in digital, different groups tend to congregate in different places. In the analog world we can see certain groups of people gathering to go for a hike or meet up at a park, a bar, or a club. Similarly, different interest groups in the digital realm, tend to congregate in different forums and sites such as Reddit and Stack Overflow.

As you are building your developer community, make sure to identify the common interests that your developers have and where they tend to congregate. You may also find out that they tend to congregate in different places for different things, and you may be able to identify a content gap that another tool could fill.

For example, in the case of TomTom we had many developers congregating and asking questions both on subreddits and Stack Overflow. However, the questions that were coming up there were relatively high level compared to the questions we were getting through our developer support channels. The questions coming up on Stack Overflow and Reddit were more about choosing which Maps APIs or location technologies to use, than about how to integrate a certain API endpoint and which parameters to use. Hence, we decided to launch a forum within our own developer portal that would cover content related more to technical support and the challenges that developers were facing using TomTom's Maps APIs.

What happened right after we launched the forum was very rewarding for our team. As soon as we put the forum out in the open, the conversations started to happen almost immediately. We also got very high engagement from our active developer community in helping one another when they were getting stuck in any of the steps when integrating our APIs and SDKs into their apps. It seems as if these conversations were primed to happen and we had just unlocked a channel in which they could finally happen. We learned so much from this experience. Not only were our support costs lowering because members of the developer community were helping each other, but we could also see when most people were getting stuck in a certain integration step. All very valuable feedback to improve our products, integration, and ease of use.

What's in a Name?

Each one of us has "a name". Depending on where you are from, that name could be very short or very long. Some people have only one name, some have a first name and a last name. Others have also a middle name. Some of us have two last names as well: in Latin America it is very common to have both your father and mother's last names. In Argentina we usually have a first name, middle name, and last name, but in Venezuela for example, or Spain, in addition to a first name, middle, and last name, people use a second last name from their mother's family. I've heard stories where people coming from Latin America or Spain to the United States have had issues getting an ID or driver's license because their "full name" would not fit in the fields and maximum characters allowed on ID cards.

If we are trying to build an inclusive community, and we take into consideration how many forms a name can take, we can see how designing a form that forces the user to put a "first name" and "last name" could make some of us feel excluded. These "standard" fields may not be able to accommodate someone else's full name.

One of the ways to tackle this challenge is to have a "full name" field – which is more culturally inclusive. The full name may include first, middle, last, family, and other given names. It allows users to type in their name without splitting them into first and last. This approach makes the text field usable for every user, no matter where they come from or what culture they identify with.

At TomTom we also explored adding a "preferred name" field. While some of us have long full names, we usually go by a nickname or short name. For this purpose, you may want to parse the user's full name so that you can address them as they would like to be addressed on your platform. Since the full name field doesn't parse their first name, you can give users a "What should we call you?" field or a "Preferred Name" field on your form. These fields allow you to address them in the way they prefer without having to identify the first name from the full name field.

Making the name registration process easier for the end user reduces friction, saves time, and improves registration and activation rates. It removes barriers that might otherwise hinder your developers from using your product, even if this means having to do some additional work in the back end to allow for this kind of user interface and user experience (UI/UX) flexibility.

Build an Inclusive Team Reflective of Your Community

Now that we see and understand how the developer communities are evolving, we need to make sure our own Developer Relations team reflects the community we want to build. If you want to make sure that your messaging resonates with your audience, your team members must understand and identify with that audience as well.

Hence, once you have iterated on the personas and understand them well, and it is within your mandate to hire for the Developer Relations team, make an effort to look for candidates that reflect and mirror those inclusive personas you created. In addition, look for candidates in places you do not usually look, so you can add more diversity to the mix. When people have different perspectives, you can have more creative and richer conversations. This in turn, can help enrich both the product and experience that you bring to your community.

Conclusion

In this chapter we discussed different factors to build an inclusive developer community. We learned how developers are becoming more influential in decisions to select technology tools and services, and why we want them to be aware of our offerings early on.

We looked at how the "typical developer" with a computer science degree is diversifying to include people from all over the world who have gone through different types of training, and how we need to build documentation and tools that are helpful to all of them when they build their applications. Each developer needs to feel like the community is both welcoming and beneficial to them. As part of this, we learned that developers speak different languages and while most programming languages are represented in "some kind of English", writing the documentation around it in the developers' native language, can help them understand the concepts faster and hence make it easier for them to adopt your technology.

We also explored the need to meet developers where they are, even if that journey doesn't start on your development portal, so that we can potentially invite them to join the community on our portal. More generally, we need to understand where our target developers are active and be active there as well. And to accomplish this, we also need to make sure that our team reflects the community we are building. This means we need to make sure we hire for, create, and maintain an inclusive community within our team.

Last but not least, just because some of us have a first and last name does not mean we all do. Make developers feel included from the beginning of the journey with your tech, by creating a "Full Name" registration field if you must get their name, if not, just do it directly with email.

I hope you found the information in this chapter helpful and that it has inspired you with some additional ideas on how to build an inclusive developer community.

Additional Readings

If you are building a developer community, there are some additional books that can inspire you and come in handy. Below is a short list of the books that I have found most relevant in my Developer Relations journey. I hope you find them helpful too and if you have more readings to add to this list, from books to blog posts, reach out to me on Twitter at @leanmarg with the hashtag #DevRelReadings so we can all share in the wisdom.

"The Art of Community: Seven Principles for Belonging" by Charles Vogl

Charles has been building developer communities since before his time at Yale. I had a chance to meet him in the San Francisco Bay Area where he still builds communities. His seven principles for belonging and his definition of communities has helped me define and build developer communities as well.

"The Art of Community: Building the New Age of Participation (Theory in Practice)" by Jono Bacon.

Jono was the original community manager for the Ubuntu and Linux communities and we can learn a lot from his journey, for developer communities in general and open source communities in particular. This book was originally recommended to me by the GitHub community team at GitHub Universe conference in San Francisco.

"People Powered: How Communities Can Supercharge Your Business, Brand, and Teams"
by Jono Bacon

This is Jono's latest book related to communities. This book was also recommended to me by the GitHub community team at GitHub Universe conference in San Francisco.

Sources

Why Your Form Only Needs One Name Field by Anthony @ UX Movement (https://sdata.me/B3LM1)

Stack Overflow code of conduct by Stack Overflow (https://sdata.me/B3LM2)

Measuring success in Developer Relations, a 3-part framework by Max Katz (https://sdata.me/B3LM3)

We are rewarding the Question Askers by Sarah Chipps (https://sdata.me/B3LM4)

Chapter 5 | Starting from Scratch: How to Build a Developer Marketing Program

Luke Kilpatrick: Senior Manager, Developer Marketing - Nutanix

Running an existing developer marketing program is challenging, but starting from nothing within a company that has never previously marketed to developers brings a number of different challenges and experiences.

Introduction

This book is filled with great stories of successes, failures and long established developer marketing and developer relations programs, many such as Microsoft and Atlassian, on their second decade of existence. However there are many companies where getting developers involved with their products is a very new and very scary thing.

I started working in developer communities back in 2007 when I joined and ultimately became the co-manager of the Bay Area ColdFusion Users Group (BACFUG), an Adobe program that was done on a volunteer basis. It was here that I got my feet wet in community building, and from there I started up several other

Adobe user groups, eventually resulting in a shift in my career path to working full time as a Social Media Producer for VMware. In this role I took my first steps in marketing to a developer and technical audience rather than writing the code to power those experiences. I built my first website in 1996 and worked as both a graphic artist and web developer for various companies from 1998 until 2010. I then made the shift into working to build communities for VMware, Virtustream, Sencha, Atlassian, and currently, Nutanix, and I have not looked back.

During my time at Atlassian I was able to create a very successful event called App Week which brought the community closer together, building deeper connections among established players. My colleague, Neil Mansilla, and I described this in "Growing Up by Scaling Down", which you can find later in this book

My role at Nutanix is very different from my previous role at Atlassian. I am quite literally starting the developer marketing program from almost nothing. While it's exciting to start from scratch, this can be daunting and I have learned some valuable lessons along the way. The developer marketing team at Nutanix is about 1 year old as of May 2019. It is still growing and learning, but I believe that this start up story can help you build your team to serve the goals of your company and community.

Nutanix, a leader in the hyper converged infrastructure (HCI) space is one of those companies who have had great success in an area of the industry but due to a recent pivot and creation of new product lines, developers have suddenly become a key part in its current and, more importantly, its future success.

Nutanix is in the process of shifting from a hardware focused company to a software focused company and has brought out a suite of products that require development work to implement in production or which would be a key part of an automated DevOps stack. Realizing this at the highest levels, they needed to figure out how to talk to this new audience and how to get the right kind of attention from the right kind of developers. They decided that a developer marketing organization would be the best way to get this done.

To build a developer marketing organization you need buy in from the highest levels of the company possible. If you don't have a champion who is at least a VP, or higher, the time you have to prove your success will be very short. The amount of time that it takes a developer program to be successful from baseline to growth is measured in years, not months or quarters.

Building a Developer Marketing program is hard...where do you start?

Start first by asking two questions to figure out what type of developer program you need to build. The goals and activities for different programs have great variety depending on who you are trying to reach and what you want them to do.

Who are you trying to reach?

Figuring out what type of developers you need is key. Are you building a marketplace where folks can sell apps or extensions to your products? Do you need integration developers that use your product and who need to write code to make it work with others? Is your product a tool to help developers do their job better? Do you want to reach the DevOps folks who will use your APIs to automate things? Correctly identifying what type of developers you are trying to reach is step 1 in any developer program. There is nothing worse than doing an event and getting the wrong folks in the room. I have made this mistake and will share how it happened and how to avoid it. But, firstly, let's consider the all-important question...

Why do you want to reach developers?

Everyone wants to developers to be part of their product. Getting external folks engaged with your products at a deep enough level to want to code something for it is in some circles the holy grail of their product. But to do this well you need to understand why developers would even care about or engage with your tools or products. Also there are many different types of developers, before you can engage them you need to figure out a few things, also you need to always keep in mind what is in it for them. Without a clear understanding of what is going to drive developers to your products, your developer program will look like a dying open source project that no one participates in.

There seem to be a few broad categories of why you would want to start a Developer Marketing program, they are:

- **Marketplace based developers** - your company's products are extensible and you want developers to help build out features that some but not all of your customers would use. Atlassian's Marketplace for Jira and Confluence or Apple's App Store are examples of this. One of the primary motivations for this group is financial and businesses are often built on this.

- **API consumption** - Your product has APIs that allow your products to interact with other products and to programatically accomplish tasks that users would use a GUI for. Nutanix's Developer Marketing program is focused here, other examples would be Cisco, VMware and other companies in the infrastructure space. The developer for this type of ecosystem is primarily working for someone else that has adopted your products and needs to get them to work well and quickly with other products. This is where DevOps lives as they try to automate workflows and systems.

- **Developer tools** - This type of Developer Marketing is closest to the more traditional marketing practices where the actual product is being bought by the developers. IDEs, Testing tools and other frameworks would be in this category. Sencha, Atlassian, New Relic, Sentry and others are examples of developer tools being marketed to developers to get adoption in a bottom up way.

- **Developers are needed to use the product** - Anything headless that requires development for adoption would be an example of this type of ecosystem. Twillio, Contentful and others who are smaller parts powering a greater whole is where these companies need to rely on developers for adoption to solve their problem.

Support from above

Once you have identified your target developers and the type of ecosystem you are building, you need to get support from above. Executive buy-in is critical because building a developer ecosystem is a slow process, taking a minimum of 18 months, if not several years, before you are able to show bottom line financial success.

To help your case, set early metrics: measure attendance at events, mailing list size and developer portal visits for example.

Unless you are selling developer tools or running a marketplace, tying directly back to sales early-on is difficult.

Spend the first 3-6 months establishing baseline numbers. If the company has been around for some time, interview power users and sales engineers who are already using your products to learn why and how developers use your tools.

This is key. You need to find developers already using your products. Chances are that you already have them, whether it is the developer team, customers or just hobbyists, you need to talk to these people once you have identified them. Find out what they need. And find out where the strengths and weaknesses are currently so you can put them in your backlog and address them.

What does your team need to succeed?

Developer marketing is different at every company but your priorities will have an impact on how you hire and what roles you hire.

After I joined Nutanix, my first priority was to create great content to get developers swiftly onboarded and working with our APIs.

I prioritised hiring a technical content person, as we needed content to share before we could do anything else. If your engineering team has already created great content and that is ready to publish, you can evaluate other roles. However, when you are starting out, it's a pretty good strategy to make your first hire someone who can build out your developer portal.

After your content person begins to populate your portal, you need someone to go spread the word about it. Often as the leader of the team, you will fill the role of evangelist or advocate to start with, but to accelerate growth and success, you need someone else who can get out to industry events to share your product in a dedicated and visible way.

For the first hire in both these roles look into the internal sales engineering and engineering organizations as chances are there is a rockstar or two looking for a change and joining the developer marketing team could be what they are looking for. This gives you a big head start as they can hit the ground running rather than spending several months coming up to speed on your products and APIs. After the first initial hire in each role, look externally as you will need new ideas and fresh perspectives from people who are not drinking the kool-aid already.

Another important role for this team is a community manager, marketing specialist or marketing manager, this person will focus on social media, newsletter creation, analytics and metrics collection, logistics and many of the standard functions of a marketing team that are found in any type of marketing organization. Again as your team is just starting out, you might be doing all of this but as your success grows, bringing this person on board can expand your reach and get you out of the tactical and into the strategy which is where you should be as the team leader.

Once you have your team, or plans for it, you need to figure out what to do next. I recommend getting your developer website in great shape.

Creating your developer portal

Often the first place where you can get an easy and highly visible win is launching or re-launching the developer portal or the website that will be your primary communication platform with your community. Learn what your developers need from your portal, which in most cases will have, at a minimum, the following:

- Searchable API Reference documentation - typically this is created by your engineering team, although you may be responsible for publication.

- Developer blog - your blog should not be focused on marketing, but on using and experimenting with your products.

- Getting started - there should be a great big button that leads to a page with all the current information needed to get people up and running quickly, ideally within ten minutes or less.

- Labs or tutorials - while onboarding is the primary goal of developer marketing, having great tutorials on how to use different areas of your APIs, or other products, is vital.

- Contact system - you need some place for developers to reach out for help and give you feedback on things on the site, such as forums or a Slack channel.

Optional things your developer portal should ideally have:

- Code samples - Having a source controlled set of code samples and examples of the top 10 use cases for your API in your most common languages helps lots of folks solve their problem quickly.

- Community forums - Building a community is hard, you need a place where the crowd can hang out and discuss things, these should be moderated and monitored.

- Events page - Let people know where you are going to be next.

- Social media listing - learn where your community is, are they on Twitter? Reddit? Stackoverflow? Find that out and go participate with them.

Make sure you have a CMS behind your portal, I recommend WordPress as it is flexible and it's blog and page system are great - unless you are selling another platform using this will allow for flexibility and for the portal to live beyond your tenure. Other systems for different parts of the site should be used, pick best of breed rather than try to shoehorn everything into WordPress. At Nutanix we use a combination of WordPress, Stoplight.io for our API reference documentation, an in-house LMS system that is used by our sales enablement, customer enablement and education teams and inSided for our community platform. This works well for us, talk to your web development team and work with them, look to adopt company and industry standards rather than going and building your own. The less you need to build and maintain the more you can be focused on reaching your developers.

Launch your first event

Once you have your developer portal and at least one lab you should look at going out and getting people to try it. There are several ways to do this, I have found the most effective is to piggyback on someone else's event for either your customers or the larger ecosystem. In your first event I highly recommend a hands on lab for 15-20 people and see what their feedback is. This gives you data for your next iteration. You want to grow your events slowly, matching your community size.

After you have had a few small events look at joining larger ones, this can be done by joining a larger user conference held by your company or by working with a more generic event. Sponsoring a booth, getting speaking slots and holding happy hours are great ways to start exposing the audience to your ecosystem.

Running a full day event at a User Conference

More and more user conferences are holding developer days either before or after the main user conferences. Salesforce, Oracle, Atlassian and Nutanix are all following this pattern recognizing that the content developers would be interested in is not the same as the content in the user conference. Developers tend to be much more hands on and want to see real world code being shown. Live demos are preferred and this audience will be more forgiving when something goes wrong.

There are several formats you can use for a developer day or conference but the three different formats that are most common are the following

- **Hackathon** - Everyone build a team, pick something to build and then show it off in competition at the end

- **Coding Lab** - Work through a series of labs with help in the room for when you get stuck

- **Conference with Breakouts and Keynotes** - Traditional trade show format, lots of listening on both sides, lowest risk.

Case Study: Nutanix Developer Marketing Program days at .NEXT

We have had 3 developer type events tied to our large 5000+ person user conference over the past year. We have tried a hackathon, a lab day and a more traditional format with labs, these have had some success, but for our audience one has stood out beyond the other two.

New Orleans Hackathon - May 2018

Nutanix is an infrastructure company so most of our attendees at our user conference are administrators and managers, since one of Nutanix's primary strengths is its excellent GUI interfaces, very few of our users use the APIs or code.

To get the right people from deep into our accounts we paid for attendees' hotel rooms and made special efforts to get people who can code to this event. We also made sure we had at least one technical person on each team from Nutanix.

The overhead on this event was significant, and several things were built, however no code from the hackathon ever made it into production. This is why in many cases external facing hackathons are not a great use of resources, the teams tend to focus on things that present well rather than what they need to help them do their jobs.

Fun was had and the feedback from the attendees was positive, but it was hard to track back this activity to growth or sales. Hackathons have been the default "Let's get developers to write code for us" events for the past decade. However, due to there being so many of them and the simple fact you are asking professionals to work for almost free, they stopped hitting the right notes with the right people you need to be growing the use of your platform.

If you are trying to fill your marketplace with apps then they can be great, but for API adoption, and tools adoption they do not hit the mark as the code produced in a hackathon is rarely ever used afterward. Internal corporate hackathons like Atlassian's Ship It can be amazing for new products and tools, but external hackathons outside of the marketplace use case are rarely good for teaching people how to use your products or APIs.

.NEXT on Tour - September-November 2018

With our new developer portal launched and our first lab live we needed to get the word out to the community that we wanted developers and DevOps folks to take interest in our APIs. To do this the Nutanix API Accelerator program was born.

The .NEXT on tour was a collection of 11 events in cities across North America for Nutanix customers with prospects to learn more about HCI and Nutanix in general. This year we added a breakout track where folks could select between 2 lectures and an introductory lab using our APIs.

The lab was a simple one where folks built a PHP web application that monitored a cluster of servers. It was written in a way that allowed someone with no programming background to understand and be successful in building it. For many it was their first time building a web application. I'm a big believer in a hello world is not enough for a first exposure to an API, your labs need to build something worth taking home and showing to their boss. What better way than having them build a wall board, customizable report or boss screen.

Once they were done with the lab they could use the end result as a test harness to try different API calls and learn more about the power available to them.

This program was highly successful at training over 400 people with an average lab time of 90 minutes. We received positive feedback, and we learned the level that most of our customers were at in their programming and DevOps journey.

One of the key things that made this lab work so well was using virtualized desktops available in a browser. By having everyone bring their own laptop, but not having to install an IDE, connect up PHP and so on, we were able to get folks working on the lab in only minutes, compared to the first hour being lost to setup issues on everyone's laptop. If you are wanting to do labs with people's own hardware, virtual desktops are amazing.

London IoT Lab - November 2018

After the success of the On Tour labs we thought we would just expand it and do a full day version in London at November's .NEXT. As we were just preparing a larger wall board lab we learned we had an awesome new product that we thought our developers would love to try out. However something else came up that looked to be more exciting.

Xi IoT is a new platform that allows folks to run machine learning and AI software out at the edge, processing it locally before going to the cloud. Our developer marketing team thought this was awesome and we pivoted our lab from being focused on our API to being focused on IoT.

This was our first mistake as we had already advertised it as the API Accelerator and had folks expecting one thing but we prepared and delivered another.

The next mistake we made was going super hardware-intense in this lab. We had a full 4 node cluster, 23 small PCs to act as edge devices and 100 cameras to act as sensors with all the networking and wiring as well. Due to the newness of the platform and our inexperience with the product we added so much complexity to the lab that things that we tested with two to four folks started failing in the real world when we scaled beyond 10. To add on top of the extra stress, the shipment of all our hardware was lost for 8 hours and the team was up until 5am trying to make it all work.

Things snowballed even further when we ended up with horrible weather on the day of the event. Due to this of the 110 people signed up for our day, only 46 people showed up. It was easy to add API accelerator to your .NEXT registration as all people had to do was check a box. We filled up in just a few weeks from this, however checking a box doesn't make people value your content leading to people attending who didn't get value out of the event.

Most people who attend .NEXT are managers, system administrators and operators - not developers - so trying to find the developer needle in the haystack with a check box failed completely.

Of the 46 people who showed up 5 were actual developers! We missed this by a long shot and because of this our deeply technical content went right over our audience's head and interest level. By the time 11am rolled around we were down to fewer than 20 folks participating.

Our plan was for the morning to be a lab teaching about IoT and building a facial recognition application then in the afternoon to turn folks loose to see what they could create with their new skills. Since we had the wrong folks in the room the afternoon program became more systems design and brainstorming applications rather than building something.

After the event was completed we got hammered in our feedback with one person even saying it was the worst event they had been to.

89

Key learnings from London:

- Don't change horses in midstream.

- Don't be tempted to showcase the new and shiny when it is not relevant to your audience's day to day yet.

- Developers are a trailing indicator. In most cases you are better off teaching them how to use the products they own already rather than something that isn't relevant.

- Add more friction to the registration process. Checking a box gave us the wrong people in the room.

- Don't ship critical pieces of hardware unless you have easy ways to replace them.

London did result in some sales prospects for the IoT team and some great learnings but we needed to do a major retool to figure out what our audience needed and wanted.

From these learnings, feedback from the event and discussion with others we decided that we needed a more traditional conference type event with content that would appeal to both the manager, admin and developer but also bring home the message that now more than ever, to be relevant in the IT industry you are going to have to know how to code.

Developer Day at .NEXT Anaheim- May 2019

Between London and Anaheim the developer marketing team attended an internal event called Tech Summit. The purpose of this event was to train our sales engineers on our products as well as to build bridges across the organization. With over 700 sales engineers in the company, across 3 theaters, it is a huge process. The tech summit format was a combination of lectures, panels and labs. While learning from the team that built out the tech summit events, we decided to adopt a similar format for an external-facing audience for our Developer Day at .NEXT Anaheim.

The format for our Developer Day was 2 keynotes in the morning, one focused on the present APIs and then a second focused on culture and the future of DevOps. We also added a customer panel, as people will believe their peers more than they do the folks in marketing, and finally we added a hands-on lab component with technical staff supporting the attendees.

The more people with whom we discussed this format, the more validation and excitement for it we received. With any new event it is tough to get the word out, but in this case we introduced some friction to make sure only the people who would get value from the event showed up. This was the single biggest issue we had learned previously in our London event.

We used a few methods to do this.

- Everyone who wanted to attend developer day and came in via the .NEXT website had to fill out a form telling us why they want to come to it.

- Everyone had to have a code added to their registration when they signed up, they got this code directly from their salesperson or sales engineer, or by being accepted from the sign up form.

- Direct marketing campaigns with the code in it were targeted at developer-focused sites (Stack Overflow, Developer Media).

The direct marketing campaigns completely flopped with only 1 person showing up from a 2 month long campaign that generated over 25,000 impressions. We won't be doing those in the future! However, a direct call out campaign to the sales engineers of our biggest accounts created great results. We found that many of our sales engineers wanted to bring their customers to our tech summit (Sales Engineer hands-on training event), but could not due to it being internal only. With Developer Day we were able to give them that opportunity.

Lunch time was a key part of developer day as we endeavored to get as many of the engineers and technical people attending the conference to sit with the customers to build relationships. In many companies these people are kept away from the customers, especially engineers and product managers. I think this can lead to some problems whereby folks build the wrong things. By having the users and the builders share lunch together there is a greater chance of building empathy and understanding. My favorite result from these is when long standing bug #4920 becomes Matthew's bug that is stopping him from implementing his new system the priority of it shifts. If you are not bringing your company's engineers to your developer events, start doing so. This is hard to measure as value but in some cases these relationships can bring more to your company than a big sales deal.

As a final addition we brought on an industry leading keynote speaker. This person has a large following in our industry and his talks aligned with our goals and products well, so his talk ended up being the highlight of our event. It can be risky if your speaker is not relevant or trusted, so make sure you know your audience well enough. Look at the keynote speakers of other events and ask your sales, product marketing and engineering teams of who they think would be a great speaker. Sometimes this might even be an internal player, but someone you don't know yet.

Slowly but surely our event started to fill up, going from 4 people signed up to over 80 in just 3 weeks. The word got out; even better, most were coming in via our form so we could filter to make sure the right people were there. By adding this extra step the folks became more committed to attend and it felt more exclusive We had over 60% attendance from pre-registration which is high for a free event. We also kept the door open so more folks could drop in on the day of the event, and we had almost 40 people do just that.

Most of the day, the room was completely packed with over 140 people in it for the two keynotes and lunch. After lunch it thinned out a bit for the panel, and by the time the labs rolled around at 2:30, we had about 80 people left. These are still good numbers as we had a number of people very interested in the keynotes who had other meetings in the afternoon, and the non-technical folks do not have much interest in the labs. The labs covered our API and several of our products to give people a chance to go hands on. Technical people don't trust marketing, but by giving them access to work with the tools and products directly they can apply what they learned in the keynotes directly in the test environments.

Our feedback for the event showed 89% of the folks rating it a 4 or 5 out of 5 which is a great number for a first time event. Even more importantly several of the sales engineers who brought their customers were able to greatly expand the deals they were working on based on their developer day experience. At the end of the day, marketing is about building sales pipeline in most cases and our developer day event did just that.

.NEXT Steps

This format of keynote, panel, labs works well for our community and I believe it would work well for many others. For a marketplace based ecosystem replacing the labs with a hackathon might be an option but the real key is giving people who work with the product time with the people who make the product.

For our next event we are going to move the panel before lunch with our headlining keynote in the afternoon to keep the engagement high, also giving folks the opportunity to have lunch and further the discussions started from the panel. Lunchtime is one of the most important parts of the event as it is where the networking happens.

Our team has recently grown to a team of five, including myself, this enables us to start to actually walk and build more value rather than just keeping the lights on for a documentation site. Our team is now composed of an internal hire of an evangelist/advocate who will be taking the bulk of the travel off of my shoulders, our content architect who will continue in his role of making nutanix.dev be amazing - he was also and internal hire, a marketing specialist/researcher who was an external hire, who handles much of the email and social media along with doing surveys and collecting feedback to share with different parts of the company. Last, but not least, we hired an external developer who has experience running developer events to back up the other roles as well as focus on building applications for us and customers to use.

Getting the team you need to go to the next level is much easier after you have had a successful event that brought value to the company. With this expanded team we are moving beyond starting from scratch and now are working to show business value to the sales, engineering, marketing and other organizations in the company and beyond.

Chapter 6 | The Developer Relations Council: Leading and Aligning Developer Messaging within a Large Company

Arabella David: Senior Director, Global Developer Marketing – Salesforce

How do you reconcile many developer messages across one company, all targeted at the same audience, especially if they are not all in the same team?

In this chapter, I'll recount successful efforts to align global marketing initiatives across a large company to developer audiences. While reading this, I hope you gain relevant information you can immediately apply to your own initiatives and achieve greater success. If you are in a smaller startup or have a short portfolio of developer offerings, parts of this chapter may not be immediately applicable, but maybe you'll find a tip or two that will help you power up your programs nonetheless.

Before we dive in, a few words about how I got into developer relations while not being a traditional developer. In my career, I've been excited to create great projects and programs for developers for more than 15 years – and it all started because I showed up to a really great community festival in Helsinki, Finland. If you are not familiar with the demoscene community, and to be fair it'is extremely niche, I'll cite Wikipedia for the description:

"The demoscene is an international computer art subculture focused on producing demos: self-contained, sometimes extremely small, computer programs that produce audio-visual presentations. The purpose of a demo is to show off programming, visual art, and musical skills. Demos and other demoscene productions are shared at festivals known as demoparties, voted on by those who attend, and released online."

Inspired by the energy and enthusiasm of these coders, I became a demoscene festival organizer, volunteering with the festivals where these competitions took place. Although those days are long ago, the passion for building alongside developers is still with me today. I love working with developers simply because I love working with creators – seeing people's excitement when sharing the latest tools and creating the right environments with which people can innovate groundbreaking technologies and applications.

This affection and empathy for who developers are, and the respect for why people become developers, has served me well in some companies you may recognize including Microsoft, Nokia, Google, and Salesforce. This chapter primarily focuses on a specific time at Salesforce when our team created an internal program – the Developer Relations Council – and how we strived to strengthen community developers working on the platform using this initiative. The Developer Relations Council was built by the team in 2018 and, as of the time of writing, still functions as an influential entity in the company.

The role of Salesforce developer marketing

Salesforce is an enterprise customer relationship management platform that currently serves over 150,000 companies worldwide. I'm proud to work for such a robust company with a visionary CEO like Marc Benioff. Founded more than 20 years ago, Salesforce's primary code base has recently been opened up to developers with the addition of a web components framework, enabling anyone with JavaScript development experience to immediately customize the platform using industry-standard code. My Salesforce developer marketing team strives to effectively communicate to 6+ million Salesforce ecosystem developers about the possibilities available when they take advantage of this range of extensibility. In addition to the core Salesforce technology that underpins Sales Cloud and Service Cloud, there are several other frameworks and resources available for developers under the Salesforce umbrella. These include Marketing Cloud, Commerce Cloud, Heroku, Tableau, MuleSoft, NPSP (Nonprofit Success Pack) smart solutions such as Einstein, and beyond. Some of these offer developer related resources, while others have yet to surface in-depth code customizability.

To raise awareness of these tools and resources, there are several developer marketing channels primarily utilized, in addition to key collaborations with other marketing teams across the company. In order to get the word out to the world, we use industry-standard channels that include paid media, email, webinars, streaming, and events. Because the company is large, the team also coordinates with other key teams across the company who have different audiences and objectives.

The Salesforce developer marketing team builds an accurate understanding of developers and works from marketing knowledge of how they experience Salesforce, particularly from a coding perspective. We help guide them through their onboarding journey with the platform, especially when it comes to how to use their existing toolsets and resources for Salesforce, and help to solve their specific development needs. We seek to understand them through quantitative and qualitative surveys, and advocate for their pain points when working with product managers to improve our overall offerings.

The business challenge: everyone can talk to developers and say whatever they want

The story of the cross-company Developer Relations Council begins with the fact that, to paraphrase Douglas Adams, "Salesforce is big". You just won't believe how vastly, hugely, mind-bogglingly big it is. With 50,000 people at the company at the time of writing, and the products I listed above, you can only imagine the range of different initiatives and objectives that need to be accomplished.

A number of products at Salesforce are targeted towards developers. While this group comprises a diverse range of constituents – a group that ideally becomes more diverse every day through the efforts of STEM outreach – what unites developers is an insistence on assets with which they can immediately begin building. Coupled with this is a demand for marketing language that is low on hyperbole and high on delivering clear facts and immediate implementation.

As the Salesforce developer marketing team, it is our responsibility to internally advocate on behalf of this audience. For example, other marketing teams might focus on the positive impact that items like ROI or sales cycles have for audiences, but those concepts would not resonate with developers who seek to build robust, scalable applications. In the worst case scenario, any given developer could concurrently receive several different, potentially conflicting, messages regarding different products, all under the same master brand.

The Salesforce developer marketing team, on paper, "owned" this audience, but were seeing other teams attempting to publicly market to developers. This is a natural result of all of us living in an interconnected world and working in a matrixed organization, where, through the power of social platforms and the plethora of channels available, anyone in the company can talk to anyone else inside or outside the company, about anything. While this is great for communications as a whole, it is not an ideal scenario for companies who are trying to align their messaging to specific audiences like developers while leveraging aspects of independent initiatives that resonate with this audience. Our marketing surveys were showing that, as a consequence of this widespread bilateral communication, developers were experiencing a range of messaging and becoming confused. To put it bluntly, we were shipping siloed messages to the same people. This was a delicate challenge that needed to be solved cross-functionally.

In summary, different groups within our company were producing different marketing outputs about different products, possibly offering conflicting or misaligned benefits that potentially targeted the same developer audience. The potential consequence to the company of this misalignment is that the audience, who is already sensitive to marketing that does not resonate with their needs, might react by tuning out the entire brand. How would we go about improving this and get to a successful state of aligned, resonant messaging for developer audiences?

Establishing an internal council; discovering who talks to developers and listening to their needs

The Salesforce developer marketing team's conclusion was, in order to lead and align on developer marketing across the company, we needed to establish a Developer Relations Council. The decision to form a council was due, in large part, to the core values of trust and collaboration; two values which are vital to the corporate culture. As a company, establishing core values is an integral part of forming each new initiative and underpins key decisions throughout any project or program. Based on these values, one early idea that was discussed but discarded was to define a set of core messages and rules, then pass them to all other teams for integration into their materials. The reason for setting aside this approach was that it would minimize contributions of other teams across the company, and, in addition, it felt dictatorial, when there was a clear opportunity here to build trust and increase productive collaboration.

The council was envisaged as a group of people within the company with the same objective: to effectively connect with the developer ecosystem and deliver targeted updates about the tooling and resources that help them most in their efforts to be productive on the Salesforce platform. The group would have key representatives from all relevant teams and products that had a stake in communicating effectively with developers. If you're familiar with the Lord of the Rings, this Council would be similar, except instead of disposing a bit of jewellery, we would have the task of establishing and maintaining cross-functional collaboration.

However, as anyone who is even slightly familiar with Lord of the Rings and the fact that it is a hefty set of tomes knows: *one does not simply form a Developer Relations Council.*

As this chapter doesn't include images, imagine for a moment the above sentence in Impact typeface, overlaid upon an image of Sean Bean in full medieval garb, dramatically gesturing.

This meme repeatedly popped up as our tiny, five-person developer marketing team at Salesforce sought to bring about what some may see as an overwhelming quest: effectively align and drive worldwide developer-oriented marketing across multiple teams, products, and initiatives.

Now that we had landed on the concept of forming a council, the next step was to sort out who would be in it. We already knew of a few people across the company that were passionate about developers and would be willing allies. However, there were developer initiatives that our team simply weren't aware of until they were in the later stages of pre-launch – that is, making their projects known widely across the company, but not yet public. Our approach to clarifying this challenge of discovering who was planning developer initiatives was a jump-start audit – we set about compiling a list of all existing and upcoming offerings and researched within the company to find the relevant teams and if they had any relevant developer offerings in the works.

The importance of executive advocacy and understanding stakeholder needs

Finding the correct stakeholders in those teams and getting them to respond to our inquiry sometimes turned out to be difficult, simply because people are busy. I'm not sure how many emails you usually have coming into your inbox throughout your workday, but unexpected emails from someone you've never heard of before, from a totally different team, asking what, to you, is a question that may not connect with any of your projects, might not be of the highest priority for you to respond to. To both discover the right people to talk to AND to ensure a response, we needed executive-level support. In this instance, this is where the great program leadership of Jacob Lehrbaum, then Vice President of Developer Relations (check out his chapter on *The Power of Community*), recruited the assistance of an Executive Vice President at Salesforce. In order to gain this support, we concisely summarized the impact of doing nothing and continuing with the current status quo of misaligned messaging, and presented the hoped-for benefits of establishing a single forum for alignment. Once they and others at the executive level could see the confusion resulting within developer audiences if this were to continue, it was an elementary exercise for executives to connect their teams in the company to our team, and help prioritize responses.

As Salesforce has multiple teams developing dozens of offerings, and we were meeting several of these teams for the first time, the process of discovering and engaging with these key stakeholders throughout a matrixed organization easily consumed several weeks. Once we knew who the right people were, and got them to talk to us about their developer offerings, what next?

We knew with the executive advocacy we had secured that we could ensure introductions and responses to a few emails – but that is not a way to collaboratively achieve the larger objective of sustainably leading and aligning developer messaging. In order to build, and continue to have, an effective Developer Relations Council, there had to be internal incentives to maintain a productive dialogue. We needed to answer the age-old marketing question when targeting any audience, internal or external: "What is in it for me?"

To uncover these incentives for productive dialogue, we designed and implemented an internal survey that had two components: quantitative and qualitative. In the quantitative component, we asked how the teams were positioned to developers and where their perceived pain points were. In subsequent individual, qualitative interviews, we discovered background motivators, added additional detail to their survey responses, and explored why they had answered certain questions in surprising ways.

One line of inquiry focused on our developer marketing channels, discussed earlier in this chapter, and dived into how we could better partner with them through these channels to deliver better value to developers. One example is this question: "Do you have an interest in delivering content such as videos/developer newsletters/events featuring your product?" Other questions lent themselves to in-depth discussions, such as, "What are your pain points regarding reaching developers?" or "How do you measure success with developers of your initiatives, and how does it compare with your overall metrics?"

What we learned fairly quickly was – particularly with the people that we had never met before and with whom we had little previous contact – it was difficult to get thoughtful responses and the reasons why varied considerably. Some teams did not talk directly to developers and thus were not equipped to answer, whereas others were not yet in a state to form metrics. Oftentimes, what was then needed was a meeting, wherein one or two developer marketing team members would both administer the quantitative questions and then dive into the qualitative interviews in real time. From my experience in corporations, it is easy to forget to respond to, or depriotitize, responding altogether to a survey email, but it quickly becomes a matter of etiquette to fail to respond to a politely worded meeting request – particularly when you have been connected by higher-ups! To get useful information, it was helpful to really consider the positioning of the questions and approach to stakeholders – that is, getting engaged answers from participants rather than quick responses. Many of these questions had a strong internal customer service slant, with the questions positioned as, "How can we help you better achieve your Salesforce goals so you can rock your/your team's work?" Overall, beginning with the initial email questionnaires, continuing with the face-to-face meetings, and finally by compiling internal data, our team needed a few weeks of time.

All of the discussions were interesting; some were surprising. For example, some teams only wanted to stage hackathons as they knew "that was something that you do with developers", but once we dived into detail about metrics and the larger awareness objectives they were driving towards, we were happy to partner with them and share our experiences about what initiatives could be most impactful to their particular objectives, depending on where they wanted to work in the marketing funnel. In one particular case, there was an objective to raise awareness and initial usage of an API. Rather than provide the resources for hackathons and judging infrastructure, a more scalable impact would likely come through providing more documentation and how-to resources in small, short formats like videos and blog posts. Both tactics used the same resources - people - but the latter was far more valuable to overall strategy and metrics, and in addition, scaled far more effectively than the in-person hackathons that were originally proposed.

Networking, thought leadership, and planning: the need for an in-person workshop

Survey responses, while interesting and sparking immediately valuable conversations, do not comprise a Developer Relations Council. It certainly does, though, help to establish the baseline of problems stakeholders have and provide insight into what might start to define success. Once we had discovered the relevant groups and representatives across the company who could speak for developer interests, we ended up with about 60 people. In order to fulfill the vision of leading and aligning messaging for our developer audiences, we thought the next step was to organize an in-person workshop. This workshop would serve two objectives: one, to bring together those we had identified across the different products so they could all meet each other, learn, and share best practices; and two, to help establish the thought leadership of the Salesforce developer marketing team.

After we decided on the event of the Developer Relations Summit, we crafted the agenda. We created a day-long program designed to share and address the shared challenges that we had unearthed through our surveys. The surveys had established that these challenges were regarded by the participants as high priority and the event was a brainstorm on how to solve those challenges together.

Building the full-day workshop, which we dubbed a "summit" instead of just a workshop, to provide additional visionary positioning, was a lot of fun. I love both getting hands-on with projects and connecting people and it was great to have a reason to build an environment where, together, we could set aside time to build a leading vision for developers in the medium and long term.

Here's a quick rundown of what we designed for the Developer Relations Summit, in case you're interested in creating something similar.

- Cap your number of attendees. It's hard to remember so many faces at once, especially if you are meeting so many new people for the first time as an attendee. We had 60 people, but I would have preferred a smaller group of 50 if possible, as it would have provided more opportunities for in-depth, one-on-one conversations.
- Seats were assigned and the room itself was set up with a number of what are called "8-top" tables, but we seated 5 people at each so everyone could have personal space for the workshop. Every table had a developer marketing or developer evangelist team member to help facilitate. No two people from the same product team were sitting together and, where possible, each table were entirely new faces to each other. This

helped attendees network, with facilitation to keep their heads in the room.

- We started the day with coffee and breakfast so people who knew each other could catch up, others could meet each other for the first time, and everyone could grab a bite to eat.
- After breakfast, we began our program with structured introductions. We asked all attendees to each spend one minute introducing themselves, the product they were associated with, and their top three developer related concerns, which we had also compiled beforehand in our survey interviews. This enabled attendees to note who they might want to chat with later. This is a great setup for effective networking during breaks.
- Even though every attendee had one minute - the time scheduled added up to an hour - people tended to go over their allotted time, so time management was important. Since we had so many attendees, we needed a break after this segment.
- After the break, an executive in the room gave a short talk and reinforced the vision of why everyone was selected to join the council. This also helped everyone in the room to refocus on the day's objectives.
- Results from our survey were shared out to the group and from this information, we built the groundwork for the collaborative segment of the workshop. This alignment of our shared challenges was key to a productive, interactive session. All of the ranked challenges, discovered in our survey and research, were coded – we used numbers but you can easily use colors – and assigned to each of the ten tables. Then, they were tasked with generating ideas to solve the challenges. The ideas were segmented into three categories: what can be done now, what can be done this year, and what will take longer than one year.
- These ideas were then presented to the attendees. Afterwards, every participant was given a set of colored stickers. Each of these stickers were "spent" on the ideas that the attendee considered high priority, and they could place the stickers on any of the ideas from any of the tables in the room.
- This was a nice transition to another break in the afternoon, and, while attendees were networking, the

core team conducted a rough count of what was voted on with the colored stickers.

- Coming back from the break, we shared the counts and held an open discussion on the top items. Did we have alignment on what we can do right now and for the medium- and long-term? We established working groups, each with a volunteer lead, to discuss how we would build and execute on these ideas.
- Happy hour! We all had casual, less structured time at the conclusion of the day, and reflected on how the workshop helped us to align, meet each other, and set the social groundwork for further collaborations with an aligned intent for the future.

Hopefully this will be helpful to you if you find yourself needing to design a similar workshop to kick start alignment.

The Developer Relations Summit accomplished two critical goals: 1. Prioritizing the importance of the workshop via executive sponsorship, and 2. Establishing buy-in from across the company to address problems, while benefiting from the solutions we designed together.

Continuously leading and building, together; council cadence and communications

The 60+ Developer Relations Summit attendees left the day with a new feeling of solidarity and shared intent towards developers. More importantly, they knew who to turn to for best practices regarding developer interests and concerns within the company. We then began to collaborate together to co-create new initiatives and increase stakeholder buy-in for projects. How do you keep that kind of momentum going after just one workshop?

This was one of the questions we made a point to discuss during and after the Developer Relations Summit, and if you establish a Developer Relations Council along similar lines I strongly recommend you survey your participants to see what is best for your group. Other groups in other companies may decide to establish slightly different cadences and formats – for example, perhaps once per quarter in person for a half day to align with strategic planning and overall corporate realignment, or virtually, twice a month to account for large initiatives. For our Developer Relations Council, as the company is globally distributed and all participants wanted to stay updated in a live session rather than through an asynchronous or offline format, we agreed the next best steps were to have a monthly, hour-long council meeting session. A clear agenda is shared beforehand that participants can choose to attend, send delegates to attend or present, or watch the recording of the session after it is over. As the company is so large and geographically distributed, it is not feasible to repeat in-person sessions on anything more than possibly an annual basis. These meetings were to be held at specific times, so that everyone could make sure to book time to attend and come prepared with any questions. This format has been working since inception and in a recent survey with attendees, continues to be the best format for productive interaction.

Two weeks prior to our monthly Developer Relations Council session, we call for content from our attendees and curate specific topics that we think might be relevant for the group. The agenda usually starts with our team where we set the tone by presenting the latest relevant information such as results from our quarterly developer ecosystem surveys, or deliver a keynote preview for an upcoming developer conference. If there are larger initiatives that will consume more time, we provide additional sessions just on that topic, and if needed, call for topic-specific working groups. This segment of the session is usually followed by an update from one of the products in the portfolio that has relevant updates for others concerning developer relations – for example, Tableau's approach to hackathons, or a new developer center from Commerce Cloud. Questions are asked online via chat, or asked at the end of each segment by participants. This structure not only sets the tone for what we message to developers as a company, but also how we align on messaging with each other, share the latest news, and exchange tips on what might be most effective for developers in the industry.

Council challenges: content, churn, and communications

While I believe the model of the Developer Relations Council is solid for our business needs of effectively messaging to developer audiences as a unified Salesforce, there are some challenges. These can be described as content, churn, and communications.

The first, content, arises when the product content that the different product teams are making may not be the best fit with the developer audience. One example of this is when the content simply isn't perceived to be of relevance by these developers, who, as noted before, have little tolerance for vague benefit descriptions or lack of resources they can immediately "get their hands on" – that is, documentation or sample code. Oftentimes, in these cases, there are strong business needs to push the product and the related messaging out, so we need to advocate strongly while pushing against a high risk of poor message-audience fit. This risk of low fit coupled with the fact that the company is a highly matrixed organization, means that developer relations is not in a position to block release of content, but must instead register strong recommendations before release and record any results for reference in future initiatives.

Churn reflects the fact that Salesforce is a large company and, as with any company, there is a certain constant cadence of employee turnover, structural reorganization, and differences in product offerings. What this means in regards to the council is that different people may be different stakeholders for a given product at one time, and maintaining clarity of who these stakeholders are, and keeping these new stakeholders continuously invested in a council and its benefits, is a challenge. It can be challenging to assume that a specific set of people representing a certain set of products accurately reflects the current set of products. This is a challenge we continue to struggle with, and to help address that we are implementing recurring formal and informal surveys with our key stakeholders to ensure the right people are always in the loop. Another step we have taken is to open up attendance and participation to the Developer Relations Council to anyone in the company. Previously, there were venue constraints for the Developer Relations Summit planning and kickoff. As the council continues to evolve, "big tent" positioning is more productive, where all activities are internally public and all employees are encouraged to join, no matter what their role or product.

Communications is the final major challenge when it comes to the Developer Relations Council. As with every other large company, Salesforce is quite large and all the employees are quite busy. Keeping the large number of stakeholders we have updated with the latest relevant information and making sure they see what is best for them to use in their developer-oriented practice is a continuing challenge, and this is where we rely on the internal marketing aspect of developer marketing. We need to ensure that we have several communications channels active to reach out to internal stakeholders about our external communications at any given time. This includes channels such as email, Chatter - our platform tool for communication - Google Meet, and more.

Getting alignment for developer programs in your company: a final word

Moving forward with your initiatives in a large company for the benefit of developers has quite often been referred to as herding cats. Through this chapter, I hope you can learn from the actions we undertook and the lessons that we learned in our efforts to align messaging and form the Developer Relations Council. While overall it was great to get executive buy-in, a venue, and time for an in-person summit, one of the guiding lights throughout this exercise was a clear focus on our core values in the exercise - trust and collaboration - as well as agreement on related, high-level, strategic needs. Once you approach others in your company with this assumption of trust and building together, and couple it with the need to move in an aligned strategic direction, in this case, improving the experience of developers on our platform, the rest of the work is simply execution - organization, communication, and getting it done.

Special thanks to Andrea Trasatti who inspired the idea for this chapter.

Chapter 7 | Structuring Developer Relations

Dirk Primbs: Developer Relations Lead - Google

Introduction

Things were easier when I started my career at Microsoft's Developer Relations department, in September of 2001. I was an engineer by training and I had a passion for developer communities, so I became what the industry back then called a "developer evangelist". I only cared about my little technology bubble (distributed systems) and sharing knowledge with other developers. The team I joined had 8 members. One was a freshly hired marketing program manager, everyone else was an engineer, focusing on a few selected products.

We presented our knowledge on stages large and small and were on the road 3-5 days a week. When new products, such as Windows, Office and Visual Studio were released it was on us to do everything from answering support questions, hosting training, channeling partner questions, flagging bugs to our engineering team and everything in between.

Yes, things were easier. Whenever the question came up, "Who is responsible for X?" the answer very likely was, "What technology?" followed by, "Oh, that's me then!".

Of course the downsides were obvious as well. For starters, passing on sales leads was never our forté because we usually did not attend events based on their lead generation potential. We went wherever passionate developers were found. Decision makers were someplace else.

The next challenge was workload: We were busy. Always. In my first year as an evangelist I boarded 80 planes. And at the same time, there were teams like our consulting department that complained about us taking away their business, or teams like our partner group who fretted about our lack of alignment.

But there were two assets that always worked for us and made all the difference: we knew the ecosystem and the ecosystem trusted us.

After all, we didn't follow a sales agenda, instead we brought gifts and knowledge and were known to participate at all levels of discussion.

Famously, developers were the strategic focus at Microsoft, and our team was expected to grow and integrate into the wider organization. We became audience-centric and a breadth team, a depth team, a marketing team and a partner sales team were founded in addition. We were told that, instead of specific products, our focus should be on *who* we worked with. What was lost was our focus on technology. Suddenly we were responsible for a broad range of technologies and it was the type of engagement that mattered in selecting our activities. Our two assets of course stayed the same, largely. But what suffered was our technical edge.

This was the first of 5 reorganizations that I participated in at Microsoft, and every one had a different theme. But the most interesting one was the last in the cycle. Just before I had decided to move on to Google, another tech giant with its own growing developer relations effort, Microsoft decided to move engineers into separate product centric groups that focused on developer relations from a product perspective. Full circle!

By then I had started an online degree in business science and reading the theories of Mintzberg and G. Morgan's essay on organizational structures (check them out on Wikipedia for some further information). I decided to make developer relations within organizations the subject of my master thesis at the University of Liverpool, UK.

So let's start this chapter with the most basic question of all…

What is the definition of developer relations?

We have barely started with the chapter and here it is: The million dollar question! And since you're reading this, I bet you have an intuitive answer to this question. So what would it be?

Some are quick to answer: "Developer relations is what software companies call their marketing department." Others would beg to differ and insist that developer relations is a critical part of engineering and tech support. A third opinion may be that it is the role of developer relations to turn a technology platform into a viable platform business. But maybe they are all wrong and actually it is about selling technology products to engineers? Or is it all of the above?

The answer depends on the organization that asks the question, but one aspect is common: developers interact with products beyond their initial scope and build their own solutions. The ability to extend a product is what makes the difference between regular support, marketing or engineering groups on one hand and developer relations departments on the other. The moment developers start co-creating, they are not only customers but become participants and often partners, who are critical to the organization's success.

The result is a two-sided market. Such a market has two distinct user groups that provide each other with benefits and often allow for greater scale than regular product offerings. At Google, the Android platform is a very good example of such a market. Instead of being a standalone technology product, it is used and enhanced by developers who extend it by engineering products of their own. To the regular user, Android almost merges with these enhancements; it becomes infinitely more valuable as it is customizable to even the most exotic requirements. This allows Google to co-innovate with developers, and developers benefit from a scaling market opportunity and from technologies that work better together, unlocking scenarios that would otherwise be out of reach.

In such two-sided markets, developers are occasionally in the role of the customer and are marketed to, but more frequently it is not the marketing and potential sales that provides the scale. Instead, the providers need to offer the correct incentives and enabling technologies. Those providing the technology often depend on developers to provide feedback, use available resources and cooperate. What's more, developers are a creative force that make or break technology products, and it is a strategic imperative for a provider to understand the requirements and trends that emerge.

Companies that manage to co-create and strike a balance between listening and broadcasting are those that are at an advantage and will often benefit from the collective knowledge and innovation of an engineering force much greater than their own.

One can argue that good marketing is about close relationships with customers and developers could be framed as customers as well. While this holds some truth, there is a crucial aspect in most companies, if not all, that often keeps marketing-centric views from successfully embracing developers. Marketing is ultimately about products and about positioning those towards a customer base. But in order to collaborate with a community of volunteers and to co-create technology with them, the scope becomes much broader than this. After all, many tools, content pieces or activities in developer relations do not sell anything, and sometimes it isn't even about products but about entire technology strands. Furthermore, often developer relations creates tools that benefit the ecosystem, and with it maybe even competitors, knowing that developers expect a degree of flexibility and connectivity.

Developer relations is about bridging between heterogeneous developer communities and technology engineering inside the actual company and is the interface that allows for true collaboration.

Developer communities in a nutshell

I was one of those kids that grew up in the eighties with a home computer and parents that would have agreed with the statement: "Our kids grow up with all this stuff, it is native to them". "This stuff", of course, referred to anything electronic, including the video recorder and the answering machine, but what did I care? Everything that was programmable was mine to conquer, and when my father finally gave in and spent what was for him half a month's salary on a Sinclair ZX81, I finally arrived in nerd heaven.

I wanted to tinker, solve puzzles, control technology and, above all, to learn new things!

But there was a very real limit to how much you could learn on your own. There was no YouTube, barely any written tutorials and very few in our school with similar passions. In a nutshell it was the perfect genesis for our local little hacker club, which later formed the very core of a still active developer group in my former hometown.

It was in this hacker club that I received my community socialization and learned everything I needed to venture into the growing and fascinating world of technology. We would meet and develop projects together, sometimes we would just hang out, and on occasion we would help each other to solve puzzles and problems.

It is precisely this learning experience that drives literally every developer community out there. It starts with fascination, then evolves into a growing appetite for knowledge, but the final ingredient is always the fun of solving problems together and the joy of shared learning.

If you structure a developer relations department, these communities are your most important resource, partner and audience. There are two parameters that govern how you're likely to interact with them:

- The accessibility of your company's technology. Can hobbyists successfully master and use it to create value? Or do they need to be experienced engineers?

- Your business priority. As I'll discuss in the next section, it makes a huge difference whether you're in it for the few or for the masses. You also need to consider the stage your technology has reached. Are you introducing something brand new to the market or is it an established framework that already has a strong community?

Also a word of warning. It is very tempting to confuse developer communities with the type of activity they often enjoy. I've seen many cases where community builders look at the market and think if they just create enough events with developers in the audience, the result will ultimately be an active community just because active communities tend to organize a lot of events. But doing so means you confuse cause and effect. One may lead to the other but more often than not your so-called community will dry out as soon as your organization stops running these events.

Here we have a crucial difference between **developer marketing** and **developer relations**. The former creates a channel and tries to send information that hopefully leads to action to a defined audience. Developer relations, on the other hand, is about creating and growing social groups and their relationship with your business. And these groups are not bound by the events they show up at. They share an interest and a passion.

Here is something that may surprise you: In most cases this passion is not the technology. The passion almost all communities share is a passion for learning and teaching!

People who enjoy learning new things in company and love helping each other group together and form relationships. And these communities are generally much more scalable and have a better return on investment than groups that are only temporarily bound by an event series.

Why? Because these groups tend to contribute without your prompt, scale exponentially and often do so in a self-sustaining way. And they serve as a center of gravity for others.

Sharing the workload - roles and responsibilities

Most companies stumble into the world of developer relations without even noticing. It starts with the idea to add some API and extensibility to a product or share parts of the core platform. As soon as developers start working with it, requests start coming in.

- *Can you provide more documentation?*
- *We have this event, would you be willing to speak?*
- *I tried x and ran into problem y...*
- *How can I report a bug I found? Here is a sample that demonstrates what I mean...*

Depending on how technical the requests are and how deep the engineering ethos runs in the company it is then either a product manager or an engineer who will answer these requests and nurture the resulting relationships. Event invitations start coming in, customer evangelists emerge, cool projects and ideas from the community surface. This network and its interactions then forms the core of the future developer relations operation.

In the beginning it is probably a part-time role but very soon it'll become evident that there is a need for full engagement and the two unique roles are born that exist in almost every developer relations group:

- **Developer advocate or community manager**
  Developer advocates are normally engineers working part time or maybe even full time with external developer communities. Speaking at events, creating demonstrations, writing documentation or articles are all tasks that fall into this role's typical profile.

- **Developer relations program manager**
  As I wrote earlier, most companies start with either engineers or product managers as community contacts. Those who start with engineers will quickly discover that the model will not scale very well. There are only so many hours in the day where you can travel around, give presentations, hold events or write sample code. Sooner or later it will become necessary to scale. So sooner or later you'll either hire a program manager to support the advocate or the advocate will turn into a program manager and ask for another engineer to run the show…

Over the years I've seen many developer relations organizations, large and small. Interestingly, most companies tend to start with an emphasis on engineers and consequently run into a scalability challenge that leads them to hire program managers and form partnerships with marketing or sales eventually.

These internal partnerships (or additions to the organization) are critical because developer relations is often the main interface to the developer audience. As such it may be responsible for a variety of tasks which usually overlap with fields such as Support, Marketing or PR:

- Event organization

- Documentation (including sample code)

- Content creation (e.g. videos, walk-throughs, codelabs)

- Representation (in events, in PR settings, in media, as social media contact)
- Tech support
- Tech consulting
- Relationship management
- Engineering of bridge technologies (e.g. SDKs, Toolkits)
- ...

Generally organisations diversify as they grow. Developer relations departments typically start with a single engineer, followed by a "band of two" before they turn into a functional structure. Then a matrix is very common.

As the above list clearly demonstrates, in most companies there is more than just one organization working with developers. Often there is a technical support team, maybe the task of documenting APIs sits within the engineering teams, sales may have a few engineers that want to talk with selected developers too, etc.

Therefore the quite obvious question is: "Why have a developer relations department at all?" or alternatively: "Why not reduce overlap by concentrating said tasks in DevRel?". And the answer is in both cases to look at the work that is unique for developer relations:

- **Supporting communities** of learning and practice
- **Participating** in the developer ecosystem
- **"Growing the cake"** by supporting the larger developer ecosystem.

It turns out that these tasks tend to be long-term engagements and are on the surface contradicting the typical business requirement of short-term ROIs. We're talking essentially about relationship work and trust is the currency developer relations deals in. Trust is created by showing up, demonstrating real interest and by supporting people when they need support. A good friend once said it better than I could,

"Developer Sales and Developer Marketing is about what's good for us. Developer Relations is about what is good for them."

Relationships at scale

If you tried to reach every single developer in the world and if you'd define "developer" as those who regularly write or design source code for use in software products, then at the time of writing this text your activities would need to interact with roughly 20M developers (IDC).

Very few companies really have that aspiration or the resources. After all, this audience includes engineers who develop software for your car as well as those who animate a bunch of pixels on your phone. Some focus on web pages, others wrestle with distributed server infrastructures. It takes companies with an unusually broad scope to span all of these audiences, most of us will aspire to address a much narrower group. So it goes without saying that the true and tested tools of marketing that allow you to segment and understand your customers also help to identify motivations, segmentation and needs of your developer audience. In other words: Before you think about building or changing your developer relations team, understand their audience first. This effort starts of course with the developers but it should also include parties that work with your audience as well, like partner organizations, competitors, service offerings, trainers, event organizers etc.

You'll find yourself in relation to all those and you will likely need to support their growth as well. Healthy ecosystems grow as a whole and developers are often just one element in a bigger landscape.

Once your analysis is completed, it is time to map out the sizing and interaction depth that is required to work with the groups you identified. It depends on your ultimate goal of how these interactions will look. Is your product new to the market so you are in need of a committed and active group of early adopters? Then your mapping will include other players and tactics as if you'd map out your activities and audience for a product ecosystem that is established and where you, say, plan to introduce an architectural change. No matter what you consider when mapping your audience, don't forget to plan full circle. If you're only planning to reach developers but do not consider a way for them to channel their feedback, then you're considering only half of the equation.

But back to our exercise. From size and interaction depth you can derive a type of interaction. Generally there are three options:

- *1:few* (for instance, you know there are 10 key universities researching in your field of expertise and you plan to work with them)

- *1:many* (you want to interact with as many developers as you possibly can)

- 1:few:many.

If you look at your mapping and at the models, it is almost a matter of math to figure out how big your teams need to be and what to expect. These models scale in a linear way. If one partner manager can manage 10 partners, then 2 will manage 20. The same is true for *1:many*. The more people you reach, the less interaction you get. It becomes a one-way street. If you maintain a bidirectional mode, then you'll hit a glass ceiling and need to increase your resource investment. For every type of *1:many* programs you'll find a sweet spot, a compromise between investment and reach, and from there on you'll scale linearly with the need for more communication, events, content etc. Also, let's not forget that even for *1:many* programs we're talking about the relationships we aspire to form. This is why developer relations programs differ fundamentally in their scale dynamics from marketing programs, because human relationships cannot scale indefinitely.

The observations above are exactly why **communities** are such an attractive vehicle to scale developer relations. After all, we talk about a network of individuals that are passionate about collective learning and growth and communities tend to be active on their own because they often form around individuals who make organizing communities almost a lifestyle decision.

Hence, instead of working with each developer individually (and hitting the mentioned glass ceiling), **1:few:many** models focus on the multipliers in the relationship network.

There are three main types of *1:few:many* programs commonly found in the industry and they differ in objective but are similar in methodology:

- Communities - These programs are about scaling the kind of social groups that are also known as "communities of practice" (there's more about these on Wikipedia). Examples include Google and Mozilla's developer communities. Companies often aspire to form these groups but it turns out that those groups are much more sustainable when organic growth is fueled by adding resources like content and other support thoughtfully instead of building them artificially. The "few" in these programs are the community organizers and trainers, the "many" of course are the members.

- Influencers - Every technology space has its recognized experts and opinion leaders. You want to work with them, you want to listen to their feedback and keep them on your side! While this may feel like a *1:few* approach at first, it is important to recognize that these experts themselves reach many developers, often thousands, through articles, social media, PR work and so on.

- Partners - A healthy tech ecosystem forms scalability partners that allow your developers or customers to build solutions faster or better. Think about agencies that implement your technology stack in key accounts, consider trainers who make a living enabling others to skill up.

Look back to your analysis now - which audiences do you think need your direct management and do you need to scale in a linear or in an exponential way? Most developer relations teams will likely have a portfolio of programs. Google for instance is proud to have a high quality content production team that is constantly producing excellent video content, documentation and supporting materials. Of course this type of effort follows a *1:many* and has the advantage of reaching large numbers of developers. Contrast this with Google's partner programs where we help individual software companies to develop flagship solutions based on cutting edge technologies. You could see that as a clear *1:few* type of approach. Finally, we also run the world's largest developer community program GDG, (see sdata.me/qNiZNF) and an one-of-its-kind developer experts program (see sdata.me/pOYRxY), both of which literally reach millions of developers although we focus most of our work and attention on having really close relationships with the group organizers and the market experts specifically which are in comparison much lower in number and much easier to scale.

You can't have it all. Efficiency, agility or accessibility? Take your pick!

Large departments in big companies seem to restructure quite regularly, developer relations are no different and with the proverbial speed of the IT industry as a whole, organizations tend to move in even higher frequencies than in other sectors. I've been in developer relations for 18 years now and I can't remember a year when there was no organizational change affecting my team or the organization my team was a part of. Some of us even took pride in the number of manager changes or how many reorgs they outlasted. Often these changes are driven by necessity. A fast moving market, new products and growing silos are strong motivators to rethink what you're doing. Of course, sometimes it may simply be that the new manager demands a change.

Whatever the motivation for a change may be, once you've been through a few of them you'll realize that the themes repeat themselves, and after a while you may even be able to guess what major theme the next wave of changes will carry. On one hand the dimensions these changes circle between are defined by the type of business you're in, on the other they reflect the decision and control structure implemented in the company itself. Externally oriented teams may align with their company's portfolio today, base their structure to match their main customer segments tomorrow just to take a detour into a purely functional setup after that coming back to a product focus where the cycle begins anew. But while the external team keeps moving between these bases, the internal structure will be governed by different priorities such as information flow, decision making, reporting and control. With a growing organization these aspects become more important and get their own representation.

No matter the specific situation you find yourself in. Chances are very high that you structure around common principles as organisational models tend to fall into one of the following four categories. Most companies structure into mixed forms of these.

The table lists examples per category:

Functional	Audience-centric	Execution-centric	Product-centric
Advocacy/ Evangelism	University relations	Breadth outreach	Cloud team
Program coordination	Enterprise relations	Depth outreach	Backend team
Business development	Community relations	Marketing & communications	Database team
Audience marketing	Small & medium business relations		
Sales	Startup relations		

Each of these models has its strengths and weaknesses. For example, some models are better suited to interface as closely as possible with developers in the ecosystem but run the risk of friction when translating this into internal activities within the company. Or to use another dimension, we may group the models into those who are moving fast, but risk some double work or resource waste, while others are known for better efficiency. When should you pick what model? Aside from your internal motivations, new leadership, silos etc, your primary motivator should be your developers and the very nature of your technology platform. Let's take the broad space of cloud technologies as an example: assume you're Google, with a massive developer ecosystem, strong competitors and enough resources to live with some redundancy in exchange for better market fit and speed. Given all these factors, a structure that focuses on execution and understands the market by splitting it into segments based on your engagement type may give you what you need.

As a counter example, maybe you're starting a new product that has an initially small user base. Instead of working with the masses you'll need to focus on selected developers. Maybe this calls for a product-centric focus as it allows you to work closely with your internal product groups and allows for a better use of resources.

If you'd draw these models on a graph you could come up with a two-dimensional diagram where one axis is labeled external vs.

internal accessibility and the other marks efficiency vs. agility as opposite poles. When planning a developer relations organization this is a critical consideration. Do you need to be efficient or agile and is it your internal structure or the external ecosystem you're optimizing for?

A word about location

The name says it all. Developer relations is about **relationships** and relationships are built one way and one way only: through multiple in-person encounters that are used to build mutual trust. How do we build trust? By keeping promises and by staying in the game long term, not only just for the duration of a short transaction. So in other words, we'll need to bump into each other from time to time, have fun during those encounters, and we should all have skin in the game.

These factors are really hard to accomplish without at least some "boots on the ground". Much of the work a successful developer relations organization is involved in is about forming opportunities for interactions. Community summits, flagship events, roadshows and so on. These provide opportunities to "meet the gang". It goes without saying that in a world of global markets, multiple time zones, and diverse cultures, maintaining meaningful relationships becomes a strain if the team is too centralized.

When you build your developer relations team, location should therefore be an important consideration. Your advocates and your local community managers benefit a lot from shared cultural contexts and local networks. Yes, it is harder to manage distributed teams, but considering your organization by its relationships first means that you may need to invest in a local presence or otherwise in significant amounts of travel and late hours for those who are expected to emulate that presence.

On the other hand, distributed teams put strain on collaboration and decision-making structures within the company. This is why larger organizations tend to form hybrids with a strong headquarter team consisting of those who are focused on either support roles or on functions that can be executed independently, and a field organization with people who are present in cities and countries with the largest developer populations.

While this is often a very effective compromise I like to give a word of caution: make sure you include your field teams in central decision making and information exchange. Many headquarter-centric teams lose their connection to their developer facing teams due to time zone differences and communication habits. That will lead to additional friction, and potentially you'll start breaking promises your people gave to your communities, something you do not want because it will cost you the very thing you built this team for: your developer relationships.

Bringing it all together

As I mentioned earlier, it is a very simple world that most developer relations departments are born into. Your company is either focused on engineering-first or on marketing-first and you're likely to see engineers or program managers taking the lead initially. Because you're reading this, you have likely outgrown that stage, so the question becomes how to thoughtfully approach the task to form a successful developer relations team that can serve all your needs and grow your ecosystem.

Thankfully it is actually not that hard to map out the steps you have to take. From top to bottom:

1. Decide your product strategy. What type of developer interfaces do you have? Do you have an idea what an ideal developer engagement might look like? Do you want developers to work with you on your platform or rather extend it through defined APIs?

2. Map your ecosystem. What are the players? Who is your audience? What parts of it are easier for you to reach? Which elements do you want to see growing? What is the level of resourcing you're prepared to invest?

3. Now you should be able to identify a handful of key programs and their nature (*1:few*, *1:many*, *1:few:many*).

4. If your team is large enough, consider your local presence as an alternative to a large centralized team. If you can have both, then maybe a headquarter team with supporting functions and distributed smaller teams in key markets can provide efficiency gains.

5. Now structure your teams. You have four general ways to distribute work (functional, audience-centric, product-centric, execution-centric) but it is always a compromise between efficiency and agility and between external focus and internal alignment. When you did your mappings in steps 1 and 2 you'll have found some options present themselves as better than others.

6. Your developer relations department is neither marketing nor sales, so don't consider outreach or adoption as the main metrics! Instead consider those such as community activity, community growth and contributions to your platform. Why? Because relationships and trust in your community are not expressed immediately in money but in self-initiated activities. Your organization will make money from your work down the road but it is a long term investment, not a short-term transaction.

Chapter 8 | Repositioning Your Brand To Developers

Siddhartha Agarwal: Group Vice President, Product Management and Strategy – Oracle.

This chapter describes what Oracle has been doing to reach a new generation of developers. Our goal was to change the perception of our company in the eyes of software developers outside our traditional customer base, those who think of Oracle as an enterprise mission-critical software company, but not one that can help them build modern cloud native applications. We wanted to raise awareness of our cloud platform for building microservices, and container/serverless applications, our support of open-source projects, and our innovation in areas such as chatbots, artificial intelligence and blockchain. Our goal was for these developers to see Oracle's Cloud Platform as a rich canvas no matter what languages, databases, or tools they wanted to apply.

Our strategy included building a personal connection with developers via a series of intimate developer events around the world (branded Oracle Code). We have found that offering many, relatively small opportunities for engagement, and bringing content and connections to where the developers are working, affords us an effective way to engage and learn along the way. We also created a new online web portal focused on developer needs, created lots of content to provide continuous developer education, built an external champions community, and launched an innovative program for engaging developers at startups.

Introduction

If there is a general theme throughout this book, it is that the cloud era has changed the nature of software development, and developers face the twin challenges of creating new, cloud-native applications, and migrating existing applications to the cloud.

Developer organizations inside companies often go through their own evolution of cloud adoption. Among the first uses for the cloud is development and testing (dev/test) environments, which developers can license, provision, and use instantly without the bureaucracy, delays, or capital costs required for going through the IT department.

From there, developers use cloud resources for building more sophisticated applications, and experiment with new technologies, tapping into free trials, pay-as-you-go services, and vibrant idea-sharing communities, including lots of code sample sharing.

Once new applications are written for the cloud, companies often find it easy to bring those applications into production simply by expanding and scaling up those cloud resources, adding testing and security, and integrating those new cloud-native applications into their existing IT infrastructure.

Reaching a new generation of developers

Since its founding, Oracle has nurtured and supported Oracle database, Java and developer tools communities, via Oracle-led technical online forums, and community led online and offline engagement. There are also a range of initiatives around Java, which Oracle acquired along with Sun Microsystems in 2010, culminating in the annual, multi-day JavaOne event.

We realized that we needed to encourage developers to experience Oracle Cloud – especially those who had never worked with Oracle beyond using Java or Oracle Database. We needed a new approach to reach out directly to developers who are building cloud native API-first applications, and who are embracing containers, AI, and serverless computing.

The success of Oracle's cloud platform and infrastructure depends on these developers. The technologies they choose in development are the ones that de facto become the production environments on which their businesses are built. Oracle wanted to win the minds, and then the hearts, of these developers.

As one of the largest software companies, we may have no shortage of name recognition as a database, Java, and middleware company. However, in this cloud native era, our goal is to connect with developers who weren't already using Oracle products. We knew Oracle's traditional means of marketing, branding, and customer engagement would not work on these modern developers, who don't often respond to messaging that emphasizes ROI and discusses market share.

So the initiatives we pursued were all based on this understanding: developers are not like other individuals involved in product specification, evaluation, and purchasing. They must be engaged-with directly, with a free flow of information in both directions, and with opportunities to try the products.

Who we are

I lead the Global Developer Initiative for Oracle, in addition to Product Management and Strategy for the cloud platform, with responsibility for defining and executing strategy and revenue growth across cloud services for application development, mobile computing, chatbots, Internet of Things (IoT), API management, and integration. My team serves as the key leadership interface between engineering, sales, and marketing, and is responsible for driving Oracle's global developer engagement and ongoing relations. In my experience, a small core team of individuals are best equipped to define the direction of ongoing developer engagement, and to make rapid decisions to ensure that the engagements are successful. I put together a team of just five core cross-functional leaders to drive the developer marketing effort.

In past roles, including a previous stint with Oracle in the early 1990s, I've worked as a developer, founded companies as CTO/VP Engineering, and run sales and field operations in managed services, security, and application server companies. I know from experience the defining role developers play in deciding the fate of technologies – and technology companies.

The rest of this chapter will describe how we approached developer marketing through online and in-person engagements, and the lessons we learned in doing so.

Strategy for developer engagement

We knew very early on that successful engagement with modern developers required the following:

- Significant online content
- In-person engagements
- Quality free education
- An external champions community
- A program to engage developers at startups.

Ongoing online engagement

We created a lot of online content to demonstrate the value of cloud-native application development. We launched developer.oracle.com, a website designed to let developers jump right into the technology areas most of interest to them – from databases to chatbots – and get practical content including peer-written articles, hands-on labs and workshops, videos from sessions on the Oracle Code tour, code samples, and GitHub links.

The developer.oracle.com site is meant to reflect developer interests and trends, not replicate or replace Oracle product specification and documentation pages. Each technology page on developer.oracle.com is run by an Oracle developer community manager, who keeps the page fresh with the latest content and ideas from Oracle sources, product managers, and from around the web.

In addition, developer.oracle.com also has become a deep well of developer-focused video content, a lot of which sprung naturally from the Oracle Code event tour. By videotaping many Code sessions, Oracle created a steady stream of fresh thinking from experts around the world that developers could access online.

We also aggregated all the various Oracle blog sites targeted at developers, into a single Oracle Developers Blog, to allow Oracle technologists to communicate directly with the developer community about the latest trends and products.

Our community managers interviewed experts on site at Oracle Code events (which we explain later), streaming them live via Twitter and recording them for replay from developer.oracle.com. We also held three Code Online events in 2018 that drew inspiration from the live events, including the inclusion of non-Oracle speakers, who brought real-world use cases and peer-to-peer credibility to the attendees.

We also started sending out a monthly developer newsletter to stay in touch with the community on an ongoing basis. Like developer.oracle.com, the Developer Newsletter focuses not on product pitches, but instead on the issues and news developers care about, and it includes practical, actionable links to resources like workshops, and code samples, blogs and how-to videos.

Here are the lessons we learned about online marketing to developers, in some cases, through our own trial-and-error, and in other cases, from observing best practices from other software companies:

- Put everything online. Developers could be working at 2 pm or 2 am, and when they want something, they want it now. For example, you can't take a day to provision downloads of demonstration or trial software. If that developer is working at 2 am, he or she wants to try something now.

- Provide rich, constantly refreshed educational content, including articles, code samples, videos, how-to's, and structured classes, and make it easy to download them. Nothing says "cool" like having classes taught by experts in the field on the latest technology. Nothing says "old-school" like highlighting yesterday's buzzwords.

- Make it easy to find a community of like-minded developers with forums for questions and discussions. The whole industry has seen that the success of communities like Stack Overflow shows the best, most trusted experts are the developer's peers who have solved the exact same problem.

- Newsletters can add value, but only if they are true newsletters with technical content and links to new material. Faux newsletters that are nothing more than marketing pitches will not only fail, but can also backfire and leave a bad impression. We're careful to make sure that our outreach to developer includes how-to's, code, more code, and even more code.

- Embrace developers outside your ecosystem, and invite them inside the tent to provide feedback in exchange for early access to technology and events. Many of them, if impressed with your offerings, will help evangelize your brand and share their credibility with their fans and followers. It was new for us to put local developers on-stage at our Code roadshow events; at most Oracle events, the stage is dominated by Oracle executives and partners. While many developers are introverts and would never go on stage, others enjoy the limelight, and find it rewarding (and beneficial for their reputations) to present in front of their peers.

Continuous developer education

Oracle has always offered educational opportunities for its customers, and developers are no exception; we provide beginner, intermediate, and advanced-level courses that can be taken online. It's essential to allow developers to learn at their own pace, whether it's snacking on a quick lesson, or sitting down to attend a series of formal classes, with their employer's backing. We created a wide array of educational programs including:

- Non-product-oriented MOOCs (Massive Open Online Classes), which are taught on both fundamental and cutting-edge topics. Right off the bat, we offered MOOCs for free; we saw from other industry offerings that trying to turn MOOCs into a money-making business would be a turn-off for developers. Our goal isn't to make money from developers directly, and we don't want any barriers to learning from our experts. Rather, we want to embrace anyone who want to enroll in a MOOC, which takes a real commitment, since a typical MOOC runs over a period of weeks, and requires a 4-6 hour commitment to review videos and take quizzes. Adding to the incentives, certificates are given for those who pass the quizzes. For some attendees, those certificates may have value at their current or future employer.

- Product learning. We brand many of our product-oriented training and education sessions 'Oracle University'. Many of our Oracle University sessions are on developer topics, and with emphasis on the cloud, we're continuously expanding our new offerings with developer training on our cloud services. Oracle University classes can lead students to professional certification, which can be essential for career growth, and perhaps, lead to more trials of Oracle products by developers and their employers.

- Free trials and usage credits are powerful tools for developers – far better than webcasts or scripted demos – so they can try offerings in their own time, and on their own projects, either at home or at work. We are continually removing the friction that it takes for developers to sign up for online accounts and try software; we have learned that developers aren't patient with red tape or bureaucracy.

Engaging with startups

Another step in the educational direction are customer startup accelerators. Providing resources to developers working at startups can be essential for their success, and, in-turn, provides precious product feedback from cutting-edge users. For example, if anything is unclear with an API or its documentation, or if an API needs additional functionality, we want to learn about it sooner rather than later. Developers working in startups tend to push the envelope on using cloud services, and are not shy about providing feedback and new-feature requests.

Such programs are expensive to create and operate, but can lead to deep and lasting relationships with creative, growing companies. Oracle currently offers two accelerator programs, which are unusual in the industry in that our company does not take an equity stake:

- Oracle Startup Cloud Accelerator is a residential program enabling early to later-stage startups with a hands-on and immersive six month program. It includes co-working space, credits for technology services, mentoring, and – perhaps most important for these nascent companies – access to some of Oracle's enterprise customers, and its global partner network and investors. Our accelerator is sited in nine cities around the world, from Austin to Bangalore to Sao Paulo.

- Oracle Scaleup Ecosystem is a nonresidential, virtual-style program designed for mature startups and venture capital and private equity portfolio companies to enable rapid growth and scale. This is a newer program for Oracle.

External champions community

It's critical to engage external communities to communicate with developers on your behalf. This provides access to new audiences, and leverages the authority and credibility of partners. For example, in 2017 we launched the Developer Champion advocacy program, to complement the existing Java Champion program. Developer Champions are not Oracle employees, and are, for example, contributing to our open source projects, or are authors on contemporary development approaches, or speakers at prominent Oracle and top industry conferences. Developer Champions (like our Java Champions) enjoy a close relationship with Oracle, and often evangelize our initiatives to the broader developer community and ecosystem.

Oracle code events

Oracle put live events at the center of the developer engagement initiative so that developers could build a personal relationship with each other and with Oracle, and us with them. We created a new global program of dozens of intimate developer events, called Oracle Code, around the world, to augment our large annual JavaOne developer conference in San Francisco. Offering many small opportunities for engagement – and meeting developers where they are – afforded the most effective, and affordable, way to engage. And it provided for rapid changes and iterative learning that let these events continuously improve as they progressed. The events have been essential for bringing together local developer communities, letting them share ideas, and giving them a place to get hands-on with Oracle technology. Thus was born Oracle Code: a series of free-to-attend, one-day events that would traverse the world, with 35 events popping up in 31 different cities in 17 months, from Buenos Aires to Bengaluru, from Chicago to Shenzhen to Paris.

The Code Events were unlike anything we had produced before. The team deliberately chose to create relatively small events, for us, with only 300 to 500 attendees at each.

One guiding principle of the Code events is that they would not be all about Oracle. The event team published a call-for-speakers for each and every Code event, giving local experts (and even our competitors) a chance to speak to their peers about their work. Many speakers shared insight on open source projects they're working on, showing how these innovations could be applied to enterprise development. That call-for-speakers meant there was no cookie-cutter agenda for these events. Instead, the sessions were shaped by the interests and expertise of the local development communities.

The Code events traveled the world from March 2017 through July 2018, passing through cities in Asia, Europe, North America, South America, and the Middle East. While each event was relatively small, with only a few hundred in-person attendees, the reach was huge, both from the live events and from the web, through streaming during the event and on-demand video afterwards. Overall, Oracle Code notched up more than 600,000 developer registrations, from more than 31 countries.

A related initiative is what we call Oracle Code @ Customer, where we create and produce Oracle Code events for specific customer accounts, as well as to top ISV partners and global systems integrators. These provide access to different developers, many of whom have not had previous contact with Oracle. Our goal is to ensure that the Oracle Code @ Customer events are as engaging, exciting, and effective as our broader road-trip events.

In some cases, the Code @ Customer events were requested by the customers (through their Oracle representatives) because they had a large number of developers who wanted to be trained, or because they had specific technology topics that needed to be addressed, such as specific competitive technology they were migrating away from, and embracing Oracle. We were happy to satisfy those requests! In the case of integrators, this allowed them to host or co-host developer events for their biggest customers (or prospects), and also allowed them to highlight their own capabilities, product lines, and service offerings. These proved to be very popular, and we believe successfully positioned both the integrator and Oracle as innovators in cloud development.

There were several ways that the one day Oracle Code events were different than traditional multi-day Oracle conferences – and all these changes were designed to fit developers' interests, improve the on-site experience, and provide diverse viewpoints and technical insights. We knew that developers don't want a heavy-handed marketing pitch. We wanted them to hear many voices, and we wanted to receive their input and hear their stories too.

There were 200+ speakers rotating through all the Code events in 2017 and 2018, and many were developers from local companies. This provided a local flavor and air of authenticity that a pure Oracle-based speaker roster couldn't deliver. For another, there was a tremendous emphasis on hands-on workshops, going far beyond what Oracle had tried in the past.

Knowing that developers often learn best by playing, the Oracle Code events offered ways to combine tech learning with tech fun. At some Code events, developers could take a coding challenge in game form of an adventure in deep space, complete with Star Wars-style lightsaber sound effects. Completing the mission – which involves shooting down an enemy spaceship, hacking into the enemy's database, and identifying the coordinates of the evil empire's reactor core – required using languages including Java, Python, PHP, and JavaScript.

The affinity of many developers for brewed beverages is legendary, and so the Code Events provided several fun ways to engage with delicious libations – from coffee to beer – while experiencing practical applications of cloud computing. We presented it as follows:

Got a few minutes to try the IoT Cloud Brewed Beer from a local microbrewery? Extend manufacturing processes and logistics operations quickly using data from connected devices. Tech behind the brew: IoT Production Monitoring, IoT Asset Monitoring, Big Data, Event Hub, Oracle JET.

Robots Rule with Cloud Chatbot Robot: Ask NAO the robot to do Tai Chi or ask "who brewed the beers"? So how does NAO do what it does? It uses the Intelligent Bot API on Oracle Mobile

Cloud Service to understand your command and responds back by speaking back to you.

What we learned about events

In planning Oracle Code, the events team needed to rethink a lot about the look-and-feel and type of events the company runs – which were quite different than our huge annual Oracle OpenWorld conference, or for our smaller events focused on executives or senior managers in vertical industries. From attending developer meetups and other conferences designed for developers, we knew that developer events should look different than buttoned-up C-level conferences, which affected not only the topics presented, but the nature of the speakers, and even the timing of the event, and its agenda.

The events team had to present a unified view across lots of cloud services to developers. It had to reassess the type and format in which we produced technical content, the type of people to recruit to our Developer Champion advocacy program, the user experience within our cloud trials, and the nurturing programs we used once developers engaged with us.

This also required changing the mindset of sales and field marketing teams, to not just invest in programs that generated immediate pipeline. This required explaining that realizing the benefits of developer-focused programs requires patience; it's unlikely to pay off in deals closed this quarter, or even next quarter, for developers who have never engaged with the company before.

After all, developers are not prospects. They are certainly influencers, and in some cases, they may have formal or informal sign-off on platform adoption. However, metaphorically speaking, you don't take developers out for a round of golf, and try to close the deal on the 18th hole. Instead, you give them knowledge, you give them tools, you give them trials, and you let them work with your products at their own pace, on their own projects, at their own time. Developers don't want slick marketing collateral; they want code that works.

They want to be their own judges of whether you're a market leader or a tech innovator, thank you very much. They don't care about analyst reports; they care what their peers are thinking and saying.

In addition, unlike many prospects, developers aren't contacting us because they are in a buying mode. (Many don't even have purchasing authority for enterprise software like ours.) Instead, the developers attended our in-person and online events because they were curious. Curious about meeting Oracle people, about learning about a giant company, about cutting-edge tech like AI and blockchain, about cloud services that might advance their business or career. They came to learn, not to buy – and not to be aggressively marketed at.

Once up-and-running, the pace of production for the Oracle Code events was grueling – in some stretches events came once per week, often many time zones removed from the previous event location. Fortunately, Oracle's management committed the resources, both at corporate and at the local level, to assist with marketing, promotion, logistics, and recruiting local sponsors and presenters.

Essential to successful software development are frequent project meetings and code reviews, and the team took that same practice to heart for Code events. There was a full debriefing, debugging, and learning review after each one to fine-tune the events, such as assessing which sessions really resonated with developers, which were 'meh', and which fell flat. There were some of each, and to roughly summarize: Developers don't like anything that's vague or fluffy. They want to see the product, not hear about it. They want to see the code and touch the code. They want to see the actual running platform, not screen shots in a slide deck. And they don't want to hear from anyone who isn't technical.

Oracle also continually refined how to reach developers who weren't already part of Oracle's developer ecosystem, and how those developers best wanted to engage with Oracle before, during, and after the event. We paid rigorous attention to detail in order to understand the broad content concerns, and also the small details that matter in building close connections. For example:

- Developers work late and don't want to be dragged out of bed for an 8 am keynote. While sessions at Oracle OpenWorld and other major tech-industry events often start that early, we saw that wouldn't work for this audience. The kickoff talks at the initial sessions were sparsely attended, despite great speakers, as attendees

136

straggled into the venue. We now begin the first presentation at 9 am, with much better results.

- On a personal level, I had to change. Initially, my appearance fit the corporate habitat I'm often in: sport coat, button-down shirt. I immediately realized this was not the best fit for this audience. But the t-shirt-and-jeans look wouldn't have been authentic for me either. After several iterations, I settled on slacks and a nice zip-up sweatshirt.

Each of the Oracle Code events turned out to have its own characteristics, and provided unique opportunities for the Oracle team to learn about the local developer community. For example:

- At the Austin event, we had a lot of excitement from the entire region's development community. Several attendees woke up early in the morning to make the 160 mile drive from Houston in order to attend the keynotes – and drove back the same day. Austin was one of the most engaged audiences of the first year. We saw engagement and enthusiasm very different than events located in the usual huge tech hub cities. It demonstrated why a road show model is great to build and connect with the developer community.

- Some things only work in specific locations or countries. At the recommendation of the local Oracle team, we often tried some experiences that sounded a bit odd at first to the people at headquarters – but really worked. One example of this came in India, where we set up a "selfie booth" where we had some of our advocates and speakers engage in technical discussions and take photos with attendees. It was amazingly popular – with a full queue all day even when technical sessions were running.

- Local events are a great way to discover hidden talent in your organization. Some of the local sales consultants who helped staff the demos turned out to be highly skilled and passionate about our products, and crafted ingenious new ways to connect with developers. One example came from a London staffer who helped us on the Internet-controlled CNC Router demonstration in 2017. The demo showed how to use a computer numerical control cutting machine to manipulate building materials. The employee went on to create some cool attendee demos that were showcased in San Francisco at Oracle OpenWorld later that year.

Some additional lessons we learned from the Code Events include:

- Smaller global events can be more successful than huge mega-events, because they allow for more engagement with diverse audiences who might not travel to the mega-event, especially those who aren't already customers but might be willing to spend a day kicking the tires.

- The logistics for a road trip can be significantly more complex than for a single annual developer conference. Even the process of choosing dates for visiting cities world-wide can be a challenge, avoid local holidays and other big events in those cities – and tying them together into a single trip that doesn't destroy your staff. It helps to have a local presence in the geographies considered for the events who can arrange venues, find well-respected local speakers, figure out what will be fun activities, and highlight local preferences.

- Some developers are serious and all-business. Others learn through coding contests and games. Some are extroverts who will engage with speakers; others will never look up from their laptops. Be prepared for all types of attendees.

- Keep the price low. "Free" is a good price. Many developers lack budgets for attending paid events, or for travel outside their city. One-day events also minimize time out of the office so are attractive to employers and employees alike.

- Pay attention to details: Good food, good coffee, plenty of cold drinks and snacks. Have a party, if that fits your style.

- Bring in many voices, going beyond your own experts. Have perhaps one-third to one-half the speakers be from your own company, the rest from local experts and partners.

- Leave the sales pitches at home. That's not what developers want to hear. Beyond a short introduction, developers don't want to hear from your sales or marketing staff. Keynotes should be from techies, not from marketers.

- Have a casual style. Developers wear jeans and T-shirts, not suits. Also decide how much you want to tailor the developer experience to the local market, compared to, say, having a uniform, American-style look-and-feel.

- Be authentic and honest. Developers have a keen sense about when they are being patronized, or if flaws in products or technology are covered up. To win their hearts and minds, be candid with them.

- Provide free access to demos or trials. Again, although they are vital influencers, developers don't have large budgets themselves. Particularly if they are not already your company's customers, do everything possible to give them access to the product – before, during, and after the live event.

Oracle is now considering the next moves for developer engagement events. With all the lessons of Oracle Code in hand, we're ready for the large-scale, multi-day developer event we initially held off on.

Overall learning and best practices

Developers are essential to the growth and long-term success of Oracle's cloud platform and infrastructure service business, and we will continue to broaden and deepen our engagement with this critical audience.

By putting the developer in charge, offering excellent content and treating developers according to their preferences, we have found a way to help developers discover our company's technology, the side that's relevant to their goals.

One final best practice: Relentlessly listen to developers both inside and outside the ecosystem, and inside and outside the company itself, to get the best view on your evolving audience. What developers want is constantly changing. And thus, engagement must always grow and evolve to meet developers' needs.

- Understand that developers don't like to be sold to, and need to be engaged, not pitched. Anything that's purely a marketing effort will fail.

- Get executive buy-in and support for developer engagement, from the highest level.

- Define a small core team (handful or less) that defines direction, incorporates input, and makes fast decisions, and most of all, isn't afraid to make changes in mid-stream.

- Engage online and in person. The key is back-and-forth engagement and continuous education – not presenting one-way marketing messages.

- Think big, and execute in small increments showing some value in each increment.

- A lot of small activities can be more effective for reaching diverse audiences, as well as allowing for rapid changes and iterative learning.

- And always remember to be authentic, open, and honest in your developer engagement.

Chapter 9 | Connecting Developers With Experts

Thomas Grassl: Vice President, Developer and Community Relations – SAP

When software developers using your platform or tools need answers or advice, you might think that your company would be able to provide the perfect resources for them. And you would be partially correct. While developers do seek guidance from their vendors, they often prefer to get information from their peers; meaning from your community, particularly from external developer experts within it.

Serving up expert access from your company's workforce alone won't be sufficient. You'll need to encourage a network that provides expert advice from external sources. In this chapter, we discuss the key elements of an expert developer program and describe how to attract evangelists, product managers, and other highly skilled and motivated developers to provide their expertise to the broader developer community. We will discuss how to find experts, how to position them within the community and how to reward them.

Introduction

Founded in 1972 by five developers, SAP is now a leading provider of business software. Initially focused upon on-premise solutions that covered everything from customer relationship management to enterprise resource planning, we have expanded into the cloud and technology space.

Whether installed locally, or enabled via the cloud, our solutions depend on the developers who implement, maintain, integrate and extend SAP software. Providing those developers with an expert network is essential. They need to be able to connect, to ask questions, to share information, and to give and seek feedback from SAP, and also each other. This information exchange explains why nearly 3 million developers visit our community every month to get the most from our solutions and their development efforts.

Fortunately for me, as the head of the company's developer and community relations organization, development is near and dear to my heart (pun fully intended).

I took on my role at SAP in 2012, but my expertise in development started long before that. I was a developer for years; I built development tools in C++ and worked with Java for Web Application development in the early days of the Internet. I still continue to develop to stay sharp.

In addition to development, I have covered other technical aspects, such as product management. I know how a developer works and thinks, which comes in handy when building and evolving the best possible channels for expert access.

Humility helps. As much as I know about development, I know there are experts who know more. Most developers recognize this truth, and while the very best may come to a community or expert group in hopes of spreading their knowledge (and building their reputations), they realize that these outlets can also teach them and make them more successful.

How to build a network of experts

Your network should be a good mix of internal and external developer experts, ranging from specialists to generalists, who act as educators and role models. They are positive representatives for your company and brand, but they aren't just

142

cheerleaders. They're professionals who can teach and influence developers who are using your software. Moreover, they're professionals whom the developers will actively seek out for input and collaboration. Providing access to these experts will be seen as a valuable service to community members. It's also valuable to the company providing the community, as members can provide real-time feedback about the company's products in terms of what works and what doesn't.

At first blush, building a group of experts and a community for developers may seem like a classic Catch-22. A community without experts cannot succeed, but a community cannot succeed, and draw experts, unless it already boasts experts in the first place. In reality though, all facets are equally important and must be executed in tandem. It's not a matter of build it and they will come. You must build something that gives a reason for developer experts to come. And participate. And stay. And return.

A vibrant community depends upon both attraction and interaction. It depends upon a diverse group of experts for that reason.

Finding experts within your company

Typically, your network of internal company experts splits into two categories:

One group will consist of **Developer Evangelists** who are most likely to sit directly within your developer relations team. They are often (if not always) developers themselves, and they possess first-hand experience with the broad range of solutions that outside developers use. Given their direct experience with diverse solutions, these evangelists can speak knowledgeably to developers about a variety of technical topics.

The second group comprises **Product Experts**. They are more specialized, yet still gifted at relating to developers. Internally, they are your product managers and product engineers. Their contributions come from their deep know-how in their product areas; offering up information and insights to developers who focus on their products.

Internally, it is easy to spot some prospects for your expert network because you'll know the rock stars in your product and developer relations departments. Peers speak highly of them. I'm talking about product managers and evangelists who show initiative and speak at internal company and department events, as well as at external conferences, sessions, gatherings, and other get-togethers that developers frequent. Many are active in social media, and you'll see them tweet (and get retweeted) about relevant subject matters – a good sign of a potential candidate who will act as a company expert publicly. They may already be participating in other types of communities or writing for relevant sites. For example, if you visit StackOverflow, you may see them answering and asking questions about the solutions your community covers. A pro tip: generally speaking, you should check StackOverflow regularly. Monitoring other communities and sites is a must for spotting experts and even for getting ideas for improving your own community.

Other potential developer experts within your company may not be as visible, or may need nurturing. A call for experts is a good place to start. Post and make announcements within your company. The people who reach out to you might not have the chops yet, but by contacting you, they have demonstrated drive and enthusiasm. You certainly won't need to worry so much about incentives. The motivation for many internal experts is a desire to further their careers. Getting their names out and being seen are great motivators for anyone seeking advancement. You can entice them further by providing support for them to engage with external customers and developers in focus groups. Invite them to speak at events and pay for their travel. This support goes a long way – both literally and figuratively.

If you'd like to give your internal experts additional status, consider putting together a formal group that employees can strive for. At SAP, we're launching SAP Technology Ambassadors. An offshoot of SAP Mentors (a group of external experts, explained in more detail in the next section), this initiative is limited to employees who can serve as true ambassadors: the crème de la crème who are the best company representatives and speakers for developer topics.

Whether new recruits or veterans, your internal experts will need coaching and training so they are consistent in their presentation. For example, you'll want to encourage them to be visible contributors within the community, and you'll want to prepare them to meet the expectations that you set. Start simple with a list of responsibilities and a code of conduct so the experts know what they should do (investing a certain number of hours per week answering questions about their topics for example) and how they should do it (appropriate behavior). Your internal experts can make great presenters for hands-on trainings and labs on the products they cover. In return, they get to interact with the external customers and learn more about them, their needs and their priorities.

A developer program builds your external network

Finding developer experts outside the company may be a little trickier, but you'll apply criteria similar to those applied to building your internal network. You'll spot external experts speaking at events, participating in other communities, and generally establishing themselves as professionals who are knowledgeable about your technology. External experts will typically fall into the specialized areas that are either related to your company's products, or to a specific domain. That's because experts tend to specialize themselves. Even those familiar with a variety of software experience will tend to feel most comfortable with a core set of solutions.

Your job is getting the attention of the external experts you spot and giving them a reason to share their expertise.

This is where your developer program comes into play. A program for evangelists, product managers, and other highly skilled and motivated developers – like a broader developer community – is a method for providing expert access. But whereas the community is open to all types of members (developers primarily, but certainly not limited to that audience), the developer program is, not surprisingly, geared to the developer audience.

To break things down even further, our developer program concentrates heavily on three areas: awareness, engagement, and adoption.

Awareness, as the name implies, makes developers aware of products. Engagement educates developers more deeply about these offerings. Adoption includes tools and content that developers require to build and implement solutions.

Some members of the developer program may specialize in one area – for example, evangelists are great at engagement, but the experts often straddle all areas. Take our SAP Mentors initiative, launched in 2007. The mentors are the best and the brightest developers from outside our company. They provide a valuable service by guiding other developers and offering feedback to SAP, and they're capable of addressing each phase of the developer program's progress (i.e., awareness, engagement, and adoption). More specifically, they collaborate with SAP on topics ranging from products and features to go-to-market efforts, general strategy, and partnering. In exchange for their participation, they receive access to SAP events, invitations to meetings about special topics, recognition in the community and at conferences, access to our executives, and swag (such as individualized SAP Mentors shirts).

We've capped the SAP Mentors at roughly one hundred participants, all of whom are highly recognized experts in their fields. Naturally, a developer program requires far more than that, so while you can use initiatives to highlight certain experts, you'll want an extensive network of outside professionals.

To encourage external experts to join your developer program, you should have a strong online presence, for example on social media. Use it to make a positive impression and highlight your community and your developer program. For example, in the online community, look for new members who have written their first blog post or have taken a stab at answering questions. Encourage them. Give them positive reinforcement. You could promote their post through your social channels and within the community itself.

Offline, you can find experts at events, introduce yourself, tell them a bit about your program, and explain why their expertise could be a boon to it. A little flattery never hurts.

As with your internal group, you can't expect to survive with one crop of outside experts. Even as you're bringing in experts, you should be prepping the next generation. An established name isn't a prerequisite for program participation. To be sure, it's beneficial if your target audience recognizes your experts, but don't be short-sighted. You want to be on the lookout for future talent too. Remember: No expert – even popular ones – started as an expert.

The developer community

Your developer community combines everything from online destinations to in-person activities. The former includes your own community site, but also extends to StackOverflow, LinkedIn, and any other site where your audience can share information. For SAP, in-person activities include SAP Inside Track events (where developers can network and learn) and local, informal meetups. We also support an activity called CodeJam, upon request from developers. We host these CodeJam events and provide an expert who can work with attendees to solve problems or work on coding together for a product.

A developer community provides a perfect channel for two-way communication with developers (who are also customers). Most developers seek communities where their peer members are not only company employees. They do, however, appreciate information from your internal experts, so I'm not suggesting that you exclude your employees from the community. Just make sure that they understand what your members expect, which shouldn't be a problem for your product managers and evangelists, who handle developer relations on a daily basis anyway.

Both a community and a developer program need focus, and focus comes from defining what they are. This may seem somewhat contradictory to what I noted earlier – emphasizing the need for a group of experts who cover a wide range of topics. But even a diverse group of experts requires a firm strategy for the program that gathers them together.

The importance of planning becomes evident when you connect the experts and the community. As you define the community, you'll find that you'll be defining the parameters for your experts as well. Your developer experts and community must complement each other. That's impossible if you define your community as a destination that provides areas of knowledge which don't match the talents and skills of your experts. This disparity would be disastrous.

With this in mind, consider how your experts should cover the complete range, from product specialists to evangelists with a broader base of knowledge. Your community should be equally comprehensive, but without getting too generic. Calling it a community for developers is a fairly broad statement. Does that mean developers can wander in and post about whatever they want, where they want? That invites chaos.

To help maintain order, we have established rules of engagement and moderation guidelines for our community site.

On top of that, our seasoned members may kindly call out simple questions from new visitors (ones the rookies might have been able to answer themselves via a basic search). Having a community that polices itself can cut down the noise, but you also need to appreciate the fine line between strict enforcement and lax policies. It's not always easy, and we continually look for the right approach that welcomes all members while also maintaining quality content.

We also maintain order through the structure of the site itself, which gives direction. Think of the community in terms of the areas of a developer's expertise. (This shouldn't be too hard, considering you're doing essentially the same thing for the experts in your developer program!) These areas could range from products to wider topics to industries to specific functionality. When developers join a community, they will be joining for different reasons. It's important to think out these reasons and map them to the topics that interest developers,- which, as you probably guessed, should also be fairly close to the topics that the experts in your developer program cover.

In a way, the term "community" is actually an umbrella for smaller groups who are devoted to one or some of the topics within the community, not to the entire community itself. We discovered the layout logic of this strategy early on by building spaces that served as sub-communities, an approach that eventually evolved into tagging content and topic areas.

I should add, however, that we have revisited the tagging concept, because tagging is not always conducive to the tribal feeling of a dedicated space. The advantage of tags is that it flattens the site in a way which simplifies navigation. The downside is the lack of centralized sections for topics where like-minded developers can connect and enjoy a one-stop location that aggregates all content related to their specific area of interest – not just tagged content such as blog posts, but also relevant tips, a list of experts who can provide additional guidance, a breakdown of all topic-specific news, and so on. In short, visitors need a section for each topic that makes information more accessible and easily consumable.

Defining the community isn't simply determining which topics belong in it, though. The topics are part of what the community is (a destination for information about x, y, z, etc.), but the definition also needs to cover what the community does, or more appropriately, what members do in it. If you think of the community as a grouping of forums, then each forum should offer an identical experience. Typically, this experience amounts to sections where people can ask questions, provide answers, blog, collaborate, make connections, and so on. Ideally, your product managers and outside experts should monitor the sections corresponding to their areas of specialization, while evangelists can keep an eye on the bigger picture, chiming in to discuss general development trends and similarly broad topics that might cross multiple products and industries.

As an aside, even if you limit your company's contributions to the community, you still gain a major benefit, as community Q&A can lower the burden on your support department.

With all of that in mind, you could define the developer community as a place where members can get and share information about the topics you've identified as most relevant to your audience, and that can be supported by your developer experts. However, information is another broad term. What information precisely?

A company must understand what the community needs, and what it wants from its experts. It's tempting to turn the community into a marketing tool to churn out company-generated messages. To some degree, this will be unavoidable. For example, your colleagues may want to post something promoting one of their upcoming webinars, an action that qualifies as marketing, and members will accept this content, as long as the webinar covers a topic of interest to them. But if the webinar strays from the area of interest, their comments will be less than kind.

The trick, then, is finding a balance, which is one of the many things we learned when we launched our community nearly 15 years ago as SAP Developer Network, which evolved into SAP Community Network and is now known simply as SAP Community.

And what of the content itself? As I noted above, a community can give a company an outlet for promoting their events and product release details that developers need to know. But most developers come to the community because they're stuck and they need questions answered quickly. Active members – the experts you want to draw and keep, and eventually introduce into your developer program – will keep an eye out for questions and jump in to answer. They may also blog about their areas of expertise, sharing knowledge that may answer questions before a developer even asks.

But why would the experts have an incentive to do any of that? They could be paying it forward by helping to educate developers in a way that they themselves were once educated. They might be doing it for their careers. Someone who is a recognized expert, especially a consultant, becomes a desirable service supplier. They might be doing it for the rewards (some of which I mentioned earlier, many of which I'll explain in more detail shortly).

And they might even do it to learn more themselves. Many experts will tell you that, when answering a complicated question or writing a blog post, they will research the topic more deeply and thereby expand their own expertise.

That should give you a sense of how to define the community: what it should cover, what it should provide, and how it should operate. It should also help you understand the motivations of why people participate. But I've not yet shed light on how you establish the community, so that developers will see it as a go-to destination for information and guidance, and so that experts will feel inclined to participate actively.

As I noted near the beginning of this chapter, these activities do not, nor should they, follow a set sequence, where step A gets you to B, B gets you to step C, and so on. Everything should happen in parallel. Even as you're laying the groundwork for a community: building out areas where members can ask and answer questions, publish blog posts, and collaborate and socialize; your internal experts should be involved and serving members. At the same time, you should be looking within and outside your company to bring in more traffic: increasing the number of developers using your resources when they are in need of answers and increasing the number of experts capable of providing the answers. Some cynics might dismiss this philosophy as attempting to build a plane while you're also trying to fly it. I would counter that no community is ever truly complete, and the actions required to build and maintain it are ongoing efforts. If you ever think your community is finished, then it is indeed finished: but not in the way you intended!

Rewards and recognition

Once you have an established base of developer experts and a mechanism for finding new ones for your program, then what? Make sure that your program gives the experts a sense of identity and purpose.

Your experts add up to a major component for your online community, but always remember that a community extends far beyond the online world. Community is everything, from informal get-togethers to formal events. You should encourage these, promote them, host them, and make participants feel welcome. If budget allows, help fund the events or offset costs so your experts can attend yours.

SAP TechEd is our biggest annual event for developers, in fact we host three SAP TechEd conferences each year in the autumn: one in the United States, one in India, and one in Europe. They provide our program with an excellent opportunity to give expert access on a global scale, and our product teams are particularly active in these intense sessions, bringing their knowledge directly to the attendees.

During SAP TechEd, we roll out the red carpet for our developer program members, the SAP Mentors. They have their own space on the show floor, they have their own special events, the SAP Mentors get free tickets to the event, they are given special speaking opportunities, and they even get front-row seats at the event's keynote. We make every effort we can to thank our experts and show appreciation for their efforts. Our Developer Heroes and Community Heroes place the names of exceptional contributors front and center, by introducing who they are and what they do and why that's important.

However, if we limited expert participation to SAP TechEd, we'd be missing out on a big chunk of the year. That's why we have other events: our internal experts hold SAP CodeJam events where they conduct hands-on sessions with developers. Our external experts hold SAP Inside Tracks (SITs) to give developers a deeper dive into topics. In all cases, the experts often conduct these sessions locally. Since SAP is a company with offices around the globe our internal and external experts come from many different countries. We truly do share our expertise around the world.

To handle these events successfully, your experts will require effective public speaking and teaching skills. The shy ones might limit themselves to the online community, but wherever possible, you'll want experts who can operate both online and in person. If they're comfortable standing in front of a room of developers, they'll likely be comfortable on camera as well. So if you have a YouTube channel, use it to interview your experts and promote the videos. You need to invest in support since it must look professional. At big events, we have a studio and we invite them in to discuss a topic, but alternatively, it can be a roving reporter at the event or an online interview, such as recording a video chat. Let them shine and show off their expertise. They'll appreciate the opportunity and you'll promote your community as a destination where visitors can benefit from the interviewees' expertise. The videos also provide yet another way to access experts. Our SAP CodeTalk series of interviews in our SAP Community channel on YouTube could give you some food for thought for shooting your own videos.

We also make sure to salute the community's efforts. For example, our popular Member of the Month feature shines a spotlight on up and coming community participants, to show our appreciation and encourage them to get more involved. We also have a system of badges and points that we have implemented in a gamification system which allows members to build their reputations.

Motivations for community participation are similar to motivations for participating in a program for experts. In both cases, the experts are volunteering to share, but they also understand that they'll be reaping benefits as well. It's no surprise then that a program for developer experts and a developer community fit together so nicely.

Lessons learned

I've established what goes into offering access to developer experts, but you're probably wondering where things can go awry. Beware hubris and deaf ears. Your program gathers experts with the expectation that developers will listen to them. You should listen to these experts as well!

In many ways, the experts know what developers need because they're developers themselves. You can provide the tools and support, such as the formal program and the various aspects of the developer community, but don't ever assume you have all the answers. Be willing to learn from your experts when they come to you with ideas to improve the community, the developer program, and so on. That doesn't mean you'll change and implement everything they ask for. But you must keep the channels of communication open so they can comment about the program and the community experience itself. If they don't think you're taking them seriously, they'll stop taking you seriously. And they'll drift away. Considering that you want developers to mimic the experts' behavior, you don't want your program participants to leave!

We learned from this mistake with our developer program and community. We're still learning. After introducing changes to the program that our most vocal experts didn't accept, we had to step back and re-evaluate. At the same time, we decided to overhaul aspects of our developer program to bring in new perspectives while giving our long-timers a chance to continue to contribute as alumni. This is important. You must scrutinize your program and community constantly, so that you don't fall behind future trends.

Looking forward

Speaking of future trends, you will likely have noticed that my advice about finding and nurturing experts, building community, etc, requires a lot of legwork. In the future, this work doesn't need to be so manual and nor should it be. AI and algorithms already exist to connect the dots for like-minded people – bringing together groups of people with similar tastes or pointing these people to things that might interest them (based on previous behavior). The same logic can be applied to experts and communities. With the right automated tools, you can more easily identify experts in specific fields and connect people more quickly to the content that might apply best to them.

Regardless of the approach: whether you set up tools to find experts or rely on good old-fashioned investigation or some combination of these, one thing is certain. Your developer program requires a solid base of experts and a bullpen of up-and-comers. You must find them, coach them, keep them. Your developer program and community, and all of your attempts to provide expert access, cannot succeed without them. So look for the experts within your company and outside of it, and never stop searching.

Chapter 10 | "Build It and They Will Come" May Not Work
Investing Early in Developer Success

Lori Fraleigh: Senior Director, Developer Relations – Samsung Electronics

In developer marketing, we invest a lot of time in attracting developers to our platforms and, in developer relations, we educate those developers about what they can do, and then help them build products. However, we do not always invest much energy in making sure that the products they build are successful. While developer marketing and developer relations are usually not part of a profit and loss calculation, the success of our communities often ties to revenue somewhere else in the company. Whether we get a direct cut of their revenue in an app store, or they make our base product appeal to a wider audience, we cannot thrive without them.

Introduction

In this chapter, I'll explain techniques to ensure your developers see a return on their investment. I'll describe both technical and marketing programs I've implemented at various companies along the way, and how we've recognized and mentored developers to help them achieve success.

Developers are my customers

Developers have been my customers for the duration of my career. I started my career as a software engineer building tools for other developers using embedded and real-time operating systems. I worked for many years in Developer Relations and Developer Marketing at Samsung, Intuit, Amazon/Lab126, Palm, and Motorola.

I joined Samsung in January of 2018 with three jobs: to co-lead the global Samsung Developer Program with my counterpart at HQ in Korea, to lead Developer Relations for North America, and to co-produce the annual Samsung Developer Conference.

I plunged into my new role and soon found some areas to achieve quick wins while I also built up the team. We launched new tools for developers, including the Cloud Device Farm, which allows developers to test their apps remotely on Samsung Galaxy phones. We merged two competing developer portals into one, and we also kicked off a series of Designer Day events, including engaging with design schools for the first time.

The Journey

Most marketing effort, especially at larger companies, tends to be reserved for large strategic partners. However, it pays to engage all types of developers, and in order to attract and retain smaller partners, indie developers, and even students, you have to show how your program helps them find success. I'll share some of the programs and tools we've created to help a range of different types of developers be more successful, as well as the ways we use to reach out to these audiences.

Best of Galaxy Store

During my first year at Samsung, we devised a program to recognize the top apps in Samsung's Galaxy Store and the developers who created them.

We picked winners based on the number of downloads, the quality of the app, and the user experience they delivered across five different categories:

- Best Theme
- Best Galaxy Watch Face
- Best Galaxy Watch App
- Best Android App
- Best Game.

To highlight the winners, at the 2018 Samsung Developer Conference (SDC), we announced the "Best of Galaxy Store" winners, who had produced the top content in our U.S store (although the developers could be from anywhere). Winners received a variety of benefits including:

- A physical award to show off to friends, family, and colleagues
- Recognition in a public ceremony at SDC
- Mention in a press release timed during SDC
- Banner promotions and other premium merchandising in the Galaxy Store
- "Best of" award badges and imagery for use in their own marketing channels and events
- Features in communications to Samsung Developer Program members including an interview-style blog post and social campaigns.

The most impactful benefits to developers are the press release and the promotions and merchandising in the store. For small companies and indie developers, being featured in a press release from Samsung, a top 10 global brand, is a huge win because it gives them immediate credibility. The promotions and merchandising in a store seen by millions of consumers provides a real opportunity to grow a business. For developers and designers of multiple pieces of content, especially watch faces and themes (content that allows the consumer to personalize their device), there is the chance to grow ongoing revenue streams as consumers return to buy more of their content in later months.

One of our winners is from Uruguay and their embassy in the US even picked up the news and shared it on social media! Another winner from Indonesia was featured in a variety of online news channels in his region, which also helped boost his reputation. These types of awards, and the various publicity for the authors and the content that results, reward the current developers and helps attract future developers. When new developers consider whether or not they should build with the platform, it helps to see that they too, can be successful.

We expect to grow the "Best of" program to recognize top content in even more categories and expand from the United States to many other countries.

Beyond Awards: Improving Sales

Outside of these awards, the team also focused their time on the top sellers that were generating the most revenue or were otherwise off to a strong start. We wanted to see how we could help our top indies get to the next level. We analyzed the performance of each seller on our app store. Many of our sellers have multiple pieces of content in the store, so we looked for patterns as to which of their content did better than others, how strong the app/content descriptions were, the quality of the screenshots, and any reviews that existed. We also explored how their content performed in different markets compared to the United States.

Based on our analysis, we provided developers with feedback over email and phone consultations on how we thought they could grow their business. We advised on how to improve their screenshots. We helped people rewrite their content descriptions, which can make a big difference for those who don't speak English as a native language. On average, the sellers who implemented our recommendations saw their revenue grow as much as 179%.

As an example, we observed that some developers and designers struggled to create good screenshots for the app detail page in the Galaxy Store. Not only were some of the images of poor quality, some of them were in visual formats that looked out of place next to the top watch faces. We knew we needed a more scalable approach from our pilot of working with the top sellers, which required individualized coaching and many back and forth conversations. The team brainstormed how we could turn our advice into a resource that would help many more developers. After several discussions, we settled on an approach. One of our developer evangelists created a Photoshop tool that exports all the screenshots a seller needs in the appropriate file formats and sizes. It also helps properly format an app icon and a cover image for the app store. We've seen thousands of downloads of this tool in only a few months.

Our top sellers also told us they weren't sure how their content showed up in other countries. When you use the Galaxy Store, you only see the content available in your own country. The Galaxy Store is available in more than one hundred countries around the world and not only will each country have their own most popular and trending lists, but each country has the capability to do their own promotions and merchandising to feature content that is relevant to their markets. A developer may be trending in the United States but be less popular in other countries. Cute, comic-style content may do well in Asia, but edgier graphics may perform better in Europe.

To assist developers with this problem, we enabled developers to view their content as it appears in multiple countries around the world. We had previously built a Cloud Device Farm that allowed developers to test their apps remotely on different members of the Galaxy S, Note, and Tab families. We devised a plan to enhance the Cloud Device Farm by obtaining SIM cards from other countries and dedicating devices to being remote Galaxy Store test devices. Developers could then launch the Galaxy Store as if they were actually in those countries, see how their app listing looked (had they localized everything correctly?) and also see what content was successful and promoted in those countries. This is because only some of the slots are controlled by an algorithm (top and trending categories are based on the most popular downloads within a given time period). But many slots are truly promotional – they may feature time-based content (Lunar New Year, Eid Al-Fitr, etc.), topical content (New Year's, Olympics, etc.), or content that region finds interesting to their consumers. It is useful and sometimes eye-opening for the developers to be aware of these regional variations and the opportunities they bring.

Likewise, developers in different geographies have different needs. My team spoke with a designer in Eastern Europe who was disabled. Life with a disability was different for him there than it would have been had he lived in the United States. It was almost impossible for him to find employment despite his talents as a designer. By publishing his designs on our app store as an indie designer, he was able to secure enough income to support himself. He didn't need to make millions – he just wanted to create something that others valued. He relished both the opportunity Samsung provided as well as the outreach and coaching we provided.

Seeing the success of small companies and individual developers and designers has been very rewarding for our team. If we look at content that allows consumers to customize their device, including themes and watch faces, most revenue does not come from large corporations. It comes from these smaller developers. Investing in them not only makes good business sense, but it increases the satisfaction of those working in developer marketing. They get to make a connection on a personal level, understand someone else's struggles and motivations, and make a difference in someone's life.

Building Skills and a Reputation

Sometimes developers value recognition as much as, or even more than, revenue. Being recognized as a top developer on your platform may help them land a future job. It can also be fun to show off your achievements. We are in the early stages of rolling out digital credentials to our developer and designer communities. We are awarding "badges" to developers for select achievements, like winning a "Best of Galaxy Store" award or to those that successfully publish content in our store. These badges can be shared on social media, included on LinkedIn profiles, and displayed on websites. Developers can showcase their achievements however suits them best. A side benefit for us is that more people will be exposed to our developer program and may choose to enroll.

As I mentioned earlier, when I came to Samsung, we started focusing on engaging with design schools as part of our outreach. Unlike other types of apps, building a theme or a watch face does not require an ongoing investment. We coordinated with design schools across the United States to come on campus and provide a workshop for students in graphic design curriculums. These students had already learned skills as part of their classes they could apply to building content for our consumers. They could choose to publish their content for free to build their online portfolio and reputation or choose to make it available for sale and start earning revenue. When you're in college, any income can mean the difference between instant ramen noodles or peanut butter and jelly and a night out with your friends. We also found these students to be some of our most eager and creative workshop attendees. There was nothing they couldn't achieve.

Pilot Programs

During my time at Intuit, a small business and financial software company, we ran several pilot programs to help our developers be more successful. Our business was different: rather than consumers paying for content that ranged from free to a few dollars, at Intuit, small businesses and accountants subscribed to SaaS applications for tens of dollars a month. To help customers evaluate whether or not a solution was right for them, most app developers offered a free 30 day trial.

Third-party developers build and integrate a variety of SaaS apps with QuickBooks that help small businesses (and their accountants) manage their finances. These apps include apps to run payroll, manage inventory, track time of hourly field workers, and invoice their clients. It is these developers we focused upon.

Initially, Intuit awarded (very) large cash prizes to teams that won our annual hackathon. While we definitely wanted to reward creativity and hard work, we 161ptimize that the cash didn't necessarily get invested into getting the app to market or ensure its long term success. So while we continued to run hackathons to raise awareness of our program, we moved the large cash prizes to a new program: the Small Business App Showdown. Developers were eligible to enter once they published their app on the QuickBooks App Store. Ten finalists were selected through a combination of industry votes, positive reviews on the app store, the number of their users, and the quality of the integration. These finalists then pitched live on stage at the annual QuickBooks Connect conference where the grand prize winner took home a $100K check. While the winner got cash to invest back into the business, all finalists received coaching to improve their app as well as a variety of promotional and merchandising opportunities with Intuit.

During the latter part of my tenure at Intuit, we produced a variety of other ways we could help developers be more successful once they published their app in the QuickBooks App Store. Why did we do this? We had data that showed that QuickBooks customers that used apps integrated with QuickBooks had a longer life-time value to us because they remained our customers longer, and so we received more revenue. While the developer group would never be a profit center, we were still impacting the company's bottom line.

We first focused on helping developers optimize their app card, which is their listing in the app store. It is the first thing a small business looks at to determine if the app could make it easier for them to run their business. The app card shouldn't describe every feature of the app. It should focus on describing the key benefits it provides the user and how it integrates with QuickBooks.

If you've been around developer relations long enough, you're probably familiar with the TTHW metric (which stands for 'time to hello world'). This is the amount of time it takes a brand new developer to get started with your platform/API/SDK and achieve the equivalent of `printf("Hello World!\n")`. We asked our third-party developers to focus on TTROI ("time to ROI") instead. How long did it take a small business to see real ROI after clicking on the "Get App Now" button in the QuickBooks App Store?

There were many factors that could affect TTROI. How much information do you collect about the user (and is it really necessary at the very beginning)? How many different configuration options do you have? Will the default settings work for most people? Are you able to get the information you need automatically from QuickBooks or are you asking the small business to enter information that is already there?

For small businesses, time is money. They are willing to try out apps that will automate manual work and save them time in the long run, but if they don't quickly see how the app will actually benefit them, they will bail and go back to the way they have always been running their business.

To help developers understand and address these priorities of small businesses, we posted best practices in a series of blog posts, included tips in our monthly newsletters, and delivered advice at our regional QuickBooks Connect conferences. For some of our top performing apps, we performed 1:1 consultations to give specific advice. We looked for apps that were already gaining some amount of traction with our customers and asked what we could do to help them be even more successful.

We then piloted contextual "ads" within QuickBooks itself. If we noticed the small business was manually doing the same thing over and over, we'd pop up a tip card asking if they'd like to automate that task and recommend a 3rd party app. Conversion rates for apps shown in these contextual ads were much higher than the general app store listings.

Looking Down the Line

When I was at Motorola during the early days of Android, every new handset we released had a new screen size, screen resolution, default orientation, or some other change that caused select apps to have issues. We weren't introducing bugs, *per se*, but it was the early days of Android. Google itself was still developing guidelines on how to write apps that worked across different form factors.

No one was happy when an app didn't work on a new handset. Customers were unhappy if their favorite app (remember Talking Tom Cat?) didn't work on their new device. Sales teams and carriers were unhappy if customers returned devices because apps didn't work. And third-party developers were unhappy if they got bad reviews in the app store for a problem they didn't even know could exist.

While we prepped technical material that explained how to write apps that could be easily adapted to a variety of form factors, we needed to do more to ensure developers were successful on Android and didn't put all their efforts into iOS. We took the 100 most popular apps and tested them ourselves on our new handsets before they were released. If we found an issue, we reached out to the developer, let them know, and provided them with 1:1 support to make changes before we shipped our handset. Investing this time up front resulted in both happy customers and grateful developers.

As there were more than 100 apps in the Android Market, we also created an online "App Validator". We needed to scale the process of app interoperability with devices and app validation. Developers could upload their Android app to this tool and we'd perform a number of automated checks. Developers would instantly get a report of any issues we found along with a link to information on how to address the issue. This free service made it easy for developers to check how their app might perform without having to buy multiple handsets from different carriers.

We also created the "App Accelerator Program". This allowed developers who had signed NDAs to get access to information about new devices before they shipped. They could even test their application live on a real device in a remote lab hosted by one of our partners.

All of these tools became even more important with the release of the Motorola Xoom, the first Android tablet. While Android best practices had evolved, they didn't cover the types of changes needed to best utilize the larger screen size of a 10 inch tablet. In addition to our free App Validator and App Accelerator Program, we introduced the MOTOREADY program. While this program did involve a fee, developers could have their apps tested by a leading quality assurance test lab on the Xoom and receive a detailed report. Apps that passed all the tests were then eligible for special merchandising opportunities.

I'm actually experiencing a bit of déjà vu at Samsung right now. We're releasing the Galaxy Fold, the first foldable Android device. Like the Xoom, it is the first device of its kind, and is introducing new concepts for developers to consider. We're working closely with developers to ensure their apps can provide consumers with a great experience on the Fold. We're providing best practices, access to live devices in remote labs ahead of the product ship date, and 1:1 support for select apps. We know that ensuring our developers are successful will guide our own success.

Best Practices

I hope you can see that depending on your situation, you may take different steps to help your developers be successful. You need to understand what motivates them. How do they define ROI? Is it revenue? Recognition? Learning new skills? Minimizing technical rework?

Don't just listen to your top partners. Call your top indie developers; find out what is working for them and what isn't. Personal connection leads to higher satisfaction for both your external developers and your employees. Use the feedback you get to change what your program offers and how other teams within your company operate. If developers aren't seeing ROI, they'll leave your ecosystem. If they leave, your company loses out on future revenue and on customer satisfaction.

Find developers that are seeing quick wins on your platform and coach them to achieve even more. Then find ways to turn that 1:1 coaching into scalable tools and programs that can reach your entire ecosystem.

One final piece of advice. Once you figure out what works for your company, share it! It will take some trial and error, but once you learn how you can help your developer community find success, tell that story. Show your community that you don't have to be a top 100 brand to succeed on your platform. You aren't the only developer advocates for your platform; those you make successful will be even stronger advocates.

Chapter 11 | Hands-On Labs For Effective Developer Relations

Larry McDonough: Director, Product Management – VMware
Joe Silvagi: Director, Customer Success – VMware

Throughout its journey, VMware has maintained a very strong relationship with IT admins, in much the same capacity as traditional platform companies maintain an ecosystem of application developers.

As the ancient Greek philosopher Heraclitus once said, "change is the only constant in life." IT admins change. Developers change. Oddly enough, their roles over the last few years have started to overlap. Developers are increasingly taking control of the infrastructure upon which their apps are built, tested, and deployed. Likewise, IT administrators are increasingly turning to scripting and coding the infrastructure they manage.

Technology is contributing to this convergence: agile software development methodologies have led to continuous integration and continuous deployment and the "DevOps" process. Other contributors include technologies like containers, Kubernetes, Serverless/Function as a Service (FaaS), microservices, and service mesh.

In this chapter, we will describe the VMware Hands-on Labs, which are virtual computing environments that grew out of the need to bring up a trial of VMware's product stack rapidly. While the Hands-on Labs originated as a means to help existing and potential customers experience and learn about VMware's products, they have expanded and brought value to the company in many ways that we didn't originally expect, such as making the learning process more engaging through gamification.

Background

VMware was formed in 1998 and is best known as a virtualization and cloud computing company. The company pioneered the virtualization of the x86 architecture, which led to a major disruption in the IT industry. With VMware's platform, customers can run and manage their corporate workloads on virtual machines which run on fewer real computers, cutting capital expenses, maintenance costs, staffing, and even electricity bills. Over the years, our company has expanded its virtualized compute infrastructure to include virtualized storage (vSAN) and more recently, virtualized networking (NSX).

Our company has had an evolving relationship with developers. VMware's very first product, VMware Workstation, was indeed targeted at traditional developers, giving them a way to build and test applications destined for multiple operating systems on a single machine. Later, the company's core products were primarily for IT admins but, after a number of acquisitions, VMware developed a Platform-as-a-Service (PaaS) business based on an open source project called Cloud Foundry which supported application deployment and lifecycle management. When VMware spun this business out in 2013, which became Pivotal, setting its sights back on the Infrastructure-as-a-Service (IaaS) layer, one could imagine that there wouldn't be much need for developer marketing anymore.

However, that has certainly not been the case and, in fact, the number of different developer personas has increased over time. This accelerated starting at the end of 2018 and throughout 2019 with the acquisitions of; Heptio, bringing more Kubernetes and container infrastructure developers;, Pivotal, bringing more modern application cloud developers; and Bitnami, accelerating the packaging and delivery of modern applications. These critical, developer-focused acquisitions, along with the integration of container management and Kubernetes directly within VMware's core product vSphere, have together renewed and accelerated our focus on developer marketing. A great example of this is VMware Tanzu, a portfolio of products and services that enable our customers to build, run, and manage container-based applications on Kubernetes.

The one thing that has remained constant throughout all this change is that developers continue to be increasingly influential in deciding which technologies their companies use. This raises a fundamental question for our company: how do we make a complex technology accessible and easy to learn?

In the rest of this chapter, we will discuss the Hands-on Labs technologies which provide an answer to this question, and much more.

What are VMware Hands-on Labs?

Our Hands-on Labs are virtual computing environments running in the cloud, paired with some training. They help developers and IT admins get our complex VMware platform up and running in minutes, acting as a technology showcase, and allowing users to explore it easily and effectively.

Hands-on Labs are one of the main attractions at VMworld US and Europe, but are also available online, with over 2,500 Hands-on Labs taken per day, adding up to over 1.5 million taken since 2013. 730,000 Hands-on Labs will be taken in 2020 alone, with over 600,000 active users around the globe. Each Hands-on Lab has, on average, 11 virtual machines, and users average 51 minutes per session.

The platform is perhaps one of the biggest drivers at our VMworld conferences, where admins and developers take the Hands-on Labs in preparation for their certification exams. Hands-on Labs have also helped to increase the effectiveness of our beta and early access programs, and we use a similar, but slightly different, labs platform to educate our global support organization, enabling them to replicate customer environments. We've even built a robust and profitable education business upon Hands-on Labs. It's been interesting to see how Hands-on Labs has evolved from a showcase, to a tool for education, and even a sales driver.

Throughout the rest of this chapter, we'll review some of the uses for Hands-on Labs and explore each of the ways they have benefited our marketing and outreach efforts. And lastly, we're not done finding ways to use Hands-on Labs to drive innovation and add value to our ecosystem. We'll take a peek at a new developer engagement framework that VMware has been rolling out and how Hands-on Labs play a role there too.

Enabling hardware certification testing and early access programs

Like operating system software, hypervisors and virtualization software require tight integration and testing with thousands of technology partners including OS vendors, SoC suppliers, GPU providers, storage solutions, networking, and security hardware and software. The complexity and necessity of certification testing for all these hardware and software products is intensive.

With software cycles getting shorter and faster, we had to find ways to get our products into the hands of our customers without waiting for certifications across thousands of different hardware types and configurations, which can take a lot of time. VMware uses Hands-on Labs to help customers experience and test early-access and beta versions of our products. For example, vSphere 6.0 was made available for a selected number of customers, in the hundreds, who wanted to test it and provide feedback more than six months prior to its release. The long lead time allowed the customers to determine if their hardware or software was going to work early on, with plenty of time for them to make changes in time for release. It also gave us time to fix critical bugs.

The Hands-on Labs offered customers an environment that looked like a complete data center with all the software and hardware they would expect to see. It came loaded with VMware's latest products so the customer could try out all the functions, explore the new features and, yes, find and report issues which we had missed. VMware engineers and product managers could access a specific Hands-on Lab and view the issue first hand. We could debug the product and apply a fix quickly and efficiently. This included serious bugs as well as minor issues that had work-arounds. This enabled us to release the product without having a fully tested and bulletproof upgrade and installation solution, since it all took place behind the scenes via the Hands-on Labs.

Using Hands-on Labs for early access and beta programs provided such tremendous value that we continued to expand the products we'd test and the number of customers we included. In the end, the biggest benefit of this program could be measured by the results. The number of issues reported from early access via the Hands-on Labs, by a few hundred customers, turned out to be equal to the number of issues reported later by the thousands of customers who used the standard release beta binaries.

Field engineering

The initial intent of Hands-on Labs was to introduce new products, allowing customers to see and touch the new technology. There was one particular product at VMware that pushed the Hands-on Labs to the next level.

VMware's network virtualization product, NSX, had no way to download a trial and required certain physical network settings. The Hands-on Labs were the only place to try the product. As the popularity of NSX grew, not only did the VMware field engineering teams need training, but customers also became interested in this training. While real networking hardware was not easy to come by, we could easily spin up and spin down our vPods–virtual contained labs–from a Hands-on Lab to provide training to the customers.

We would give each trainee a vPod to use for the duration of the course. If they broke it, they simply logged off and spun up a new one. They could work through the manuals that were developed as part of Hands-on Lab training or go off-course and do their own thing. The Hands-on Labs provided a fully functional environment that allowed them to do that. They could experiment and try out functions, all without the worry of having to rebuild it if they broke the system. It was as simple as logging off and back in again. In a complex virtual environment with lots of applications running, it is often a lot easier to start over than it is to figure out exactly what broke and then work out how to fix it.

We discovered that, if the customer did not initially have the hardware or time to dedicate to a full-scale proof of concept, the Hands-on Labs provided an alternative way to investigate the technology to the point they could see the value in scaling up to a trial. In some cases, we kept the vPods around for days, versus hours, to allow the customer to dig deeper into the technology.·

Driving VMware's education business

VMware's education team originally provided traditional, instructor-led classroom training, typically offered as a five-day course. While classroom instruction has many benefits to customers, such as direct access to the instructor, and the networking benefits of meeting other professionals, it also has drawbacks, such as getting travel approved, rearranging schedules, and spending time away from family.

When we decided to offer the courses online using self-paced Hands-on Labs, we weren't sure how customers would react. Since there isn't a live instructor, should the cost of the class be the same? However, because the instructional content was essentially the same, we decided to launch the service with the same price as the instructor-led course. We decided that customers would appreciate the savings they made by not having to travel and the extra time they were able to spend with online Hands-on Labs. Ultimately, customers found the pricing model to be highly acceptable.

Since the training was self-paced and could be taken whenever, and as often as the customer wanted, the only question we had to answer was what should be the duration of the Hands-on Lab? As we were providing access to real hardware and software infrastructure, we couldn't leave those resources tied up indefinitely.

We considered 30 days as an option, but when we launched the first online Hands-on Labs, we wanted to be more generous, so we settled on a 45-day duration. We got no pushback on this from customers. In fact, they loved the extra time they had to run through the training and they really liked the freedom of fitting it into their schedule. However, when we looked at the data, we found that most people were waiting until the back half of their 45-day window to complete the lab. They really didn't need that much time.

We now have two options for course duration – one is 30 days at a higher price point mainly targeting enterprise customers, and the other is 20 days targeting SMB and individual customers. We did some experimentation at 15 days at the SMB and individual price point, but after some analysis, we identified the optimal time to keep a lab active was 20 days. Any less than this stressed out the customer, and any more than this meant we were paying for lab resources that weren't being used. If a customer requested an extension, we granted it. In addition, we also introduced a subscription model where a customer can buy a number of user seats for a year. The "users" can then take as many classes that are available within our portfolio as they want within that 365-day duration. The subscription is also available at different price points for different customer segments.

A problem we encountered early on as we converted the instructor-led content to an online format, was that some of the content wasn't well suited for the Hands-on Lab format. We had to redesign the courseware for a Software-as-a-Service (SaaS) framework that allows students to keep moving through the content. Hands-on components could be assignment-driven, but other components of the instructor-led courseware had to be reworked, like video-content and demonstrations, simulations, and basic instructional content.

Our content development team within Education Services made all the content updates. The team has instructional designers and learning experts who consult with instructors, take student feedback, and analyze usage data to design courses. They are constantly improving the design. At the time of launch, our objective was to test the market with a modest investment in content change, and once we were convinced of the commercial feasibility, we made more investment in infrastructure and design to scale.

Once we reworked the content, growth and the success of the online labs skyrocketed. Within two years, the online Hands-on Labs were generating more than $10 million in revenue. Although our online classes are growing at a faster rate than our in-person classes year on year, the in-person classes remain our largest segment in actual numbers. We also optimized their cost by modularizing them and making them more infrastructure-efficient, automatically putting them to sleep to preserve resources when they're not being used and reconstituting them as needed.

We have also provided an alternative, hybrid-approach, for those who want it. Students of the instructor-led classes have the option to purchase a discounted Hands-on Lab version of their course. This allows them the ability to run through the content again once they get home in their own time. We're always looking for new ways to improve the education experience and are considering new features like Hands-on Labs "office hours" where students can ask questions to an instructor over chat.

Best practices

When building a lab of this nature, it is important to keep in mind the different use cases and product features a user might encounter when using the product. This allows the lab, and the effort that went into building it, to be of multiple uses including some we hadn't considered when it was initially built. The open nature of the environment is what made it so successful.

Promoting hands-on labs to the developer audience

To promote the Hands-on Labs, we use our Twitter account (https://sdata.me/BpgPkl) and blog (https://sdata.me/pLIYzW) as part of our online and physical multi-channel strategy. The Hands-on Labs are a core element to every major marketing event, both online and physical, for VMware. It is also integrated into all of the core VMware product pages as part of the evaluation experience.

Looking ahead: driving product innovation through Hands-on Labs

Today's developer is dealing with an ever-increasing list of complex, and often conflicting and overlapping technologies. Every year, there is more to master: new languages, development frameworks, coding methodologies, and platform topologies, such as cloud-native, 12-factor app development, SaaS, service-mesh, AR, VR, IoT, etc. There is a lot to learn. Developer research also shows us that developers are increasingly self-taught with different educational foundations, many without any formal computer science training.

How do today's developers find answers to the questions they seek? Where do they go? Some may go to Stack Overflow, but overwhelmingly, the developer's tool of choice is Google.

As a platform provider, it's imperative that we make sure the correct answers to common developer questions about our platform are found easily when they are Googled. This can be improved, although not solved, through diligent search engine optimization (SEO). Is this the best we can do? No.

Often, the search results developers receive are close, but not the best. Since software technology is changing very fast, and release cycles are very short – weekly is common, but some platforms update daily, or even hourly – Google results will prioritize the volume of hits for a particular search, its popularity, over the recency or newness of the search. Even as this improves, the real winner in this scenario is Google. Whether or not your developer finds the answers which they seek, Google finds out what your developers are looking for. We find this to be an undesirable side-effect of the "Google-is-your-best-developer-tool" mentality.

To improve the accuracy of the information our developers seek, and remove any non-contextually aware intermediary search engines, we've taken the approach of incorporating "Developer Centers" directly within our products. In order to achieve this, we started by building out all our developer resources as separate services, accessible through REST APIs, and then bundling them together in a Developer Center module, making it easy for product teams to make them available in their products.

The first two tools we created in this framework were API Explorer, for browsing APIs, and Sample Exchange, an open index of VMware and community-contributed sample code. We've also cross-referenced these services so they can be used in context. For instance, when a developer is browsing APIs, we have automatically linked and made accessible any associated code samples that use those APIs. The same is true for documentation and SDKs. A great example of this can be found in a post on the "VMware {code}" blog, titled "Enabling Developers in VMware Cloud on AWS", found at https://sdata.me/VnhNnC.

Now that we have this Developer Center framework in place and it's starting to show up in our products, we're exploring how to incorporate Hands-on Labs as a developer service to augment

API Explorer, code samples, SDKs, etc. We believe that developers benefit from having a working environment with all resources available to them where they can explore and try out APIs from within a pre-configured "Hello World" app. As with the other developer services, the Hands-on Labs service will be contextually linked to our other services as well. We're still exploring the best way to do this.

Ultimately, the purpose of all our developer outreach efforts is to make it easy for developers to quickly build and innovate on our platform, and we believe Hands-on Labs will continue to help us reach this goal.

Get your game on! (Chapter Update)

In 2019 we released VMware Odyssey™ as a new, exciting way for developers to learn about the VMware portfolio, challenge their skills, and showcase their expertise. By offering users a different way to evaluate VMware products through the addition of gamification features to the Hands-on Labs, we saw a 30% spike in engagement and a renewed excitement about the platform.

Odyssey's gamification aspect is powered by a fully automated game engine that was added to the lab environment to time and validate the completion of a task. Users seek to complete what we call *missions* – these are sets of steps designed to help developers and administrators pick the learning adventure of their choice and launch their career. A mission is a combination of traditional Hands-on Labs and an Odyssey lab.

Developers can take any VMware Odyssey Hands-on Labs to challenge their skills. The traditional lab manual is replaced with a list of tasks that will test users' knowledge and expertise of VMware products. Users who have taken an Odyssey lab have their results displayed in a global leaderboard for peer recognition and to add a fun, competitive aspect. The following quote from one VMworld attendee illustrates how this competitive aspect helped correlate their understanding of the product and encouraged them to try the product for the first time:

"The competition was great, but ultimately my highest point is the take back from the competition. *Being able to leverage labs like NSX-T. Not knowing anything about it, and now understanding it like the back of my hand solely because of this competition*." - VMware customer

It can help prepare developers and administrators to pass their accreditation exams and advance their careers. While the program is still in its early stages, we expect it to also help prepare them for their certifications. We've found that, by presenting the content in the form of missions and learning adventures associated with career paths, we've given our developer and admin audience a tangible, accessible, and fun way to strengthen and target their career growth where they want directly.

Odyssey can be used at corporate technology meet-ups, hackathons, and we will be releasing new "Capture the Flag"-style games in the near future. Odyssey is available online for all developers and administrators to use. In addition, we keep changing and advancing the Lab Missions and games, so developers and administrators can return, "play", and compete with their friends and colleagues.

For more information and to check these out yourself, please visit our website - http://odyssey.vmware.com

The authors would like to thank Pablo Roesch, Andrew Hald, Nidhish Mittal, Gordon O'Reilly and Sandy Visoso for their contributions to this chapter.

Chapter 12 | Growing Up By Scaling Down: How A Small Developer Event Can Make Big Impacts On Your Ecosystem

Luke Kilpatrick: Senior Developer Programs Manager – Atlassian
Neil Mansilla: Head of Developer Experience – Atlassian

At Atlassian, we take a multi-pronged approach to supporting our developer ecosystem, including methods that you're already familiar with, such as holding a general developers' conference, hosting an online hackathon, providing a dedicated online developer community forum, etc. In this chapter, you'll learn about another, unique approach we use to take developer engagement to a new level: an event program called App Week. We have found the program yields phenomenal results, including new apps and vendors launching on the Atlassian Marketplace, improved developer relations and a strong product/platform feedback loop, plus a healthier ecosystem overall, in spite of its compact size. While this program may not be a exact fit for the needs and stage of your business, we believe you'll come away with applicable tips for improving the outcomes of your developer events.

Introduction

"Having an open platform makes not a successful platform business, nor thousands of tinkering developers a healthy ecosystem."

Over the last decade, you can find countless examples of companies that opened up their APIs to the public in the hope of sparking innovation and creating business value, but who never realized those aspirations and ultimately ended by shutting them down. However, a handful of companies have managed to succeed with their open platform approach. While there are numerous factors that separate the successes from the failures, a very noticeable difference is in how the successful companies understand, cultivate, and invest in their developer ecosystems. Developer events such as Apple's WWDC, Google I/O, Salesforce TrailheaDX, and Twilio Signal are key examples of how companies are making significant investments in this area.

At Atlassian, events have also proven to be a critical part of cultivating an ecosystem, bringing together customers, developers, Marketplace vendors, solution partners, trainers, and more. In 2008, Atlassian held its first Atlas Camp developer conference. It was small and informal, comprising of around 80 people; these days, Atlas Camp attendance is capped at around 700 people. Atlassian's first customer conference, Atlassian Summit, was held in 2009, and had just a few hundred attendees, but more recently, it hosted around 5,000 attendees.

As Atlassian's ecosystem continued to grow, it needed to find a way to continue building a healthy developer ecosystem, remaining personal and responsive. Atlassian has committed to doing this by running a new series of developer events (in addition to Atlas Camp), and this chapter describes the thinking behind the strategy, the lessons learned, and recommended best practices from the company's Developer Experience (DevX) team. The team provides support for, and advocates on behalf of, all developers in the ecosystem and supports Atlassian's developer events, from helping to organize content and tracks to providing onsite developer support.

Note that this chapter is not about how to run developer events on a large scale, but rather, how and why to focus on the qualitative aspects of an effective developer event and how it benefits the health of the ecosystem.

Why do you need an ecosystem?

At Atlassian, the tone of our relationship with developers ("open by default") was set by the co-founders from very early on. From the start, customers were given access to our source code, allowing them to customize and extend the functionality of our software to their needs. After all, being open and sharing information are part of our company's core values. Between 2002, when the company started, and 2012, when we launched Marketplace, thousands of developers were building custom apps and integrations for Jira and Confluence. From our core company value of being open, an ecosystem was born.

We build tools for teams of all sizes – from startups to enterprises. Because our customer base is so broad, building features and solutions for every specific niche is impossible. One of the purposes of having an ecosystem is that it frees product development teams from having to develop features that address every niche use case.

A good product works hard to be an 80% solution. In other words, your main product should solve 80% of the customers' problem. The remaining 20% is where huge differentiation comes into play, and where an ecosystem can get your product to be the 100% solution for your customers. Your ecosystem may have experts in respective fields that can help to extend and custom-fit your product to the special needs of your customers.

Why do you need in-person events?

Hosting and attending in-person events can be quite expensive in terms of both time and money. With all of the advancements in online communications, including virtual meetings, webinars, and real-time chat, why do we still do them? Online tools can't quite top meeting people in real life, face-to-face, for making a personal connections, building empathy, and learning from one another. All of these are key factors for nurturing a balanced, healthy ecosystem.

Physically meeting someone establishes a personal connection that goes beyond the code, and beyond the business aspects. It engenders empathy – the ability to understand and share the feelings of another. If this feels all too personal and squishy – good, you're on the right track. Understanding the motivations, challenges, and tribulations of the developers in your ecosystem can help your company make better informed decisions, and vice versa.

As Atlas Camp grew into a larger developer conference, we felt that the scale was great for making announcements about new features, and for many attendees to learn about them, but it also became more difficult for people to build connections. While only a fraction of the size of WWDC or Google I/O, the depth of the connections, conversations, and learnings at Atlas Camp became increasingly diluted.

Learning with our developers has been a key part of how we've managed to grow and build trust in our ecosystem. Learnings between developers in the ecosystem through in-depth conversations have also played an important role in the maturation of our ecosystem. The Atlassian Ecosystem team felt an alternative, more intimate event was needed to create the opportunity for more two-way dialogue and meaningful human interactions. The solution we came up with was adding a new series of smaller-sized events called App Week.

What is Atlassian App Week?

App Week at its core is a focused work week, where Atlassian developers, product managers and business people from across our company come together with the developers, product managers and business people of our third party vendor community. App Weeks have the goal of helping our ecosystem developers to create new apps (or improve existing ones) based around a theme, supporting Atlassian's business goals. The event is purposely kept small and invite only, with a maximum of around 120 developers and 30-40 Atlassian staff to support them, a very low attendee:staff ratio. This ratio provides an accelerated path to success for our attendees as often the person you need to talk to the most about an API or feature is right there, ready to help.

Any ecosystem vendor can apply to attend an App Week. Details about an upcoming event are posted in our online developer community forums, newsletter, and blog. Vendors are selected to attend based on the theme and goals of the event. Staffing is also based on the same criteria.

App Week is different from a general developer conference in more ways than just being smaller in size. There are no content tracks – just a handful of short talks that are salient to the week's goal and theme delivered by Atlassian product managers and engineering leads, and in some cases third-party ecosystem developers. There are no sponsor booths with marketing collateral. The vast majority of the time is for engineers to work together to solve problems, and for dedicated 1:1 meetings where decision makers can discuss future plans and implementations.

The first App Week

The very first App Week (formerly named Connect Week) back in 2013 was held in Amsterdam, Netherlands, with a small group of about 40 people – 25 third-party developers and 15 Atlassian team members. This was held before the beta launch of Atlassian Connect, a framework for 3rd party developers to build apps for Atlassian Cloud products, including Jira, Confluence, and Bitbucket. A successful ecosystem of 3rd party developers was already established around our server-based (on premises) products, but the launch of our cloud products introduced a different app development and deployment model.

This first App Week was critical for the Atlassian development teams to learn which features the framework needed to allow developers to port their server-based apps over to cloud. Likewise, the third-party teams wanted to learn more about what Atlassian was doing before investing in the new cloud model.

The first event was a success in that it helped lay the groundwork for the Connect platform. But the conversion of these 3rd party server apps to cloud was just the start of a five-year long journey, which in the software world is almost a generation.

From the feedback gathered at the first App Week, and the subsequent feedback gathered during the beta period, Atlassian released version 1.0 of the Connect framework in March 2015.

The birth of the modern App Week

By late 2015, the Atlassian ecosystem team noticed a lack of high-quality, successful cloud apps in the Marketplace. A number of our top server app vendors told us about their problems developing on the cloud platform: the cloud framework and APIs didn't have all the features they needed, the addressable market

183

of customers on cloud wasn't large enough, building and managing multi-tenant apps was difficult, etc.

The framework feedback was not easy to act upon, as the Atlassian product teams were laser-focused on meeting customer needs with new features and functionality, and not on the ecosystem. Unlike server app development, where the developer has broader and lower level access to resources and components, developers had to work with more restrictive sets of APIs and UI integration components when building apps for cloud.

As Atlassian product teams shifted their focus to the ecosystem and making Connect framework improvements, we decided it was time to host another App Week. More than two years after the first App Week, the second event also took place in Amsterdam, Netherlands, with over twice the number of people – 90 in total, including 60 third-party ecosystem attendees (developers and product managers from 30 different companies) and 30 Atlassian team members. Our goal was to port as many of our top performing server apps as possible over to the cloud, which meant helping 3rd party developers to work with newly shipped Connect framework components, as well having our Atlassian product teams learn what else the ecosystem needed to be successful on the cloud platform.

By the end of the week, over 30 cloud app demos were presented by vendors, including 5 of the most popular apps on the server platform. The week also resulted in new features being created for the Connect framework. Within a month of the event, the number of cloud apps in our ecosystem increased by a third, including some of our most popular server apps, which became available for the first time in the cloud.

The success of App Week had a great impact on our next Atlas Camp developer conference in Barcelona, Spain, held in May 2016. The outcomes were highlighted in the keynote, including the progress on the 3rd party cloud apps and the new features on the Connect platform. It was absolutely clear that the direction of the ecosystem was being influenced from the discussions, learnings, and work being done at our developer events.

Trust in the ecosystem was being earned, and the attendees gave this Atlas Camp its highest rating ever.

App Week had proven to be incredibly valuable for both our ecosystem vendors and for Atlassian, so we ending up holding two more in 2016 – one in San Diego, California (August), and another in Sydney, Australia (December). Both events also yielded great results, with more apps expanding from server to cloud. In 2017, we brought App Week back to Amsterdam, Netherlands (March) and then to Austin, Texas (July). With each App Week, we continued to iterate and improve the experience, incorporating feedback from the ecosystem.

Evolving App Week

The event held in Austin, Texas (July 2017) was the sixth App Week we held. At all six events, the focus was primarily on cloud app development – helping vendors port apps from server to cloud, and improving the Connect framework. For the next App Week, we applied the same formula, but set out to accomplish a different goal.

In addition to server and cloud versions of our software, we also offer Data Center editions, which is like our server version but with support for active clustering for high-availability, redundancy, and performance. Large enterprise customers were happy to find a plethora of Marketplace server apps designated as Data Center Compatible. However, some apps were not performing well, or in some cases failing in large scale clustered deployments. The decision was made to launch a program to verify Data Center app readiness, with new requirements for apps and vendors to meet before an app can be designated as compatible with Data Center products. While all of that seems logical, making changes in the Marketplace can also result in serious financial impacts for some ecosystem vendors.

In the spirit of our company value, "Don't #@!% the customer" (DFTC), the theme of our next App Week was Data Center – a departure from our cloud objectives from the last 6 events. The first goal of this event was to help ecosystem developers understand how to make their apps work well in a clustered environment, dealing with complexities like long running tasks, cluster locks, memory usage, etc. The second goal was to learn what the ecosystem needed from us, such as testing tools, clear program requirements, etc. The App Week in Amsterdam, Netherlands (November 2017) was not only interesting in that it focused on Data Center, and not cloud, but also because it was very similar to the first App Week – where the conversations, feedback, and learning were more important than the coding.

For the next App Week, we took another bold turn with a user experience and design theme. Held in Key Largo, Florida (March 2018), the event included not just engineers and PMs, but designers from the ecosystem vendors and Atlassian. The spirit of learning and sharing was in full force at this App Week, and several serial attendees expressed their surprise and delight at how much value their teams got out of it.

App Week has been truly evolving throughout the years. With each iteration, we've evaluated the outcomes, and incorporated both external and internal feedback to make the next event even more effective.

Lessons learned

Hackathons that work

Many companies have the idea of "let's just add a hackathon to our user conference and see what happens!". Without clear goals and a strategy, what usually happens is a train wreck that lasts 12 to 48 hours, with developers solely focused on putting together a fancy or funny demo to take home a glittery prize. Most hackathon projects die shortly after the event, or worse, never make it beyond the presentation deck.

App Week is definitely not positioned as a hackathon – there is no competitive element. In fact, it's commonplace to find vendors helping each other by sharing knowledge, soliciting and providing feedback, or sometimes even getting heads down with code or APIs. Focusing the event on collaboration and working together, as opposed to a competition, has brought a level of trust into the ecosystem and helped foster a real sense of community. Fostering trust and cooperation provides long term benefits to the ecosystem that's worth more than any hackathon prize.

Hackathons done correctly can create great results – but they need a specific time, theme and challenge to achieve success and ROI. Atlassian is famous for ShipIt, an intra-company hackathon held quarterly, where the goal is unbridled innovation and fun. There have been a number of really amazing things to come out of ShipIt – from internal apps, Marketplace apps, to even full-fledged products, like Jira Service Desk.

Atlassian also runs a public online hackathon called Codegeist with very specific goals of bringing new apps into the Marketplace. It's held once a year, and runs between 2 and 3 months in length. For an app to even be considered for judging, it must be live on the Marketplace, meaning that the app has to fully pass through the Marketplace app review process. Compared to traditional hackathons, where the results often range from demoware to falling short of a minimum viable product, Codegeist is aimed at delivering fully baked apps, ready to serve customers. Even if an app doesn't win the contest, the real prize for the developer is having an app on the Marketplace with an opportunity to reach Atlassian customers.

Codegeist has a proven track record of driving success in the ecosystem and Marketplace. For example, the first-place winner of Codegiest in 2007 was an app called Checklists for Confluence. The app was built by a single developer start-up called Comalatech. Today, Comalatech is a multi-million dollar business, with over 40 employees around the world, and over a dozen apps on the Marketplace that have been installed by more than 10,000 customers. Many other top-grossing Marketplace vendors got their start by participating in Codegiest, including Easy Agile and Code Barrel.

Fun developer events start with great instructions

Accurate, well-maintained technical documentation is a must for developers to start engaging with your platform at an event. Getting started should be simple, and onboarding should be measured in minutes, not hours or days. It is frustrating for developers to waste half of their time at an event struggling to get their bearings on the table stakes, such as getting an environment setup and working with API authentication. If your docs are less than perfect or your platform is a bit more complex, provide quick-start guides, or starter packs (sample apps that are easy to grok and then build upon) that help developers accelerate.

Avoid the echo chamber

Every ecosystem has its shining stars – the vendors that generate the most revenue, or seem to be making the biggest investments. While their attendance is important, events should not be focused solely on those top vendors. We believe that having between 20-40% "new blood" is important. Doing so not only helps new ecosystem developers to accelerate their development and business growth, but it also helps expose a more diverse set of ideas and problems to your product and engineering teams. Growth is important in any ecosystem, and with a good balance of experience at your event, the attendees also help each other grow.

In the fall of 2016, a solo developer named Tim Clipsham applied to attend an App Week event we were planning for Sydney in December. At the time, he had built an app for Confluence Cloud, which sold decently enough for him to start considering leaving his day job at a national bank, and focusing on running his company, Good Software Co. We invited Tim to attend because he was showing promise as a small Marketplace vendor, and he also happened to be Sydney-based. At the event, Tim was incredibly productive, putting together a marketing plan, working on a brand redesign, and starting the journey of porting his cloud-based analytics app for Confluence Server. Since attending App Week in 2016, Good Software was recognized as the "Best New Vendor of the Year" at Atlassian Summit 2017 in San Jose, California, and has added several new people to the team.

Get your staff away from their desks (and their daily work)

In an effort to save on costs, companies often opt to hold developer events at venues close to where most of the supporting staff are located, such as their own office. This sounds like a great idea, saving money on travel and venue, and having a huge pool of talent to draw from to help support the event and the ecosystem vendors. What's not to like?

In our experience, we found that holding an event at or near the office lowered the quality and character of App Week. For example, App Week in Sydney (December 2016) was held in our office, close to where the Atlassian engineering team is based. While this seemed like an ideal situation, the irony was that staffing the event proved to be very difficult. Even though hundreds of Atlassian engineers were a stone's throw away, peeling them away from their regular work responsibilities proved to be a challenge.

It's best to hold your event off site, or in an office that is not the home base for the majority of the team that is staffing the event. While it does introduce more costs, it helps to significantly improve the quality of the event. Staff members can focus on supporting the event and meeting the attending ecosystem developers, rather than being pulled back to their desk or into other meetings. Ecosystem developers, who are also making significant investments to attend, appreciate the attention and reciprocal dedication being shown by your company.

Another benefit to holding the event at a remote venue is personal networking and socializing within the ecosystem. If the event takes place close to where your team members live, most of them will just go home for the day, which results in a missed opportunity for people to connect after the day ends. At App Week, each day ends at 5 pm sharp and is followed up with a scheduled happy hour nearby. With everyone away from home, we cluster together and connect as people, creating bonds, sharing stories, relaxing, and having fun. It's similar to being a freshman in college or away at summer camp – everyone is equally out of their element, and friendships are formed quickly. Holding your event at a single venue, with both hotel and event space, is ideal, but having folks stay at nearby hotels can also work. The key is socialization after the computers get put away.

Best practices

The App Week program has been incredibly successful and it works for Atlassian, but what best practices can we share for you to apply to your own developer events?

Skin in the game

Having your product development team buy in and commit to supporting the events, to the point that they're willing to invest a week of their time away from the office and day-to-day work, is of paramount importance. Having this support allows ecosystem developers to interface directly with product and engineering teams, who have the expertise to help them accelerate development. The other benefit is that it tightens up the feedback loop, helping your product team to better prioritize and manage their roadmap by having a sharper view on the value of requested features and the impact of bugs.

Set your theme

Next, establish a theme for the event. A theme helps set the tone for what the event is trying to accomplish. If you're asking for support from other internal teams, choosing a theme that aligns with their team or department goals is helpful. Themes also help your ecosystem vendors to justify their investment of attending your event. If a theme isn't well defined, then you're signaling to everyone that you're holding a general developer event. For example, the theme for the first few App Week events was "Build your server app for cloud." Later, we set themes that were more specific, such as "Data Center readiness" and "Experience design and performance."

Select your location

The next three things that matter for your event: location, location, location. Ideally, the event is held in a place that is convenient for your ecosystem developers to attend, taking into consideration their travel and lodging costs. Choosing a location that entices people to come is also helpful. It should come to no surprise that Amsterdam, San Diego, and Key Largo were very popular event locations. Lastly, try not to be drawn into holding your event at your office as a cost-saving measure. Do not underestimate the value of having your team members stick around, instead of driving home, so they are building connections with the ecosystem after the computers are put away.

Next, you need to source a venue that fits with your event. For App Week, we typically look for a minimum of 3 meeting rooms, but prefer 5 or more. The most important room to consider is the main meeting room, where you will hold your presentations, stand-ups, and demos. We have found both rounds and class room style layouts work best. Theater seating for demos is preferred, but the seating does not have to change. The other rooms provide a variety of work spaces away from the main room – quiet spaces where developers can code in peace, a restaurant-fashion setup room with multiple tables that seat a few people for small groups meetings, etc. If you can add extra rooms, a "boardroom" or small formal space is great for private group conversations, such as business and partnership development meetings. Lastly, if you're lucky with the weather, having outdoor space where people can work is also appreciated. Just be certain that the WiFi works out there!

Finding the right venue can be challenging. Create an RFP (request for proposal) with all of your event requirements. There are services that help craft RFPs and submit bids to event venues, like MeetingsBooker and Cvent. Many hotels in the US provide a free event space if you pay for a food and beverage minimum and a hotel room block. Based on booking patterns, we generally reserve a room block for about 40-50% of the attendees, and encourage everyone to book quickly for the best rates. We suggest negotiating flexibility with the hotel for expanding the block if there is demand.

Food for thought

For catering, morning coffee service is a requirement. If you have the budget, breakfast is also a nice touch, but optional. At App Week, having breakfast does help get most attendees downstairs and ready to go for the 9 am start. Lunch, on the other hand, is essential. You don't want to disrupt the flow of the event with everyone hunting and gathering for food in the middle of the day. Also, mix it up, and ensure there's food variety between the days. It's important to ensure that you cater for different dietary requirements. As for dinner, this is something we do not recommend you provide. There too many factors to consider, including preferences, dietary restrictions, group logistics, and costs. But more importantly, dinner is the perfect time for the everyone to go out and connect with one another. Make sure to provide a list of recommended local restaurants.

A/V and WiFi

Another logistical consideration are your audio visual needs. For presenting, you'll need a projector, a screen, and a lectern to hold the presenter's laptop or notes. Make sure you have HDMI, Mini DisplayPort, and USB-C adapters on hand, which should cover most contemporary laptops. You can save hundreds of dollars per day by shipping your own company projector rather than renting one. We have found the most success with handheld microphones over clip-on lavalier style mics. We recommend having two mics, one with a stand for the speaker on stage, and one for passing around the audience for asking questions.

This applies to any developer event, but with App Week it is even more critical – you need to provide fast and reliable WiFi. We've found that it's best to secure minimum bandwidth of 100 Mbps downstream, 25 Mbps upstream, and a high-capacity DHCP address pool. You should estimate at least 3 IP addresses per attendee to account for their laptop, mobile phone, and additional networked device (tablet, smart watch, etc.) The ecosystem developers, as well as the staff, are getting work done – pulling down repos, pushing code, running tests, as well as streaming music and video conferencing. We've all been to events with awful WiFi – it's asinine. Do not overlook the importance of good WiFi, and don't implicitly trust the venue sales person – talk to the person who manages the routers and access points.

Creating your goals

Establishing goals for your event is absolutely critical. Having well-defined goals helps you to get buy-in from stakeholders and makes it easier to measure success. Only with these measures will you know how to improve your event, and justify future investments in the program.

Some common goals for developer events include: creating awareness, collecting product and platform feedback, driving adoption, building trust, training developers to use your APIs, helping developers to improve how they market to your customers, etc.

For App Week, our goals center around driving adoption, building trust, and collecting feedback, therefore we keep the event small and more personal. For goals centered on developer awareness and acquisition, sponsoring or speaking at larger developer conferences might be more appropriate (i.e. AWS re:Invent, Pycon, TechCrunch Disrupt, etc.) For goals that focus on developer training or marketing, a larger format, general developer conference, like Atlas Camp or Salesforce's TrailheaDX, might be better suited. Make sure your goals and event type match up.

Tailoring your event to your goals is key in choosing the format, staffing and location – so establish your theme and goals early, as they'll help guide you toward making the right decisions along the way.

Measuring your outcomes

Setting goals is key, as is how to measure your progress against them. At Atlassian, we've historically used Net Promoter Score (NPS) as well as a few other metrics to establish the quality of the event. For App Week, NPS can be problematic due to its smaller size. Just 1 or 2 individual detractors can cause severe negative swings of 5 or more points. Starting at the Key Largo App Week (March 2018), we shifted to a "top 5 metric" where attendees rate the event on a scale of 1 to 5 – one being "poor" and five being "awesome." This provides us with a percentage based result which we find better reflects the quality of the event compared to NPS, and addresses the susceptibility of those enormous score swings.

Every App Week concludes with a demo session on the last day where all teams get to show what they've built, and share what they've learned. Demo day serves as a tangible target and motivator for the teams throughout the week. For measuring the outcomes of the demos, we suggest having two to three staff members give each presentation a basic grade. When a vendor's demo really shines, our Ecosystem Marketing team follows up to explore ways to help showcase their new app or new features. It's also important to follow up with the vendors that did not do so well throughout the week, and investigate why. These cases require a follow up by someone in developer relations, with the goal of learning what went wrong, and what you can do to improve the next event.

At the end of the event (after the demos are complete), surveys are sent out via email – one survey for all of the ecosystem vendors that attended, and one for staff members that supported the event. The survey data helps us to understand how the attendees felt about the event – what they loved, what could have been done better, and what they actually worked on and accomplished. In our closing remarks, we kindly ask everyone to fill out the survey, and send follow-up email reminders up to 5 days after the event. Collecting this data is of utmost importance, so don't be shy about asking them to fill out the survey.

Sharing with the company

After the event, it's great to share a recap with your company to highlight what was accomplished, what was learned, and provide recognition to your teammates for their support of the event.

Doing so helps the different departments and teams within your company understand and connect with what's happening in the ecosystem, and the value that it brings. At Atlassian, this would be an internal blog post, because that's just part of our culture. In fact, it's typical to find multiple recap posts from individuals that attended. But it can take any format that your company uses – email, newsletter, town hall presentation, etc.

After every App Week, we receive feedback from ecosystem vendors stating how they were able to accomplish in a week what would normally have taken several months or longer; or sharing their gratification for Atlassian's support of the event. And while that's wonderful to hear, it's twice as rewarding to hear our internal product and engineering team members comment on what they learned from the ecosystem developers; or how those lessons have influenced and inspired them to help improve the platform, and support the ecosystem.

Summary

Intimate developer events, when planned and executed well, can drive value across multiple dimensions. In addition to helping drive business objectives, small events also promote relationship building, trust, empathy, and learning, which are all key to building a well-balanced and thriving ecosystem. Starting with clearly defined goals, choosing the right style and format, and getting buy-in and participation from all key stakeholders, is essential. Measuring your outcomes, applying what you've learned, and evolving your efforts will only push your ecosystem strategy flywheel faster.

Chapter 13 | Behind The Scenes Of Great Developer Events

Katherine Miller: Lead, Cloud Developer Relations Events Program - Google

Events are a core part of many companies' developer marketing plans, and attending in-person activities are central to many developers' professional and personal experiences. Survey data shows, however, that they are considered by developers to be overfunded compared to other programs.

How can one reconcile budget priorities and investment in events with what is important to developers? The answer is relatively simple. Events can be a platform through which to directly connect developers to the experiences and program features they most value in an authentic and measurable manner. By focusing on training, access to experts, labs, and support, events are less entities unto themselves, and more concentrated, multi-program marketing campaigns.

This chapter will focus on how to successfully plan and execute developer events to raise awareness of highly valued tools and programs, optimizing their return on investment - not only in the eyes of finance - but also in the eyes of the developer audience.

Different events serve different purposes. For the purpose of this discussion, events may include:

- Marquee company-level or product-level events with thousands of attendees such as Google I/O, Dreamforce, or WWDC.

- Broad product area events and trade shows such as O'Reilly's Strata or Velocity events, which also attract attendees in the hundreds to low thousands, although may be smaller in scale than those above.

- Language or technology-specific shows such as Kubecon/CNCF, RubyConf, JavaOne.

- Community-driven events such as DevFests, DevOpsDays.

- Local meetups, which may involve tens to low hundreds of attendees.

The objectives and tactics discussed in this chapter apply generally across event types; if something is ideal for a particular type of event, it is called out specifically.

Introduction

According to SlashData's Q3 2017 Developer Benchmark Report, only 11% of respondents ranked Meetups as a top-five developer program feature; conferences and trade shows were lower still at 10%. Conferences and trade shows, however, were ranked highest in terms of budget priorities, and meetups were also a higher budget priority than they were of importance to developers.

On the other hand, activities such as training courses and certifications (36%), access to experts (22%) and hands-on labs (21%) were ranked in the top 5 by a higher percentage of respondents, and are often considered by developers to be the critical elements of meetups, conferences and trade shows.

Upon reviewing this data, should we as marketing professionals simply dismiss events? On the contrary, so long as we target events to be part of larger, focused marketing initiatives, we can use them effectively to build positive brand affinity, humanize companies, provide direct opportunities for networking and professional growth, and be significant sources of reusable content.

Why Events?

What is it about events that makes them a compelling tactic in the developer marketing toolkit? At their core, events play a key role in engaging with one's target audience because they present opportunities for attendees to:

- Connect with like-minded people from the host company or wider community

- Build relationships and network with one another

- Deliver meaningful, constructive product feedback.

Events can also inspire, drive awareness and adoption, and offer easily accessible training and support.

The impact of an event is easy to dismiss and difficult to measure, thereby doesn't have a demonstrable return on investment to match its level of budget prioritization. However, with thoughtfulness and carefully planned data collection integrated upfront, events can yield meaningful, measurable information.

My journey to developer marketing and events took me through a number of industries and roles. Through early career experiences, though, such as hosting prospective students at a dental school, networking with advertisers at a reception, or engaging with agency leadership about product strategy, I realized the business impact that comes from bringing people together to learn, build relationships, solve problems and gain trust.

This passion, and the opportunity to use years of sales, marketing and event experience across industries with a new audience, led me to Developer Marketing at Google. Since 2012, I've led multiple work streams for marquee events such as Google I/O and Google Cloud Next, and built out global developer social media efforts, including processes for incorporating social media into events. I currently lead the Cloud Developer Relations (DevRel) events program, which focuses on how to enable DevRel to most effectively use events to achieve its objectives.

The information shared in this chapter reflects what I have learned through my experiences. The ideas expressed are mine alone, and not those of Google or the other companies for which I have worked. Likewise, I am not promoting or endorsing any specific tools. Anything mentioned is from personal experience, and decisions should be made based on budget and individual assessment.

I owe much to my Developer Relations and Developer Marketing colleagues throughout the industry, who have nurtured my knowledge of and passion for the space, and whose wisdom and insight have helped inform my practice of developer event management, and the tips shared in this chapter.

Delivering valuable, scalable and repeatable events

On reflecting upon my own journey through developer events, paired with live-event social media conversations, press cycles, and post-event surveys, I've found that successful events (of any size) deliver content seen as deeply valuable to the audience. In addition, the "extended" elements which accompany them scale the reach of the programming to have even greater impact beyond the physical event. Below I'll review what I've observed has (or has not) worked, and why.

"Serve up deep technical content"

I hear this feedback from attendees consistently, no matter how many more demos are included or code samples shared. I once pressed a product management lead to articulate what "deep technical content" truly meant, and they reflected that the best technical sessions leave the average audience attendee understanding approximately 2/3 of the content. Ideally, they are engaged, see the opportunity, and understand the next steps, yet are challenged to head home and dig into something new and unfamiliar.

The steps taken to deliver this most successfully have included engaging Developer Relations experts (advocates, engineers and technical writers alike) to advise on content strategy early in the planning process. For example, give them the opportunity to select sessions and demos, and be deeply involved in the content creation. Their core roles focus on driving awareness, learning, adoption and feedback through accessible, user-friendly resources, such as technical demos, videos, articles, presentations, samples and getting started materials. These Developer Relations experts are thus uniquely placed to drive and influence an event's content strategy.

Connecting this back to valued developer programs, technical content at events may include multiple pedagogies, such as presentations, panels, and instructor-led training courses and certification. In addition - budget-depending - recording sessions at events has been a way to scalably create an extensive repository of instructional video content. For this to succeed, it's critical to have a strong production team, a robust content curation and promotion plan, and the ability to post videos live as quickly as possible once the sessions conclude.

Do not sell to developers

"Welcome to developer marketing. You cannot market to developers".

So how can we drive developers to use our company's technology without coming across as too "marketing-y" or "sales-y?" I've approached this in a number of different ways:

- **Creating physical space for authentic conversations** - whether it be a meet up lounge at a large event, or a booth at a trade show, the right space design can create the "hallway track." Different configurations invite audiences of varying levels of awareness and engagement:
    - demo stands and lightning talk spaces draw people into the space
    - hands on labs spaces encourage learning and Q&A
    - highboy tables welcome 1:few discussions
    - reconfigurable stools accommodate larger groups.

Learn how to design with consideration for physical accessibility, as well as how to achieve multiple goals in constrained spaces. It's critical to set clear priorities up front to ensure focused, accessible spaces.

- **Having experts available** - in addition to thoughtful space design, trust and authenticity can be accomplished by including technical experts in the planning and staffing of an event. While titles and roles may vary, success can be achieved by involving individuals who are willing and able to not only advocate on behalf of an organization, but also on behalf of the developer. In addition, commit to listening to, documenting and passing along constructive product feedback. This also satisfies the desire for access to experts.

Identifying people to work at an event can pose a challenge, particularly if it requires travel, if you are a lean organization, or if events are not part of the company culture. Confirm staffing commitment from relevant teams before deciding on the type and size of event to plan (there's nothing more stressful than scrambling for staff last minute. While this may be inevitable, the level of stress can be minimized with upfront commitments).

Request help from individuals enough in advance for them to arrange their schedules and book affordable travel. Don't assume that people attending the event for other reasons (such as speaking or customer meetings) will be able to cover staffing duties. Connecting events to greater developer program goals, ensuring there's a measurement plan, and positioning the work as core to one's job function can help mitigate these challenges. Another approach to this is running fewer, yet highly targeted events to optimize the availability of in-person resources.

Create meaningful ways for attendees to connect with one another

Standard practices for connecting may include receptions and "birds of a feather" gatherings with individuals of similar backgrounds and interests. While not particularly innovative on the surface, applying a standard and well-established approach has made a significant difference in their effectiveness. For "birds of a feather" engagements and other community-oriented activities, success has come when their promotion has been deeply integrated into the event website and comms strategy. Without this thoughtful integration, these activities may feel like an "add on," and may not be as successful due to lack of awareness.

At a reception, thoughtfulness on food and beverage queueing systems, seating arrangements, and choices makes people feel more welcome and relaxed. While many of the learnings may seem obvious, we can all reflect back on well-intentioned events that missed one or more of these best practices, and resulted in sub-par experiences.

Have enough food and drink stations so that people do not need to wait in long queues awkwardly holding a glass, swag, and small, precariously balanced plates (and missing out on valuable socialization time). Make it clear in the invitation whether a meal will be provided, or if it'll be appetizers or dessert only (this way people can plan any additional dining accordingly). Intersperse highboys with lower tables and chairs for both accessibility as well as to accommodate people who wish to move about or wish to enjoy a more leisurely conversation. Ensure that there is ample food (there's nothing worse than running out of food), and sufficient selections for people of all dietary needs (protip - ask for dietary needs in the RSVP! Endeavour to provide non-alcoholic options beyond water and soda - and if there are signature drinks, create one that is non-alcoholic).

When outdoors, planning ahead for potential extreme weather conditions allows for greater comfort. If it's in a season with greatly variable temperatures, incorporate shade into a space, as well as have throw blankets and heat lamps on hand. Is there a chance of precipitation? Consider a space that isn't fully outdoors. Have bug spray and sunscreen available. When indoors, think through whether it's a conversation-driven event or a free-flowing party, and plan music choices and volume accordingly, setting the right expectations and minimizing frustrations.

For any of these, show thoughtfulness to the small gestures. Personalized name tags that allow people to share their passions, group activities such as photo booths or photo walls or "How May I?" exercises, custom shirts or pins for people to proudly express their identities. These all go a long way towards driving connectivity and a sense of belonging. If planning events globally, collaborate with colleagues in that region to incorporate in gestures that best resonate with local audiences.

Be honest and targeted

It is easy to focus on the innovation angle, particularly for the potential impact of "magic moments" on brand and press. But what may be magic from a traditional brand perspective may seem gimmicky or inauthentic to developers (how many times have we all been told that something is too "marketing-y" or "sales-y?"). Developers don't just want a slide presentation. They want to see code, touch code and break code.

In many ways, then, the magic is in showing how the innovation presents opportunity and that the developers behind the technology are trustworthy, authentic and humble. For example, not overpromising on the experience, not being afraid to have things break on stage, and being OK with feedback. Success has come from demos that truly reflect how the technology works (even with its limitations). It also comes from sponsorship sizes that reflect the story ready to be told, and a focus on content and programming that match the audience.

Show commitment to diversity and inclusion

An imperative learning to highlight on the journey is to make diversity and inclusion planning core to the event planning. Having it as its own category of content or programming can come across as lip service and not true investment. The aim should be to "show" not "tell" the audience you are committed to being diverse and inclusive, and that your event just is that way inherently. By making an event (and by way of that, the tools and programs promoted within the event), accessible and inclusive, it will broaden the reach and impact of the experience.

Strategies I've seen be successful include:

- Attention to who is speaking, and action taken to seek out and encourage participation from a range of individuals, rather than waiting to see who submits a proposal, and shrugging off a lack of diversity if few are received from typically under-represented groups. Also, if you do reach out proactively, don't make it seem like you're reaching out because that person is an underrepresented minority (URM) (e.g. "we want more women at our conference so can you come and speak?"). Instead let them know that they are an expert in X subject and you would love to have them share their knowledge.

- Thoughtfulness around images in decks and other marketing materials. People want to see themselves, and don't want to see stereotypes, such as groups comprising just "brogrammers", exacerbated.

- Having a well-publicized code of conduct and an escalation path for attendees who are not treated properly at the event, such as Google's Event Community Guidelines and Anti-Harassment Policy sdata.me/sukUxE or the Salesforce Event Code of Conduct sdata.me/SmINbq.

- Developing a strong acquisition strategy to reach into under-represented communities, including through partnerships with other diversity-focused tech organizations, meet ups and training programs.

- Creating content that empowers speakers and attendees to share how they've successfully created diverse and inclusive environments. Focus on sharing solutions vs rant sessions about the state of diversity in the tech industry.

- Thoughtfulness around language used to promote activities, with attention paid to intersectionality. For example, do not list out all the possible URM groups you can think of in your marketing materials—website, social media pages, etc. You are bound to miss folks. Instead, let your audience know that your event/meetup is open and welcoming to everyone and discrimination will not be tolerated.

- Making people feel welcome through shirts in multiple sizes and cuts, pronoun stickers, and accessible, all-gender restrooms.

- Building out all spaces to make them accessible to all physical abilities, as well as including mother's rooms and prayer rooms.

- Ensuring social activities have a range of well-labeled food and drink options as well as activities for all interests and abilities.

The Best Practices

Now that we've reviewed the value of developer events, and what I've learned, I'll highlight a number of best practices that can be used to plan and execute high-value, measurable, inclusive experiences.

Know the audience

Whether it be through global developer research reports such as SlashData or bespoke projects, dive into the data. Have a strong foundation on the motivations, decision-making strategies, preferences and sentiments of your developer audience, and build the event narrative, strategy and plans around this knowledge.

Choose the right event strategy based on goals and resources

"Developer events" represents an extensive category of activities, from local meetups with tens or hundreds of attendees, up to marquee corporate events with tens of thousands.

Knowing that companies, organizations and teams will have varying goals, budgets and human resources, it's important to select the event type to match your objectives and constraints.

If your goal is to drive awareness and engagement in established gatherings of developers, then consider sponsoring relevant industry events, partner events, or trade shows.

Tips:

- Sponsorships can range from $1K for smaller events up to hundreds of thousands of dollars. In addition, most sponsorships will have an accompanying execution cost for things such as booth design and construction, swag, printing, and rentals. Depending on the number of staff needed, and the number of complimentary passes included in the sponsorship, you may also need to account for additional pass purchases. Budget in advance accordingly, and choose events selectively if your budget is limited.

- When prioritizing events, ask questions such as size and composition of the audience, whether your company has previously sponsored the event (and if so, if it was impactful), what post-event data will be provided as part of the sponsorship, whether the event aligns with key product announcements or stories, if it is minimally staffed, and if it has a code of conduct and commitment to diversity and inclusion.

- Aim for a sponsorship level that is commensurate with the size of your offering to the community. If you're new to the space, if your technology is not yet at parity with competitors, or if your offering hasn't changed from previous years, consider a presence that brings awareness and an opportunity to engage, but without overselling.

- Similarly, plan content that is appropriate for the stage the product or technology is in the adoption lifecycle, and that reinforces the availability of associated developer programs. For example, if people are not yet aware of your offering, focus on engaging lightning talks and demos, and have accompanying materials and swag branded with program information that reinforce how to learn more.

- If planning a physical presence, ensure the appropriate teams have committed to providing staff in advance. A good rule of thumb is to have a minimum of 2 technical staff per 10' x 10' space, and have them work half the show hours. So if a show floor is open for 8 hours a day, aim for a bare minimum of 4 technical staff total. Running labs or lightning talks in the space may require a slightly higher number. For events with a larger physical presence, also have an event manager on hand for space set up and troubleshooting. If an event manager is not available for all events, provide staff detailed instructions on setup, including onsite contacts for suppliers.

- If you're unable to guarantee the minimum number of staff, consider foregoing the physical space and select other items such as sponsored sessions, receptions or diversity lunches, which allow for engagement, but require fewer people to attend from your company.

- Ask in advance whether custom booth builds are allowed or required. If custom work is to be done, estimate workback time of at least 3 months. If not, adhere to the event's deadlines to avoid late fees and the suppliers running out of certain rental options.

If the goal is to reach communities where they're at, and at scale, then consider small sponsorships ($1K-$5K) for multiple events within a network of meetup groups (e.g. Google Developer group DevFests) or a series of topical events (e.g. DevOpsDays).

Tips:

- If budget and/or human resources are constrained, develop a "priority zero (P0)" and "priority one (P1)" list. Priority may be determined by criteria such as proximity to a company's office (and associated travel cost for staff/speakers), size of community, level of technical depth, how organized the community and its leadership are, whether there is a commitment to diversity. Commit to fund the P0, and if any events fall off the radar, and P1 events remain feasible, elevate.

- Ideally at least one person from the company should attend, whether it be a previous commitment through a selected paper, or to staff a small table. Having the brand represented on the site suggests a physical presence.

- "In-a-box" the physical presence with a tablecloth and pop-up banner, small and simple-yet-desired swag, such as stickers, and materials on relevant programs, which keeps the event on-brand, should add no more than a few hundred dollars to the cost, and is manageable for a single person to set up without an event manager.

- Measurement may be challenging, depending on how formal or informal the event. If attendee data is not part of the sponsorship, then use approximate swag distribution and online RSVPs (if public) as proxies for reach, and diligently document feedback captured via conversations. For the latter tactic, this may be accomplished through shared, collaborative docs or other internal bug tracking tools.

If the goal is to have a "tentpole" moment to focus press, analysts and customers, then consider a marquee company event or a product-specific conference.

Tips:

- Marquee events are big on budget and on human resources. Planning can take upwards of a year or more, especially to reserve ample space, select and onboard agencies, secure budget, and to get buy in from all necessary internal teams. You will need to work in particular with the product teams whose efforts will be highlighted, to ensure that the timing of the event properly aligns with release cycles and narratives.

- If the conferences will include regional editions, ensure that you document processes, content, demos, and project management trackers with reusability in mind so that regional marketing teams can execute independently. If it's not financially feasible to do regional events on one's own, consider extending the content and experiences through networks of developer communities.

If the goal is to build trust and credibility with strategic developers, then consider invitation-only summits.

Tips:

- High-touch summits at first glance are pricey for their size, although can deliver a high return-on-investment, so be thoughtful in who is invited, the exclusivity of the interactions and experiences, having any customer relationship tracking set up in advance, and ensuring that associated client teams (sales, partnerships, partner developer advocacy) are bought into the tracking and instructed on the processes.

Whatever your goal, an event is only as effective as its connection to a larger marketing plan and the post-event nurture strategy. Ensure that you're able to confidently answer questions such as:

- Are objectives clearly outlined, and can they be measured?

- Do the objectives ladder up to larger objectives around the product, technology or community?

- Do the tools and resources exist to follow up with leads, whether through client teams, email or both?

- Is there a post-event plan to "keep the lights on", such as a recap email, blog post series, event content amplification campaign (e.g. twice weekly tweets highlighting session recordings), or re-engagement via digital advertising?
- For the teams involved, does their post-event workload allow for the bandwidth to execute post-event activities?

If the resources do not exist to properly plan, staff and execute all phases of an event, including post-event, it's worth scaling back plans so that you are committed only to what you can fully deliver.

Map experiences back to well-known, well-established, highly valued developer programs

Events can be a conduit and focal point to promoting and accessing other developer programs. On the flip side, developer programs can provide substantial content and structure to the event's programming.

Do you have certification programs? Consider add-on trainings on day zero or after the event wraps for people to get certified. Request space at the event for people to come and ask questions and sign up for certification opportunities.

Do you provide hands-on labs? Create self-paced learning labs spaces on site. If you have the budget to provide equipment, consider doing so (especially if the output may need testing on mobile or Internet of Things devices). If not, "bring your own laptop" is OK, but should be well publicized both in advance and on site, and space and reliable Internet access are critical. For the latter, ensure that any account creation is simple, straightforward and doesn't involve a commitment to spend (such as entering a credit card).

Do you have budget for on-site video or podcast production? Develop a content strategy that not only creates content that developers can engage with virtually so as to feel part of the event, but is also informative and instructional outside the context of the event. Particularly for marquee events, there's such a concentration of company talent, try to make the most of this as budget and time allow. From a budget perspective, opting to do live streaming, session recording, onsite video creation (such as interviews), and potential upfront video production (such as videos for keynotes) may run in the upwards of hundreds of thousands of dollars for a multi-day, multi-track event.

Do you have ample space and staff? Build office hours, "birds of a feather," or app review sessions into the agenda as a way to provide discoverable access to experts and support resources. For office hours and app review sessions, pre-event registration may be worth considering (with the availability of a reliable activity registration system). However, if budget or tools do not allow for this, be sure to clearly communicate up front what the process will be for participating in such activities.

Don't leave goals and measurement until the end

Events should be purpose-driven, and choosing to do an event should automatically be associated with broader organizational goals (e.g. if, in Q2, one wishes to reach X Java developers, choosing to sponsor a particular event, and at a specific level, will help us reach a certain percentage of our goal).

From there, ensure that the tactics used have a way of being measured. This may include:

- Hosting labs or trainings, or delivering demos that can be tracked through analytics.

- Session and booth attendance data.

- Using social listening tools, such as Sysomos, Crimson Hexagon, or others vetted and approved by your company, to track reach, engagement and sentiment of specific social media conversations.

- Administering session-specific and post-event surveys, particularly when you're hosting the event (this may be more complex when sponsoring an event, depending on the host organization's policies on reaching out to their attendee list).

- Purchasing sponsorship elements that provide data, such as virtual bags and email marketing campaigns. Not only do they provide the upfront reach data, but when links are tagged, they can provide insight into actions taken from the clicks.

To document product feedback formally, it's critical to have an agreed collection method up front. This could be a shared collaboration document, internal bug tracking, or surveys administered as part of the space's experience. As a reminder, make sure you've adhered to your company's policies on survey administration in advance of the event.

Many of these methods are "upper funnel." By being diligent about creating analytics funnels and developer journeys, and using best practices around link tracking (whether it be through email marketing tools, UTM parameters in Google Analytics, or other digital measurement tools approved by your company), you can glean considerable useful information. For example: how many people have been reached, how they feel about the experience, what initial actions they take as a direct result of the event. From this you can deliver critical feedback to product organisations.

Have a good agency[1]

Depending on the size and type of event, and the available budget, some type of third-party agency support may be needed. This could include a digital shop to build a website, app or technical demos, or an event agency to build out the event space.

When reviewing agencies, consider factors such as:

- The shop's technical expertise (particularly for web, app and technical development).

- Their understanding of your company's brand, vision and the event's objectives.

- A clear sense of how they communicate on matters such as, timelines, documentation, budget, roles and responsibilities.

- Transparency around and agreement upon who will own the technology created (if applicable).

---

[1] also referred as 'shop'.

- If development will be done, adherence to your company's privacy and security requirements.

Budget ranges will vary substantially depending on the size and scope of the project (from tens of thousands to hundreds of thousands and beyond). Generally the cost of working with more experienced shops within the developer events and developer marketing space will be non-trivial (although they may also be more reliable partners). If budget is limited, prioritize using agencies for projects for which there is limited in-house expertise or bandwidth. For industry events and trade shows, limit custom booth design to the highest priority events; for others, consider investing in upfront asset design that can then be used for printing on brand backdrops for turn-key booths.

Choose desirable swag

Swag ('Stuff We All Get') can be used at events to raise awareness (placing company or program brand on a permanent object), sentiment (delight in receiving a gift), and engagement (an invitation to approach a staff member or an incentive to participate in an activity). Thoughtful, useful and unique items are valued by recipients. We've all seen queues on the expo floor for limited edition t-shirts, socks or plushies, or crowds for a device raffle, and to a degree, these are expected. Delightful items can help inspire your next brand ambassador. It's important that items are of reasonable quality and utility, and reflect the event organizer's understanding of the audience. My best source of ideas has come from within the Developer Relations team, and asking others what they see and receive at events.

Here are best practices for planning swag for events:

- Partner with reliable vendors, and understand what they do and do not provide (e.g. design, storage, shipping/logistics).

- Plan upfront as much as possible (order in bulk to save on costs).

- Understand internal brand approval processes, and ensure that logo usage is consistent with brand guidelines.

- Request samples, ideally with your company's brand so you can confirm that the vendor used the specs properly. Place samples in a public space to gather feedback from your team.

- Avoid gender-specific items, and if ordering clothing, select multiple cuts and a full range of sizes.

- Think through storage (Do you have enough on site? Can the vendor store?) and confirm an inventory management solution.

- Understand customs requirements and tracking methods, as well as what you're responsible for and what the vendor is managing.

- If the swag is something not available in all markets, work with the appropriate internal teams on approvals, communications and alternative items.

- Know the rules around giving items to government employees and other compliance issues.

- If the item is associated with a contest or raffle, follow your company's procedures around competitions (and plan well in advance for cycles of approvals).

Don't forget the details

In the end, it's often the little things that get overlooked and cause the biggest headaches. Here's a checklist of questions to ask for each event, knowing that depending on size and scope, they may not all be applicable, or may be owned by others (making it your role to confirm that the work is attended to):

- Do all relevant teams know your plans?

- Is there ample staffing from the right areas of expertise?

- Have all items from the sponsorship checklist been submitted?

- Have all rentals (AV, furniture) been placed by the deadline?

- Has any company-provided technology (e.g. laptops, tablets) been reserved?

- Has the right level of Internet connectivity been ordered?

- Has new content been prepared if needed?

- Have print orders been placed?

- Has swag been ordered?

- Have any legal or PR requests been submitted?

- Have deliveries been sent to arrive by the correct receiving deadlines?

- Have you created a "know before you go" to inform staff of the event plans?

- Has catering been ordered?

- Is there a social media strategy? Or a media strategy of any kind (video, photography, etc.)?

Get event experience

The beauty and challenge of managing developer events is that the best way to learn is through hands-on experience. If you are new to the practice of developer marketing or developer events planning, find opportunities to attend others' events, simply to listen, observe, and engage with attendees. Inquire within your company as to whether they'll allow you to attend a certain number of events each year for professional development (and if they'll fund your attendance). Join a local meetup group. Seek out internal projects for your company's developer events. Stay informed on the latest trends and sentiment by following influencers within developer communities on social media and by paying close attention to their thoughts on the events in which they participate.

Document what you learn, and incorporate the best of what you observe into your own common practices.

Balance innovation and opportunity

Technology companies are constantly pushing the boundaries of what's possible, and have the capacity to inspire developers to create game-changing applications and businesses with cutting edge tools and products. However, for many smaller companies, seeing examples of what larger companies have built may be aspirational, but not actionable.

Inspiration succeeds when it has an eye towards opportunity for the developer. Is the technology stable? Are there communities and resources available? Will this help to grow productivity, relevance in the job market, recognition, and success? These are the questions you need to answer to encourage attendees to engage and help them get the most from the experience.

Events, the programs they promote and resources they generate (such as labs, video content, follow up emails, and extended series of meetups), present focused opportunities. They can tell stories by building brand awareness and positive sentiment, and also drive momentum around other impactful developer tools and programs.

Conclusion

This guide is not exhaustive, and doesn't go into great detail around timelines, trackers, budgeting, creative briefs, or how to work effectively with cross-functional partners. What this guide represents is tips, best practices and perspectives gathered through personal experiences. If I leave you with anything, I hope it is that:

- Events can yield a strong return-on-investment, particularly when closely aligned with other highly-valued developer programs.

- Although developers "cannot be marketed to," there are ways to create magic moments, especially if you focus on trustworthy, authentic, deeply technical experiences.

- With thoughtfulness and upfront planning, diversity, inclusion and accessibility can be interwoven into the event, increasing satisfaction, trust and respect.

- It is important that you don't underestimate the importance of budget and human resources in planning and executing events, including the post-event work cycle.

Good luck, have fun, and deliver impact!

Chapter 14 | How To Connect With Developers When You Can't Meet Them

Pablo Fraile: Director of Developer Ecosystems – Arm
Rex St. John: Senior IoT Ecosystem Manager – Arm

Imagine you are put in charge of marketing a successful, fast growing product to developers. However, your nearest competitor is about 20 times your size and, unlike them, your company doesn't make a physical product that developers interact directly with. Welcome to developer and ecosystem marketing at Arm, where our primary objective is to drive awareness, loyalty and adoption of key Arm features and technologies to create "Pull Through" for our newest products by reaching out to developers and introducing them to the latest Arm functionality.

Introduction

Our company designs and sells a series of flexible blueprints, libraries and tools, which it licenses to a vast network of ecosystem partners. These partners then use, deploy and manufacture physical implementations of our microprocessors based on our blueprints, doing so under their own brands to an

215

audience of their own developers. For our team, this is the challenge: Arm's business model means that developers rarely interact with us directly.

Arm processors outnumber humans on earth by more than 10:1: our suite of microprocessor technologies can be found in billions of medical devices, satellites, robots, drones, cars, servers, laptops, tablets, wearables, digital personal assistants and nearly every mobile phone on earth. However, our company is relatively small in size for those typical to the semiconductor industry, with a headcount of approximately 6000 employees. We tend to operate behind the scenes despite wielding a large influence in our sector. So, while Arm's influence is on a scale similar to that of companies like Amazon, Microsoft, Tencent or Google, connecting with developers is a particularly tough challenge.

Our situation is not unique. Most companies don't have the intimate relationship with developers that the Internet giants enjoy, yet still need to find a connection to their ecosystem. In this chapter, I will describe how Arm has tackled this challenge, but first I will introduce myself, and then introduce Arm.

I come from a background in product management, business development and technology partnerships, and joined Arm in 2016 to build a stronger developer ecosystem presence for our mobile line of business. Perhaps because of my relative lack of experience in the field, I've spent much of my time studying how successful companies reach their developer audiences, and how those strategies could be adapted to Arm's particular position in the ecosystem. This chapter summarizes some patterns I've observed, with real examples, and in some cases, with real names too.

You may know Arm as the company behind the mobile and embedded processor architecture. That is one of our biggest claims to fame, but Arm also makes many other products, from graphics processing units (GPUs) to server processors, and huge volumes of software to enable those products in the market.

One of Arm's roles includes building or contributing to compilers, libraries, and tools across multiple verticals. In some established markets those tools are extended, packaged and distributed by the 'tier-1' developer program owners. Examples include Android in mobile, Unity in game creation, and Red Hat in server.

The audience we aim to serve are developers who work "close to the metal" on hardware, independently of verticals or platforms. For example Android developers writing native code, mobile game developers looking for the last ounce of performance, embedded firmware and IoT device makers. A platform developer program will typically provide the platform-specific tools, software and advice, but may not address hardware specific questions in any depth.

The main challenge for us is reaching the audience, and making it aware of Arm's contribution to their developer environment despite the distance between us and their typical development platform. Connecting with those developers helps us convey the benefits of our products and tools, which, if well exploited, in turn will make their content more efficient, engaging and appealing to their users. And great content makes our products more valuable to our customers and partners.

Nascent verticals such as IoT still offer opportunities to build a direct relationship with developers. When such an opportunity exists, a direct developer outreach approach makes sense. But, in more general terms, we want to access developers further up the stack, while supporting our partners and customers. How can we connect with developers, offer valuable tools and resources, and get them to come back regularly?

An important point is how we measure the success of our efforts. There are obvious metrics, such as sentiment, downloads or followers. These are useful to measure the effect and return of investment of a certain initiative or campaign (Did anyone read our blog? Who visited our booth at the event?). The more important, harder to quantify goal is the extent to which we are influencing developers' code to run better on Arm products. There are useful proxies that allow us to gain a sense of the impact, but this would be the subject of a whole new book.

Arm's ecosystem efforts are optimized by vertical segments: IoT, Mobile, Automotive, and so on. Regardless of the segment, our approach to the ecosystem is built around some key principles that can be applied horizontally, and are summarized in 4 simple rules, which we will discuss in the rest of the chapter.

Find your angle

Okay, so another company has an outstanding developer program and accesses all the developers you want to reach. Regardless of that company's ability to connect with their audience – something that you probably don't have any influence upon – it's essential that you identify what it is that you would like to tell the developers that no one else would be able or motivated to do on your behalf. Do you have a tool that provides unique insight? Or especially good coverage for a particular configuration, or use case? Whatever it is, make sure that you can claim ownership of that particular space and be prepared to tell the audience about it.

The question we always ask ourselves is, "would anyone else in the ecosystem be able to do this job better than Arm?". If the answer is no, then we better start working on it.

Implicit in this advice is the fact that you should know your developer audience so well that you can identify a unique opportunity to serve them and, in doing so, raise their awareness of you. This would be obvious in any other field of marketing and for any other product, but when it comes to developers, the 'M' word is almost a taboo, because, as the old adage goes, developers don't like marketing.

Yet developers love a great tool that solves their problems. In our experience, time and resources spent in identifying developers' needs and eliminating their pain points has been hugely valuable. Finding out which tools to build can be achieved formally, through surveys and focus groups with developers, but often a simple conversation with a developer will throw up a lot of useful feedback. Developers love talking about what they don't like in their workflow, especially if they trust that you will do something about it.

Case study 1: Arm Mali graphics and gaming

Despite owning the vast majority of the mobile CPU market, Arm found itself with no significant contact with developers. Mobile is perhaps the most established developer segment, better served by the platform vendors than any other sector in the industry. It would seem that there is very little for Arm to contribute to the developer experience that is not already covered by the two major mobile OS vendors, Google and Apple, or by mobile platforms such as Unity, Facebook, etc.

It was clear to us that we couldn't, and didn't want to, compete with those higher up in the stack. Had we tried to offer an IDE to complete with Android Studio, for example, we would have failed miserably to gain traction – how could we build a better tool than Google? More importantly, it would not have helped support our relationship with Google. And frankly, trying to build something that already exists is not a very exciting challenge. Instead we focused on one area that we found under-served: tools and libraries to debug graphics development on OpenGL ES and Vulkan. There are tools available in the market aimed at profiling graphics applications, but they have several drawbacks for developers of mobile applications. Some are vendor-specific and don't work with other vendors of mobile hardware, while others are too high-level for detailed analysis; in some cases, they lack good integration with the mobile processor, which, in almost every case, is based on an Arm architecture. We optimize that we could build a better range of tools to help developers focused on applications with a strong graphic element: mostly games, but increasingly others such as Virtual Reality, Augmented Reality, and so on. This plays to our strengths – we have a very good position in mobile graphics – and complements Google's efforts to provide good solutions for general purpose mobile development.

Even then, there is a difference between deciding to provide competitive development solutions for graphics developers and actually delivering them. The first versions of the tools were too complex. Rather than a minimum viable product, we tried to do everything our customers asked for. With too many moving parts (drivers, operating system, devices, and the tool itself), quality assurance was a challenge and all too often we had reports of users being unable to install or use the tools. We decided to stop developing new features and focus on delivering a great user experience. But user experience is defined by the users, not the development team. To get our tools in order, it took the team multiple interviews with partners, some surveys, and our undivided attention to the problem (see below for a deep dive on this critical aspect). We simplified the product, hiding or removing information that users didn't need.

Better documentation, which was kept up to date, was also essential. However, through interviews with our partners, particularly those in non-English speaking countries, we discovered that that short videos are much more likely to be followed than long online documents, although you need both to supply all the information necessary. We also added integration with other tools into the developer workflow, to make it easier to launch the tool and remove friction. Working with our partners, we encouraged more testing before releasing new versions of the tool or any of the system components. The key was to ensure the first 5 minutes of use are problem-free, otherwise the chances are that you will have lost the user forever. Time for performance profiling is in very short supply, and it cannot be spent just getting the tool to work. We're not quite there yet, but the progress we've made has resulted in more repeated use of our graphics profiling tools by more developers, which will result in better content, more optimized for mobile.

Cultivate talented, credible evangelists

Once you have identified your unique ability to contribute in the ecosystem, you must find developers who are ready to endorse you. The chances are that there are already some developers out there who already know you and love your products. If you have a small team and a shoestring of a budget, you are going to need all the help you can get. It's all about credibility and efficiency.

A credible story comes from developers who believe in your product and think it's worth their time and reputation to endorse it. It's not unusual that a comment in social media from a respected developer receives more retweets or likes than a similar one from the corresponding corporate account.

Efficiency is incredibly important to us due to our smaller size and resource constraints. How do we maximize our efficiency in reaching dozens of different technical segments? The answer is simple: talent. We find the most talented, visionary and dedicated external teams and individuals who are passionate about solving particular problems. Frequently they are technical founders of smaller organizations who tend to be highly motivated to go out and evangelize their solutions to the world.

With tens of billions of Arm-based devices being sold into the market every year, we realize that it is not going to be possible for Arm to hire full-time experts in areas as diverse as medical, drones, robots and aerospace. The most efficient way for us to tell our story is to locate the people who have the most credibility with the developer segments we seek to target and help them accelerate and tell their story, and Arm's, alongside it.

IoT: Arm innovator program

The Arm Innovator Program is a steadily growing group of external technical experts and evangelists with expertise in a broad variety of market segments important to Arm. From a standing start, we have now almost 40 innovators in our program – reaching the limit of what we considered manageable at the onset. Each Arm Innovator is a charismatic evangelist of the products that they have built using Arm technology. We support the Innovators in a variety of ways, including co-marketing, production of proofs-of-concept, workshops, webinars, blog posts, live interviews, hackathons and more.

When executed properly, an Innovator Program can provide explosive opportunities for growth over time. We have found it to be a powerful tool to grow our developer ecosystem and greatly accelerate the innovation occurring on top of Arm technology. We have some examples below where innovators have made a substantial impact in the adoption of our technologies.

This sounds good, but you likely have a few questions such as: How do you locate and identify an Innovator? And what do Innovators get out of working with Arm?

How to identify an innovator

We see Innovators as individuals who build developer experiences on top of other developer experiences. In the case of Arm's microprocessors, an Innovator might be someone who takes an Arm processor, mounts it on a printed circuit board with a specific configuration and then produces the cloud services to turn it into an internet-connected camera to sell into the industrial drainage market. The key characteristic of Innovators is they have intimate knowledge of their own market and can repurpose our technology in a way that we would have not been able to.

Each Innovator provides us with access to developers in a new segment. Furthermore, these Innovators tend to have strong direct market knowledge and can provide interesting feedback to help you improve your own products.

Case study 2: Makerologist and DIY Robocars

In the new field of deep learning, one of the challenges we face at Arm is how to explain to our market that many deep learning and AI tasks can be performed on low-cost Arm hardware without needing to spend huge amounts of money in backend compute power. Because Arm CPUs, Microcontrollers, GPU and other IP are so prolific, if we could educate more developers on the fact that Arm processors can be used for AI, we would be able to create a major impact on the market.

Many developers feel intimidated to prototype and test AI functionality in a way that doesn't require reading white papers or spending huge amounts of time adopting heavy deep learning frameworks. This is where Makerologist and DIY Robocars came in.

When we look to market our products to pools of developers, it is very beneficial to locate communities that have already coalesced around a single niche product or application. With 10,000+ members and 40 global meetups, the DIY Robocars movement to create low-cost autonomous vehicles using Arm technology seemed like a strong fit for our objectives of efficient one-to-many developer marketing efforts. We engaged with Makerologist's Clarissa San Diego and DIY Robocars co-founders Will Roscoe and Adam Conway to launch the very first Seattle DIY Robocars event.

After much planning, we convened 77 developers to build and race 10 DIY Robocars, and were able to attract key AI technical talent from throughout the Seattle region to spend three hours building and racing Robocars and learning about AI on Arm. By embracing fun, community events with Arm Innovators, we were able to achieve high quality in-person connections within the demographics of developers we targeted.

What's in it for the Innovators?

An important characteristic of an Innovator is that they are small business that is not yet fully established. This is important because the primary motivation of Innovators to work with us is to raise awareness of their product offerings so they can grow larger. Innovators frequently have stockpiles of talent, domain knowledge and motivation. What they lack is exposure.

The goal of a well-run Innovator program is to shine the spotlight directly on each Innovator to give them more opportunities to tell their story. The faster these Innovators move, the more they grow and the more they benefit your company.

We provide wide ranging benefits to our Innovators including funding their workshops, webinars, conference travel, inviting them to special internal Arm events, helping spot fund proof-of-concept ideas and much more. Helping our Innovators grow their market share is directly beneficial to them, and to us.

Case study 3: OpenMV

When Arm Introduced our CMSIS-NN software for deep learning on low-cost microcontrollers, the market quickly forgot the announcement. With an opaque name and highly technical white paper, the true value of the CMSIS-NN libraries was not understandable to many of our developers and not accessible. We sent OpenMV to a small team of just two developers who both have day jobs, a casual one line email mentioning CMSIS-NN and asking them if they could use it. Two weeks later, OpenMV released support for CMSIS-NN on their IoT cameras and demonstrated in a 4 minute video exactly how developers could use the project to create immediate business value.

After circulating the video internally at Arm, we began to be inundated with requests for access to OpenMV and introductions from customers wanting to use the functionality in their own projects immediately. All of this from a two person team and a one line email. This is the value of Arm Innovators, for themselves and the Arm ecosystem.

Leverage partners' channels

As we described at the start of the chapter, we optimized that there are other companies with a closer relationship to developers. Arm's goal is to help those developers build better applications by using the architecture features, tools and best practice, and work with our partners to offer an excellent channel to communicate our value. When the content is relevant and brings actual value to developers, it's in both Arm's and the partner's interest to ensure it reaches the widest audience possible.

This builds brand recognition. If you can, join your partner's booth in an event, or invite them to a webinar. Your audience will optimized their name alongside yours, something particularly important if your name is not well known yet. It's amazing how powerful those associations are, and your brand will be reinforced as a result.

Partner blogs

Arm has a blogging channel in our forum and collaboration site called Arm Community. In our traditional hardware domains, the Community is the place to go to find news and subject experts in the Arm ecosystem. In other areas, such as multimedia software and tools for graphics, its reach is much smaller. When we have content of particular relevance to an audience in those areas – for example, a new algorithm for Virtual or Augmented Reality that offers material benefits for the end user – we try to publish somewhere else outside the Arm Community. Buying sponsored content in a technical publication is an option which works in some cases, but for technical content it can smack of inauthenticity, and you may not have the budget, in any case.

Whenever the piece features some of our partners' technology, a better approach is to try to publish it in their blogging channels. This has worked very well for us. On one occasion, a piece on VR reached 10x the number of views and engagements than we could have possibly achieved in the Arm Community. The partner also benefited with a relevant, engaging and original piece that they would have never have written.

Of course, this approach only works if the partner perceives that the content is going to benefit their pool of users, and the message aligns well with their own. In another instance a different partner refused to publish a similar piece because we were 'hacking' the platform to build a new feature that it wasn't intended for, and which would never be officially supported. It is important to understand, even internalize the partners' developer strategy and objectives, ensuring you are well aligned with them. Your content needs to expand the partner's developer outreach, not take it over.

Put your heart into it

Let's be honest: developers don't have time for us. They are busy getting their product out of the door, or responding to a demanding customer. They will not become your beta testers free of charge, or be expected to take something that almost solves a problem and have to figure out what's missing, filling the gaps themselves. If you have identified your angle – what it is that you can do for developers better than anyone else – it doesn't matter how big or small, broad or narrow, make sure that you can solve that particular problem completely, and do it better than anything else in the market. Think about whether your enthusiastic developer evangelists will shout about it, and whether your partners will be happy to promote it in their channels. If you don't think you can delight your users, don't waste your time on it. It will fail to rise to the surface amongst the rest of less-than-ideal solutions out there.

Case study 4: mobile compute with Arm NEON

Not all mobile applications are the same. In compute-intensive tasks such as sound or vision processing, or machine learning, developers need to make the most of the hardware available to them. In 2010, Arm started to include a vectorized engine called NEON in their CPUs. A few years later, virtually every mobile application processor is NEON-accelerated.

Modern compilers do a reasonably good job of optimized code for available NEON hardware, but they won't achieve the optimum performance for a given routine. In those cases where compiler output is not enough, it is necessary to optimize the code by hand, or have someone else do it for you.

Ne10 was Arm's first attempt to create a developer answer to the need for optimized NEON code, in the form of a library of primitive functions for applications such as computer vision. In 2011, a few engineers set out to build an open source project that would combine some of the most commonly used primitives in compute-intensive applications, opening a hosting page and sharing it with their contacts in the industry. Despite a promising start and a good degree of excitement amongst partners, Ne10 ultimately failed to live up to the principle of putting your heart to it: the library was incomplete, providing only some functionality that the user was expected to complement with their own. In addition, it was not very well documented and in some cases not as well optimized as other open source functions already available. While the library enjoyed some success in certain computer vision communities and research labs, it eventually fell out of official maintenance and now only survives in GitHub thanks to the contributions of a small number of individual industry advocates.

Building on the learnings of Ne10, Arm released its new compute library in 2017. This time we considered it to be a central element of our success in mobile compute. A product owner travelled the world for over a year meeting with tens of developers and partners to understand their needs, and prioritized work based on it. A team was set up to work on the project full time and support ongoing requests and issues, creating a careful outreach plan to ensure that the benefits and repository updates were clearly communicated to the developer audience. The library was embraced not only by the mobile business unit at Arm, but by many others, such as embedded and automotive; and so on. Since it was launched, the Compute Library has become the most starred project amongst the more than 60 open source Arm repositories in Github. Today it still has a team working on this library full time and has added other key use cases besides computer vision, such as deep learning, to the list of functions optimized by the library. Thanks to this work the team has been able to engage with a large number of new developers, building trust and gaining access to new opportunities for growth.

Summary

Whilst every company would love to have a developer program that reaches millions of passionate advocates, unless you have bottomless pockets, it's unlikely that you will ever be in that position. However that doesn't mean you should give up your developer program, or that you should settle for a vague sense that people are aware of you and your product.

With a systematic approach to understanding your value proposition, your audience and the developer landscape, it's possible to find a unique angle that both your developers and your partners will love to endorse and promote, amplifying many times any effort you could make on your own. They key is to put all of your energy into identifying your angle and then committing to it for the long term.

Chapter 15 | Hardware Is The New Software – Building A Developer Community Around A Chip Instead Of An SDK

Ana Schafer: Director of Product Marketing – Qualcomm Technologies, Inc.
Christine Jorgensen: Director of Product Marketing – Qualcomm Technologies, Inc.

You are the head of developer relations for a program that has been focused on software development. Now, you are tasked with building a community around a solution that requires programming and building in the physical world with a combination of hardware and software. What's different about marketing to software developers versus hardware developers anyway? And what is different when it comes to events, support, content and logistics? How do you acquire, educate, engage and retain hardware developers? How do you continually drive toward commercialization for yourself, your developers and everyone in your ecosystem?

Whether your goal is to start a developer community from the ground up or encourage your existing developer community to

follow you into new areas and opportunities – or a little of both –
this chapter is for you.

Introduction

At Qualcomm Technologies, Inc., we create many of the
inventions behind wireless communication, and we've been
facing these questions in our efforts to get our technologies into
the hands of more developers in different areas. As our
company's business strategy takes us beyond smartphones,
we're focused on encouraging developers to work with our new
hardware, which leads to two main developer marketing goals:
encouraging a large community of mobile app developers, who
already know us, and attracting an even larger community of
hardware developers who are new to us.

This chapter describes how we introduced a new hardware
development tool – the DragonBoard™ 410c – a small, single-
board computer that is accessible to almost any software or
hardware developer and compliant with an open-source
hardware specification. It is designed to ease developer
engagement with our technologies by allowing developers to
prototype and invent in myriad directions, supporting our growth
in Internet of Things (IoT) and opening the door to brand-new
use cases. Critical to the adoption of the DragonBoard 410c has
been a focus on making hardware the new software: accessible,
affordable, expandable and easily programmable.

The task for our marketing team at Qualcomm Developer
Network (QDN) was to build a community of followers ranging
from our longtime, multinational customers, to newcomer
startups, makers and educators. Along the way, we learnt some
lessons about developer marketing around hardware, which we'll
share as we describe the journey.

New business opportunities beckon

Long before the term "Internet of Things" became a staple in our
vocabulary, our product management team had been making
development boards built around our mobile processors,
populated with the connectors and physical interfaces needed by
component vendors to integrate their hardware into smartphones
using our processors. As companies began exploring the
combination of computing and wireless connectivity in new
applications, manufacturers in a wide variety of industries saw

potential for our processors far beyond smartphones. Qualcomm Technologies began fielding requests for development boards to evaluate use of our mobile processors in areas such as robotics, drones, home automation, appliances, toys and media servers. The opportunity was clear, but our company needed to build a new commercialization approach as we diversified our business.

In the Internet of Things, most embedded systems have modest product requirements compared to mobile communication devices like smartphones and tablets, and Qualcomm® Snapdragon™ processors[2] meet the most important of these such as high performance, low power consumption, and wireless connectivity.

However, we had to build a new commercialization strategy for IoT that met the requirements of an array of embedded devices that, for example, have a much longer lifespan compared to the typical, one to two year lifespan of most smartphones. Other requirements included an ecosystem of hardware vendors who could provide off-the-shelf or custom modules as well as system integration services, and a mature distribution channel to scale from dozens to thousands of customers. Customers would also require an evaluation board, and our approach was to provide an open source, low-cost (under $100) community development board for potential customers to evaluate our processors.

To meet these needs, Qualcomm Technologies focused on the Snapdragon 410E (sdata.me/RuZDzs), a mobile processor optimized for mass production in IoT, and alongside it, an easily accessible prototyping platform, the DragonBoard 410c (sdata.me/XgqRgw), a development board compliant with an established open hardware specification, accompanied by product information and support resources. The business goal was that developers would use the DragonBoard 410c to build prototype designs that they could then commercialize in products based on the Snapdragon 410E processor by using off-the-shelf modules, or purchase the processor for a chip-on-board designs.

While the product team worked on rolling out the DragonBoard 410c, the developer marketing team set its own wheels in motion. Before long, we encountered our first speed bumps.

---

[2] Qualcomm Snapdragon is a product of Qualcomm Technologies, Inc. and/or its subsidiaries.

At Qualcomm Developer Network, our focus had previously always been on mobile software developers. However, we now needed to build a strong, engaged community of both hardware and software developers around the DragonBoard 410c. We had many years of experience working with smartphone engineers, but we needed to target developers in a broad array of new and emerging IoT segments.

The smartphone business involves a very small number of very large customers, each one with a Research and Development group staffed by experienced engineers. The nascent IoT business, on the other hand, involves a large number of relatively small customers many with a tiny R&D staff, if any, often flying by the seat of their pants to invent first-time devices with features nobody knows they need yet.

Defining the target audience – where to start?

The product plan for the Snapdragon 410E processor was to let a thousand flowers bloom: to make it as easy as possible to use, to build up a broad community and channel, then see where biggest leads came from and tune the business approach along the way. That's a difficult place for developer marketing to work.

"Who is our target audience?" we asked. "Lots of people," the product team told us.

 "What will they make with the board?" "Lots of things. You know, for the Internet of Things."

"Can you identify a few key vertical segments to focus on for our initial campaigns?" "Why would we do that? We need to position the product as broadly as possible."

Not exactly the well-defined target audience and clear direction we all hope for, was it?

But that was inherent to the position Snapdragon 410E held in the Qualcomm Technologies IoT portfolio as a product that could broadly apply across existing and emerging use cases. It was a challenging situation to start building a developer marketing plan with high-volume aspirations and such a wide net as the product team was directing us to cast. We started by researching global developer trends as well as our own community. As you'll see throughout the rest of this chapter, tuning in to the voice of the developer was not only a good place to start, but also looking back, the tactics that proved to be most valuable during those early days of product introduction were the ones that elicited the most direct developer feedback.

Researching the space – starting our developer marketing plan

We had a strong, existing community of mobile app developers exploring IoT, but we also wanted to reach beyond that base to attract experienced hardware developers to the Qualcomm Developer Network for the first time. So, as every marketing team facing such a transition should do, we researched the differences between software developer communities and hardware developer communities.

First, we evaluated the type and quality of resources (documentation, sample code, projects, content, support) that other companies provided their hardware communities. Then we reviewed market research from sources like SlashData, comparing it to the annual survey we conduct within our own developer community. Several elements stood out:

- Developers were becoming more conscious that hardware was increasing in power and decreasing in price. The lower barrier to entry was feeding a flourishing community of hardware startups and makers ready to engage with vendors.

- Interest and expertise in programming were rising among makers, academics and entrepreneurs, outside of traditional developer circles.

- Developers were looking beyond established areas and technologies to the next ones, such as IoT, either to keep their skills up to date or to probe new sources of revenue.

- Developers were starting to place greater value on professional skill building and continuous education provided by developer programs.

- To analysts, IoT looked like a huge, wide-open frontier. To developers trying to figure out where to sink their shovel, it looked like a confusing landscape of relatively small, vertical markets. They saw a fragmented group of software and hardware solutions vying for their attention, with few unifying standards to use as a compass.

Weighing all these factors together we decided to prioritize educational content creation over promotional spends in the early stages. The developer marketing team had long since learned the lesson that comes from promoting an SDK or developer tool that has inadequate documentation. You may drive visitors to the landing page, but the number of downloads and follow-on uses will be low. We knew we had to make building with our hardware as easy as programming software if it was going to be a vehicle for developers taking their first steps into IoT and quickly prototyping new designs. Educational content would be key to making this new space accessible.

Hardening the product and encouraging community feedback

From researching the developer community and commercialization requirements, we knew that we didn't yet have everything we wanted for launch, but we didn't want the perfect to become the enemy of the good. Besides, our experience told us that once we had released the DragonBoard 410c, the community would let us know what was lacking and how to improve it.

We generated the educational content with which we would roll out the board, knowing the list would grow and change with time. In startup parlance, our minimum viable product content for launch was as follows:

- Documentation starting off with a hardware user manual, data sheet and application notes

- Getting started on projects that include step by step building instructions

- Sample code to quickly program different functions

- Short tutorial videos specific to an application.

With baseline product content in place, we then had the foundation for creating the marketing content to evangelize the product and drive calls to action to the educational resources:

- Blog posts using a three-stage editorial approach on a theme, starting with beginner-level and ending in expert blogs on technology applications, vertical uses cases, and so on

- Monthly Newsletters with project of the month feature – a feature story pulled from the blogs to highlight the new resources

- Webinars hosted with key software and hardware providers in the ecosystem

- Use cases based on commercial applications.

The community gave us good feedback about our educational content: it was insufficient; sometimes too fluffy, sometimes too far advanced. We started gathering our feedback by monitoring the questions in the forums, and as we started participating in hackathons we found these to be an even more valuable source for developer feedback. With developers working under such tight time constraints, we could immediately see what was easy to follow and where things were lacking or totally missing.

Early on, we had turned to our company's internal resources and to our vendor ecosystem for documentation. In most cases, it had been written by savvy engineers for savvy engineers and assumed too much foundational knowledge for the broad audience we were approaching. Over time, when we thought we had addressed much of the feedback and that our resources were really solid, we turned from doing hackathons that targeted mostly professional developers to Major League Hacking, which put us in front of thousands of university students and gave our content its biggest trial by fire. We got a rude awakening about how many leaps in knowledge our content took, and it was only after we started providing level-appropriate resources and sample code that we began to see a strong number of completed projects from the hackathons. The takeaway points to share from that experience are that you should always be open to feedback from the community, as there will be different insights from each new audience you reach out to. It is easy to become complacent when there are so many glaring needs vying for your attention.

Starting at home

Before we took the DragonBoard 410c to its first hackathon, we reached out to our own internal engineering community. Our company is filled with lots of engineering talent, but our developer marketing team struggles for access to technical staff the same way most developer programs do. There are always important customers commanding priority and product schedules that can't be missed. We didn't have assigned resources to help developer marketing create sample code and educational content for the DragonBoard 410c, so we invited our engineers to play with it.

Our product team vigorously promoted the DragonBoard 410c to engineers companywide, seeding hundreds of boards through an internal mailing list. The "DragonBoard Club" sprouted up, consisting of engineers who, in their personal time, are hobbyists or are involved in promoting science-technology-engineering-math (STEM) education through alumni programs and school volunteer programs, such as high school robotics clubs. This group of passionate engineers spanned San Diego and San Jose, California; Research Triangle Park, North Carolina; Toronto, Canada; Cambridge, UK; and Hyderabad, India.

What was in it for them? We rewarded employees who created projects, wrote documentation or provided support at hackathons with formal recognition awards for accomplishments that went above and beyond their normal day-to-day job, plus they were able to keep their boards at no charge. But the main motivation for the DragonBoard Club members was their love for tinkering.

What was in it for us? The DragonBoard Club contributed broadly in several important ways by:

- Testing the board and the quality of initial educational resources

- Creating demos, workshops and video tutorials that developers would ultimately use

- Evangelizing the board by sharing it with alumni groups and high school clubs

- Identifying the features and functions that would be most inspiring to developers (computer vision rated very highly)

- Documenting our earliest projects.

Their contribution of creating and documenting projects was invaluable. In the same way that case studies and customer testimonials enhance the credibility of every business, published projects are the vehicle by which hardware platforms like

Raspberry Pi and Arduino demonstrate credibility to their communities, encouraging other developers to not only draw inspiration from prior work but also replicate and improve upon it.

By starting at home, we in developer marketing were able to publicize successful DragonBoard 410c projects on the Qualcomm Developer Network website early on. Projects include a description, source code, bills of materials, assembly instructions, and often videos of the project in action, and are classified by categories like hardware, operating system, area of focus and, most important, skill level. We recognize that our community is wide-ranging in experience and areas of specialization, and we've continually tuned our resources to address both the experienced hardware developer and the beginner.

Over time and with much nurturing, we got to the point where community members are contributing their own projects unsolicited, which is a key metric for product engagement.

Driving awareness

Through traditional marketing communications techniques, we maintain a steady drumbeat of awareness and education to draw new developers into our funnel. Registered Qualcomm Developer Network developers receive email notifications of new resources in areas of interest, social media campaigns drive visits to our website, and our monthly newsletter has proven the most effective tactic to drive blog readership.

We also exhibit at events, such as Maker Faire (sdata.me/VeHzuk). We're well aware that many makers still don't know who Qualcomm Technologies is, and many more still don't know that the DragonBoard 410c is an open-spec development kit designed to be as powerful as a smartphone. Shows like Maker Faire that attract the T-shirt vs. sports coat and jeans crowd are a rich opportunity for driving awareness and education, as we get access to an audience that is interested in diving into the technology behind our demos and engaging directly with the engineers in the booth.

Our biggest reach in driving global awareness in our early days came from the DragonBoard 410c Maker Month Contest. We announced the contest and challenged developers worldwide to submit ideas of what they would build if they had a DragonBoard

410c. Almost 800 ideas came in from all over the world — from a testing device for foodborne pathogens to an under-vehicle device for mapping potholes, and everything in between. Then, importantly, we asked our entire developer network to judge the ideas and vote on them. More than 17,000 developers voted on the ideas, and the top 31 ideas won the first round. We shipped a free DragonBoard 410c to each of the first-round winners, giving them one month to build their proposed invention and send us video showing it at work. A small panel of judges, consisting of our engineers and channel and distribution members, then selected a final winner and awarded the grand prize of $5,000.

We believe that having the developer community vote for the first-round winners was an important element in the success of the contest. The conversations it started among developers all over the globe spread awareness of the DragonBoard 410c and educated prospective makers on its uniqueness as an open-spec development kit with the processing power of a smartphone. The contest also provided a huge boost to our projects page, as we posted the instructions from many of the first-round winners to inspire imitation and innovation.

From awareness to engagement – hardware hackathons

For many years, we have used hackathons as a vehicle for engaging developers with software products and we were keen to continue tapping into the creative energy the events are known for. However, we soon discovered that pulling off a successful hardware hackathon was a big step beyond.

For software hackathons we generally provide documentation, code samples and a software development kit (SDK). Since these are online resources available from anywhere in the world, there are few physical resources to transport. In contrast, almost everything related to a hardware hackathon involves physical equipment, so the hack kits we prepared for each team required much more preparation, transportation, logistics, support, and sometimes export/import arrangements.

Our first hackathon was a bit of an eye-opener on what it would take to make hardware as easy to program as software. We participated in TechCrunch Disrupt and found that attendees skewed toward software-oriented; those with hardware experience knew Arduino but not a full computing platform, and the DragonBoard 410c at this point did not have a strong complement of plug in mezzanine boards. Those who wanted to connect sensors had the additional burden of dealing with breadboards, level shifters, and soldering irons – not exactly what many of the software developers wanted to spend their time on. Subsequently, most of the projects they ended up submitting were little more than Android apps running on the DragonBoard 410c. We learned that besides the hack kit we provided, we needed to make all of the hardware components for IoT (e.g. sensors and cameras) more accessible, and we needed to provide lots of sample code and projects to allow developers to take advantage of the board's capabilities.

Developers also needed live, on-site hardware expertise. There is no substitute for an engineer who knows the board and can answer any kind of question face-to-face at half past midnight. Naturally, it took some doing to pull our engineers away from their desks (and weekends) for hackathon duty, although we benefited yet again from the strength of our internal DragonBoard club, but the effort paid off in better projects and more-satisfied developers.

An important goal for the hackathons was to demonstrate that the more things the DragonBoard 410c can easily connect to and work with, the more valuable it becomes for the developer. As we gained traction and our hardware ecosystem expanded, we were able to include purpose-built mezzanine boards and plug-and-play sensors into the hack kits. Those components allowed hackers to focus on program logic and use cases without the tedium of attaching wires to pins.

We also learned the importance of targeting more hardware-focused hackathons in order to engage with the right audience for our products. While limiting the number of events we participated in (since many hackathons are software-focused), we received a far better return on our investment in time and resources. Along the way we also learned more valuable lessons about laying the groundwork for a successful event, particularly from our sponsorship at the AT&T Developer Conference:

- Use cases – Whether we are emphasizing multimedia, computer vision, edge computing or any other use for the DragonBoard 410c, we try to tailor our hackathon challenge, and our hack kit, to align with that event's focus.

- Co-sponsors – By finding out in advance which devices, SDKs, or cloud providers the event co-sponsors planned to highlight we are able to cross-promote the DragonBoard 410c with sensors, cameras and services like AT&T M2X.

- Pre-hackathon webinars. A couple of weeks before the event, we like to reach out to the attendees with a webinar in which our engineers walk through the capabilities of the DragonBoard 410c and the contents of the hack kit.

- Resources – Hackathons leave little time for combing through documentation, so we come prepared with easy-to-follow code, shortcuts, sample projects and video tutorials aligned with the main themes of the event, highlight these during the pre-hackathon webinar and make them easily accessible on a hack-specific resource page on our website.

- Hackathon teams – Experienced hackers arrive as a team with an idea of what they want to build and the categories in which they want to compete. In addition to trying to capture the interest of teams in the pre-hack webinar, we send our staff out to promote our challenge throughout the registration time showing off all the goodies in the hack kit to increase uptake with high-value hackers.

Hackathons and similar live events play a big role in our engagement with the hardware community. Developers like these events and the atmosphere of innovation that pervades them. Although submitted hack projects tend to be more science experiment than useful commercial applications, with the approach outlined in this section we've been able to uncover some gems. Most importantly, we find them to be a great way of fueling developer awareness and interest in a new technology, and a valuable testing ground for continually making the DragonBoard 410c easier to use. We've hosted winning teams and their DragonBoard 410c projects in our booth at subsequent trade shows, including a grand prize winner that prototyped a home health automation system, increasing their exposure and ours.

Smart companies start small – for example, conducting local workshops for meetup groups or mini-hackathons with your company's summer interns – then collect the feedback they need to run large events with hundreds of attendees. Hackathons reveal what developers can do with technologies and devices, but they are not the shortest, or easiest path to achieving solid business goals. Also, hosting your own hackathon can be very expensive in terms of time and dollars, so it is often best to seek out existing well-known and well-attended hackathons that align with your business goals by looking closely at the demographic details from previous events, as well as the published entrants and winning hacks.

Building retention through commercial success

As we progressed towards a strong foundation with more and better documentation, sample code, projects, etc., and as we continued to build our hardware developer community, we knew we needed to align our growth with our goals for commercial success. The time was right to examine our approach to driving commercial wins in targeted use cases, and in doing so we had to acknowledge that in the world of IoT, our hardware is just one piece of what a potential customer would consider in an entire end-to-end commercial solution. The same is probably true for most developer programs, whatever the offering you are marketing, it is just one element in what your end customers would need to get to a final commercial product. For us, turning to our ecosystem for collaboration in developer marketing and enablement was a great area of opportunity in driving uptake in specific commercial applications.

Co-marketing with the ecosystem – a virtuous cycle

From the beginning, we designed the DragonBoard 410c to be compatible with the 96Boards Consumer Edition specification, an open standard that reassures inventors that they can develop prototypes without being locked in to any single vendor's architecture. This standard also meant that hardware vendors making add-on shields, or what 96Boards calls mezzanines, with their components (sensors, motors, displays, cameras, cellular modems, etc.) were able to support all 96Boards single board computers, including the DragonBoard. The result was a quickly expanding hardware ecosystem of components, in addition to the module ecosystem the product team had developed.

As the landscape widened to areas like machine learning, network edge and cloud computing, we also expanded our ecosystem to include software and cloud providers who can help us gain a better foothold in these areas. For example, the combination of on-device computing with wireless and cloud connectivity has become an important factor in most targeted opportunities, so we have published DragonBoard 410c projects for major cloud services including AWS IoT and AWS Greengrass, IBM Bluemix, IBM Watson IoT, AT&T M2X, and Microsoft Azure IoT.

In order to translate this ecosystem of hardware and software providers into commercial implementations, we developed win-win developer co-marketing opportunities with this community to inspire designs in targeted use cases. We turned to the ecosystem to solve the problem of how to get technical content and resources to inspire design-in, and in exchange offered valuable promotional opportunities to reach the growing community engaged with Qualcomm Developer Network. For example, we worked with Solstice, an IT services firm, who developed a facilities management demo on DragonBoard 410c with AWS Greengrass, and in exchange we showcased it in our booth at AWS re:Invent, highlighted it as a project, and featured the use case in a blog and did a profile of the lead developer in our Developer of the Month. Another example is our work with Timesys, a firm specializing in Linux development services, who created a four-part webinar series we hosted on developing for industrial IoT with Linux OS using an industrial gateway as their use case. The results were strong leads for Timesys, strong leads for us and, most importantly, a satisfied technical audience.

In engaging with new ecosystem members on co-marketing we worked to customize our approach based on mutual goals, but following is the list of possible engagements we typically started with:

- Guest blogs
- 'Developer of the Month' feature
- Posting of ecosystem project
- Hosted webinars with ecosystem company speaker
- Feature in monthly newsletter

- Hack kit loaners for ecosystem-hosted events

- Demo placement in Qualcomm booth at industry events.

We continue to nurture our developer community and ecosystem through the ongoing marketing program that reaches out to our database of engaged developers, and in exchange the hardware and software companies we work with have provided the expertise that our developers want, which has taught us valuable lessons about reciprocity and the ecosystem.

Summing it up

Here are some of the main takeaways from our developer marketing experiences in building a developer community around hardware:

- Start with what you know and do your research for what hardware developers need and want, namely quality documentation, sample code, and support. Be open to feedback on what you provide.

- When hardening a product and developing resources, start small and with a community you know so there is very open, direct feedback and they are invested in your success. In our case it was our internal DragonBoard club of engineers who love to tinker that kick-started a big part of our initial resources.

- It may still be a while before "hardware is as easy to program as software," but nevertheless, that has been an extremely useful theme for our work with the DragonBoard 410c. Almost everything we've done has supported the objective of helping people prototype their ideas and get to commercial viability as quickly as possible.

- While we started off without the well-defined target audience and use cases we would have preferred, we were hopeful that simply getting the DragonBoard 410c into the hands of the community would be a catalyst to help gain valuable feedback, and focus. By turning our attention outward and looking for patterns in what developers were making and asking for, we were able to adjust our approach to drive early successes.

- With time and more initial projects, however, we learned an important lesson: What users were making was not as significant as the DragonBoard 410c features they were using to make it. We saw them create IoT projects that took advantage of the board's smartphone-caliber technologies like camera, multimedia, gesture recognition and especially computer vision. Some users even took the DragonBoard 410c into hub and gateway applications. This feature interest directly fed our requirements for reference applications, sample code and documentation.

- Since educational content is so key for developers, we continue to look for, adapt, translate or create documentation with the instruction level and context that developers need to prototype their designs quickly.

- The ecosystem is more than a pool of customers and vendors; it is a pool of potential solutions. Whether relying on our developer community to promote and judge our contest entries or turning to our ecosystem of distributors, hardware and software vendors for technical capacity we couldn't get internally, we've enjoyed huge ROI from our relationships.

We continuously review and refine efforts, keeping in mind the entire developer journey from awareness, education, engagement and retention, to examine what's working and what's not. We think of each of our outreaches as an integrated 360° marketing campaign to get the most momentum of every event, hackathon, webinar, promoting and pushing through blogs, newsletters, projects, and social media.

Chapter 16 | Developer Relations and APIs

Mehdi Medjaoui: Founder - apidays Global, GDPR.dev

Application programming interfaces (APIs) are the interfaces for enabling the programmable economy, but to do so they must be designed in such a way that they are discoverable, scalable, and fulfil the capabilities they claim to provide to solve developers' problems. For that, companies will need to manage their developer communities' expectations and aspirations with the right approach. This is where developer relations come into play. It establishes the link between what your API can provide and the skilled people who will integrate it into other applications: the developers. In the following sections, we will explore how APIs are changing the game in the programmable economy, by providing greater reach, scalability, and ubiquity, and we will also look at the role of developer relations in the context of API management, advocacy, and evangelism.

Developer Relations and APIs: community, code, content

The role of developer relations when talking about APIs should be built around three pillars that the SendGrid developer relations team used to call the 3Cs: *community*, *code*, and *content*.

Developer relations is firstly about the community. As long as humans still integrate APIs, at least until machines can do it for us[3], the concept of a community will remain an important part of developer relations. Being where developers are, engaging with them, listening to their feedback and ideas, inspiring them, and putting a face on the API are all part of the community's mission in developer relations.

The *community* aspect is important as a soft-power to enable more word-of-mouth. As Tim Falls from SendGrid used to say, "a personal connection is worth more than a click," and sometimes he found that developers were recommending the use of SendGrid even if they had never used it, because they knew the SendGrid team was caring.

Community is also about attending developer events or API conferences to keep in contact with the community, and participating in speaking engagements which are not directly involved with what your API does. Sometimes topics might be about a cool hack someone made thanks to your API, or perhaps an open source package released for the community, or sometimes even more societal topics.

The second pillar is *code*. Integrating APIs is about code and a developer's job is to produce code that delivers value. If they can leverage code that is already provided, they can focus on implementing the business logic faster. Then, the role of the developer relations team is to provide this code as code samples, SDKs, sample applications, or API definitions that developers will be able to use directly. Code, to the members of the developer relations team, also means writing code themselves to maintain the developer platform and the API, with a nice developer experience which we will talk more about in a subsequent section.

The third pillar is *content*. Developers love transparent and honest communications and useful content. Content is one of the best ways to attract developers and maintain them as a loyal audience of your blog and ecosystem.

3https://superface.ai/

Content exists in many different forms. It can be just a technical update about recent changes; it can be a blog or email about a cool hack that your team just made; it can be more of an engineering post about a specific way to build some features; or a best practice explained in detail. It can also be broader, like the recent Stripe booklet and blog post series about how to make its company and applications carbon neutral[4]. Content is an important part of your relationship with developers that makes your company and its APIs discoverable through SEO or social media sharing.

In summary, *community*, *code*, and *content* are the three pillars of developer relations that you should strive to fulfill.

Developer relations for APIs-as-a-Product and product APIs

There is a clear distinction to make when talking about developer relations and APIs. You need to consider whether your API is *the* product, or if your API feeds and supports a product. You can then categorize it as either an APIs-as-a-Product or a Product API respectively. For instance, Stripe, Twilio, Mailjet, and Avalara are all an APIs-as-a-Product. They offer standalone capabilities for a specific purpose such as payments, SMSs, tax validation, email, etc.

On the other hand, Salesforce APIs, Facebook API, eBay APIs, YouTube APIs, and Twitter APIs are product APIs, or said differently, APIs for a product. They exist to support and customize an existing platform. They often represent more than 50% of the total traffic to the platform and product, which is quite considerable. As much as they are critical for the business to be delivered, they are often free to use because their use increases the value of the underlying business.

The role of developer relations is different for APIs-as-a-Product and Product APIs. The former is focused on generating revenue, the latter on value.

For an API-as-a-Product, the end goal of developer relations is to increase the revenue of the company, by evangelizing,

---

[4] https://increment.com/energy-environment/stripes-carbon-neutral-journey/

advocating, or building relations that will directly augment the top line business. As APIs are the product to be integrated and sold, the goal will be to maximize the number of valuable integrations according to the business model. In the case where developers are not the decision makers but just the prescribers, the goal of developer relations will be to have developers trained and acculturated about the benefits of the APIs. They can propose it inside their organization at an enterprise level, for the enterprise integrations and the high revenues that come with it.

On the other hand, developer relations for product APIs are mostly to inspire developers to build applications that will directly augment the value of the platform, but not necessarily its revenues. When Facebook opened its platform API, it was free for developers to build applications or games, and the rich portfolio of applications that resulted demonstrated that the Facebook platform was here to stay.

In the end, users will stay not only because of the social network, but for the full ecosystem of applications. This is similar for Salesforce AppExchange, which has more than 4,000 business applications. In that context, Salesforce is not just a CRM, but an ecosystem of business applications powered by a CRM that fits many use cases across many industries. For product APIs, the role of developer relations is to nurture that ecosystem, that then scales the value and the sales of the product for the user.

The eight pillars of the API developer experience for developer relations

A key role in developer relations, especially in regards to APIs, is to work on the developer experience (DX). DX is the design practice intended to ease the work of developers as they integrate APIs, from their discovery to their final production implementation.

The goal of DX is to maximize the conversion of people wanting to work with your APIs to those who will integrate them. In a world where developers are alone in front of their computers consuming your APIs, your DX needs to be at its best to make them feel autonomous and guided along the way to consumption.

You need to understand that DX can be a game changer; one that is measured by a simple formula. If the cost of the work to integrate your API exceeds the perceived value provided by the API, nobody will integrate it. If the cost of the work to integrate is lower than the perceived value of your API, developers will integrate it. This is the DX tipping-point that you enter in programmable business models.

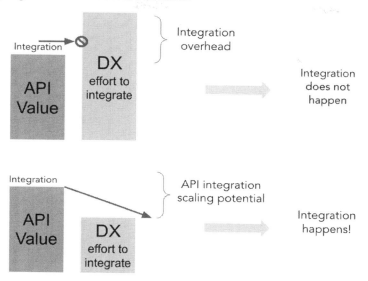

The perceived value of your API is measured across eight pillars of the developer experience: discovery, design, onboarding, documentation, tooling, management, transparency and communication, and a "no-surprise" policy.

API discovery

The way developers discover your APIs and the value it provides is key in starting your relationship with developers. How do developers find you? Since there is no search engine for APIs yet, the discovery mechanism for APIs is often described, as Bruno Pedro, co-founder of HithHQ used to say, "word of mouth + a little luck."

Of course, your communication will help a lot with SEO, along with exhibitions at developer conferences, online content marketing, online advertising, and corporate events. However, discovery is still quite rudimentary and cannot really be planned in a way where the best always wins. You will need to develop your own influence network and this is where word of mouth will be really powerful. When a CTO or a developer asks on forums, mailing lists, or social networks, "what is the best API to do something?" your API needs to be in the response provided by others. Next, when developers find you, they still need to understand the value your API provides. You will need to set up a developer portal that clearly describes the value of your API. For instance, Twilio used to market their SMS API using the slogan, "We make your application talk". Or Stripe on their first website, "Payment processing. Done right". Funnily enough, the original website was devpayments.com[5].

API design

APIs are a representation of the data or the service you provide; they are not the actual data or the service you provide. This means they offer a unique opportunity to express them from a customer value point of view. You can design your API to represent actions and resources that developers want to use instead of just exposing what you have. In this context, your API is like a restaurant menu. It must be designed to deliver the best consumption experience to delight consumers. The menu is not all the ingredients you have in storage, or the floorplan of the kitchen, it is what you want to provide based on customers' interests, and it will be the same for your APIs. This is why API design is important – to put yourself into the developer's shoes and express your internal capabilities based on what developers want to do. If you can achieve that, your APIs will be loved by developers. Let's remember here that DX is to enable good user experience by inspiring developers to build the best user experience that your API can enable.

API onboarding

Like unpacking a boxed product, onboarding is the first discovery and activation of the developer to consume your API. Just as Apple has dedicated teams to think about the unpacking experience of its boxed products, you will need to understand all of the steps that developers will have to take to make their first successful integration. We often refer to this metric as Time to First Hello World (TTFHW).

---

[5] https://www.quora.com/What-did-the-first-version-of-Stripe-look-like-How-did-they-get-it-to-work-in-production-for-the-first-users

Signing up, filling out forms, signing your terms of service, setting up their environment, getting their application credentials, downloading helper libraries, being redirected to the right "getting started" section, reading the docs, etc.; all of these steps need to be as simple and straightforward as possible. If you are in a company that requires lots of time for validation, for legal or compliance purposes, you can make the onboarding better by providing a sandbox that replicates the real API environment whilst users are waiting for their validation to complete. Another tip, based on what we used at OAuth.io – my previous company – is to ask what stack the developer is using so you can send them directly to the right SDK in their preferred language. More generally, you should try to implement every tip and trick you come across to make onboarding as delightful as possible.

API documentation

Documentation is key in every developer relations strategy, and as James Higginbotham, CEO of LaunchAny used to claim, "your API is only as good as its documentation." The focus on this part of the developer experience is key to the success of your API. Twilio and Stripe, for example, are known in the industry for having the best documentation across their topics.

Documentation should be divided into two parts. The first is a "tell-don't-teach" approach, where you provide full explanations of how things work with a clear overview of the API and how it works, what it enables, authentication mechanisms, API references, etc. This is a little bit like the dictionary part of the API. If developers are lost and don't speak the language of your API, these elements will enable them to find their path to successful integration. Others compare this part to a box of LEGO bricks without instructions, where you only present a pile of bricks and the developers build what they have in mind – if they know what to build.

On the other side, you will provide a more advanced version of the documentation in the "teach-don't-tell" section. Here, you will directly focus on making them successful through tutorials, step-by-step guides, code samples, etc. This part is a little bit like a box of LEGO with instructions, helping and inspiring developers to maximize the value of what they can build.

API tooling

The tooling provided by your developer portal is an important part of the developer experience. Tooling can include an API explorer, authentication playground, API debugging console, API sandbox, interactive documentation, an API description file like a downloadable OpenAPI specification, user personas, etc. Your developer relations team will be in charge of this experience and including all of these tools into the DX. Tooling is a pillar of DX that makes the difference when there is a lot of competition in the API market.

API management

Another pillar of the DX is the developer dashboard and API management for developers. You need to provide capabilities to developers and they will consume them, but developers need to know their level of consumption, the performance, and the error rates to effectively monitor their consumption. This is why a key part of DX planning must focus on how to give developers the maximum amount of information for monitoring their API usage. Common metrics include the number of API calls per endpoint, average response times, time to first byte, time to last byte, and the percentage of errors. You can decide to provide all the necessary metrics that your developer community wants to best manage their app with the right granularity. Also, don't forget that a good DX involves nice user interfaces and dashboards to easily follow their app and API integration dynamics. Developers love design too!

Transparency and communication

The transparency pillar is about delivering the maximum truth to developers with clear and direct communication. First, let's remember that transparency needs to be aligned with your internal culture before it can be applied outside the organization. In the context of APIs and developer relations, transparency is about communicating the roadmap, the health of the platform, the strategy of the company, and its intention towards its APIs. This is also about communicating frequently on all available channels such as the developer portal blog, email, Twitter account, and other related social networks for developers. For example, if you face a big API downtime, developers can excuse you as long as you are transparent about it, give constant and clear communication, answer complaints in real time without an embargo, and without the fear of saying that you are investigating and that you don't yet know the problem, and announcing when the problem is solved. Also, after the incident, you need to write a post-mortem to explain what happened without lying, even if it is uncomfortable sometimes, and most importantly, what you have done to avoid the problem in the future. This will be highly appreciated by developers and, contrary to what you think, it can augment the level of trust.

"No Surprises" Policy

Developers make things work. In that sense, they need to know things in advance so that their work is predictable. If you break that predictability, you break your trust with developers. There are many ways to break that trust in developer relations and APIs.

The first one is technical, and concerns breaking changes and versioning. APIs evolve, developers know it, but they want this evolution to be made with the maximum ease and the least amount of work on their side. Companies which have broken their API many times have suffered from developer disaffection over time, like Facebook for example, which at one time was breaking their API quite often. To avoid this, give time for developers to adapt to the change by deprecating the version with a long notice period – three months minimum – to respect developers' predictability, focus, and time. One way to solve this is to handle the burden of managing multiple API versions and adopt a "write-once-run-forever" policy, meaning that as long as developers still use an old version of the API, you will keep it live and running. Successful, API-driven companies like Amazon, Salesforce, and Stripe have adopted this policy and it has been an important part of their trustworthiness in the developer community. As Werner Vogels, CTO of Amazon Web Services, said, "Code can change, APIs are forever."

The other way to break trust with developers is with policy and API terms of service changes. In the past, many companies have unilaterally, and without notice, broken their legal and moral contract with developers. This was the case for Twitter, who broke their API policies many times, killing their longtail application ecosystem over time. Or Google, who changed their Google Maps pricing policy, stopping their free tier which had made it a success, and breaking millions of applications which implemented Google maps for hobbyist projects.

These pillars are not negotiable. If you apply their principles, you will be mastering the art of making APIs for developers and will take an important position in the developer ecosystem.

Developer relations ROI: KPIs for APIs and developer relationship management

Evaluating the quality and potential of your developer community is a key element of your developer relations strategy.

Many companies have tried to develop an internal tool to better understand their developer community. Many API management vendors have built what they call internally, Developer Relation Management software – like a CRM but for developers. This offers a way to better communicate, track, and differentiate developers with the most potential ROI, based on your API strategy goals which could include reach, application ecosystem, or revenues. Also, identifying and engaging developers who are on your platform is a way to reactivate them and reinspire them to build with your API.

For that, you will need what Mike Swift, founder of Major League Hacking, calls "the nuts and bolts" of developer relations. It is a mix between developer relations practices and metrics to invest and track effectively. It is split into two parts; the API usage tracking and the developer tracking.

API usage trackers: AAARRR for developer relations

"If you can't measure it, you can't improve it," Admiral Lord Nelson used to say. On the other side, as the Goodhart law states, "when a measure becomes a target, it ceases to be a good measure." How do you find the right balance between metrics and the goals of your developer relations strategy? You just have to match your KPIs with your APIs.

There are all sorts of KPIs for APIs and we have provided some here to help you get started. To get the most from each, you should couple them with the Pirate funnel, inspired by Dave Mc Lure, founder of famous startup accelerator "500 startups", better known as the AAARRR model: *awareness*, *acquisition*, *activation*, *retention*, *revenue*, and *referrals*.

API awareness

Number of visits to the developer portal's homepage and documentation: there are many ways, both paid and organic, to attract developers to your homepage. To attract developers to use your API, first they need to discover your value proposition and the capabilities you offer. Attracting the maximum number of developers is your main awareness metric.

Number of blog article views and reads: content is key in a developer relations strategy, so everything you publish must be tracked and be sure to also always put a link to the page of your developer portal to track referrals from your articles.

Number of developers registered to your newsletter: ask readers to register to your newsletter to get notified about new articles and API updates. This number is a key element to track how many community members want to keep receiving news from you and to compare it with the current developers registered to the API.

Number of speaking engagements / number of people reached by the talk: awareness comes from offline discussions and In Real Life (IRL) events. Conferences, meetups, and all public or private events where you can raise awareness of your API are important to activate a mechanic that is not measurable but that works well: word of mouth. This also serves as the foundation for kickstarting the viral referral phase, something that we will talk about later. For that, you can track the number of talks, the average audience size, etc., to calculate the reach. Also, if you have a booth at an event, you can add in the number of people you had interactions with.

Open source stars and contributions for tools: providing useful tools or releasing valuable software under an open source licence can deliver a lot of awareness for your company and API. This recently provided developer success to Strapi, who released a tool to build an API-driven CMS with GraphQL, and Hugging Face API, who released their Natural Language Processing technology as open source. Through open source, these companies attracted developers, scaled their business, and raised a lot of money from investors – $10 million and $15 million respectively – based on the success of developer relations in managing the developer community around the open source project of the company.

API acquisition

Number of registered developers: an important acquisition metric is the number of registered developers. But it is useful only at the start! Don't depend on it as an important metric in the long term because it loses pertinence when the maturity of your developer relations program evolves. This metric enables you to know if there is a match between the developer community and the perceived value of the API you provide and its associated capabilities.

Number of applications and applications / developer: most of the time, one developer account is linked to one application but when you gain popularity, or for instance, when your API has an intrinsic value that can be reused in other applications easily (i.e., it's a transactional or Business-Process-as-a-Service API), you will see two or more applications per developer account. That is important to track because these developers are probably your best word-of-mouth ambassadors since they have understood the value of your product enough to reuse it multiple times. Tracking the total number of applications and the median of developers who have at least two applications can be a good metric in the acquisition phase.

Number of API calls: in the beginning, the total number of API calls can be a good metric, enabling your API developer relations team to focus on increasing the use of the API and being innovative in their marketing strategy. The developer relations team will focus on inspiring developers into different usages, according to different common use cases. It should be tracked because it ceases to be a good metric really fast, unless your strategy and/or business model is attached to a number of API calls, for instance affiliation, pay-as-you go, or indirect models like advertisement of third-party pages.

Number of third-party integrations on other platforms: another way to scale the reach and acquisition of your developer relations is to work with existing companies which already have developer communities and build a plug-in, add-on, or integration on their marketplace to scale. For instance, Typeform, a platform to make survey forms with an API, was based on integrating a use case into third-party marketplaces to leverage their existing developer communities. Now that they have grown, Typeform can attract applications on their platform and reverse the API integration scheme of "I spend time and money to integrate with you", into "you spend time and money to integrate with me".

API activation

Time To First Hello World (TTFHW): an important conversion metric is how to transition an interested developer to an active developer. For that, you need to track the TTFHW, which is the time between when a developer registers on your platform to when they successfully invoke your API. Mark Boyd, API journalist and analyst, used to say that seven minutes is the perfect DX timing to enable developers to be successful with your API. Of course, not all internal validations and processes are possible in every organization to reach that sort of time, but reducing it to its minimum will have a direct impact on your developer activation ratio.

Number of active applications / developers: you already track the number of applications and developers as we saw earlier, but identifying the difference between developers who are just using your API for small projects and your power developers who are integrating it into business projects can help you identify where to invest more resources, or when you need to be more reactive to a support ticket, for instance. The limit between the two needs to be defined by the API product manager, but it is important to track in order to understand the difference. This difference will also help you to define your pricing plans, putting the limit of your free plan where developers and applications become "activated".

API retention

Number of valuable applications: as for the difference between acquired and activated, the difference between activated and valuable needs to be defined by the API product manager, according to the API strategy. A valuable application can be an application that provides lots of visibility into your application ecosystem, an application that attracts lots of users, or one that generates significant and growing revenues.

Number of active end-user tokens: a more specific metric in the retention phase is to track the retention of end-user tokens as the users of your API consumer applications. Applications which tend to grow their user base have less tendency to change their stack and switch API providers to focus on customers. This is why companies like Stripe can still charge high fees for their

APIs, because payment capability is probably the last thing you want to change when you are growing. This metric can be really useful if you target an application ecosystem for your strategy like the Facebook and Twitter APIs do.

API revenue

Direct revenues generated by the API: this kind of metric is pretty straight forward if your business model is directly attached to payment. Tracking revenues can also help influence an organization's internal decision makers and C-level staff on the need to continue investment in developer relations to monetize the API.

Indirect revenue generated by the API: this metric is harder to define because it requires a subjective approach, but the exercise to link indirect API metrics with business KPIs will help back internal support for developer relations. Developer relations pays off in the mid and long term, so some managers may want to demonstrate faster rewards internally to executives. Giving them a vision about the value created by developer relations, by translating API metrics into business KPIs, even indirectly, can help the developer relations team to continue to get support. For instance, if your API enables your application ecosystem to grow, and this ecosystem increases the valuation of the company by 100% to investors and to the market, the value of developer relations needs to be linked to the market cap of the company that is indirectly induced by developer relations for API adoption.

API referrals

In the referral part, the idea is to leverage your existing happy API users to spread the value and the interest to use your API in the same way they used it. Here is a set of metrics to analyze that:

Conversation activity: conversation activity is important to monitor because your developer relations team can engage developers and product managers who are actually discussing or debating about "what is the best API for that?", or debating about where to find capabilities and business-processes that have been encapsulated by an API. These discussions can happen where developers are such as on Discourse, Twitter, Medium, Hacker News, Reddit/programming, Facebook groups, etc.

Mentions from others: you can source speakers and developers who are referencing your API and its value in their talks or articles and transform them into ambassadors. For that, you must track these mentions, either in conferences or developers blogs, and begin to engage them. This is what companies like Auth0 did with their ambassador program, or Docker with their Docker Captain program based on their best advocate in the community.

API presence and use in cool hacks and at hackathons: you can only track this manually, by monitoring social networks or mentions and search engine alerts, but knowing that your API is being referred by others, where it happens, and who is doing it is also an important part of your developer relations strategy to be sure they reach you next time before actually making it.

The Story of Twitter API vs Slack API

Aligning KPIs with APIs is extremely important and can completely change the future of the platform you are building. As Jason Costa from GCV Capital said in his article "A Tale of 2 API Platforms"[6], both Twitter and Slack had great developer traction because of their important user base and their openness to build cool "stuff" and valuable applications. Twitter finally decided that its business model was not based on being a monetized application ecosystem, but to be a media platform making revenue through advertising. All the previous APIs published were now in the complete opposite mindset of the platform and this was the reason why Twitter closed their API, hurting their developer ecosystem. They worked hard to return to developers, with manifestos from Jack Dorsey himself, hiring great developer advocates like Romain Huet, now head of developer relations at Stripe, but the moral link with developers never completely recovered.

On the other hand, the Slack model was based on making an application ecosystem to enrich the value of the Slack product. More business applications increased the value of the Slack communication platform, so the business KPIs are aligned with the APIs, and this is why the Slack API never suffered from tensions in the developer community, and probably why developers love building bots on Slack. These two stories are the

---

[6] https://medium.com/ggv-capital/a-tale-of-2-api-platforms-39f8dfd77436

perfect reflection of how aligning your KPIs with APIs, and then your APIs with your KPIs, makes the difference for how you manage your developer relations strategy and APIs in the long term.

Funding API consumers

We would like to finish by sharing the original strategy used to create an investment fund for your API consumers and developers. This strategy has been used by major companies in the ecosystem like Mailchimp, Twilio, SendGrid, Slack, and Stripe. At some point, they all created investment funds especially for developer companies using their APIs. This has many benefits, but mainly it offers the potential for developers to profit from building on your platform. Even if the number of investments per year is low, it enables you to keep developers loyal to your platform instead of your competitors by showing a path of monetization and/or funding.

In another venture-friendly strategy, Salesforce was engaging developers to build on Salesforce AppExchange more than on iOS because the average revenue for an app on AppExchange at the time was $450,000, instead of $3,000 for an app on iOS[7]. Even a bank in France, Credit Agricole, proposed that developers be paid based on the API usage and traction of their app, with a monthly revenue based on active users of their applications using their APIs.

In a nutshell

Even if an API's programmable delivery model can achieve outstanding scale and value accumulation, it still needs humans to share it and developers to integrate it. In that context, you need a team that is able to match the scale of the business model with the underlying psychology and enthusiasm of a whole community of practitioners and developers. For that, you will need to focus on things that scale with the power of APIs: community, content, and code.

You will also need to communicate the difference between your API and those which are in direct competition with you, and even against the do-it-yourself approach. For that, you must

---

[7] Offline quote from a Salesforce developer marketing manager in 2015

implement the eight pillars of API DX under the guidance and constant feedback of your developer relations team.

To build support for your developer relations work amongst your organization's managers, you will need to match the APIs metrics with business KPIs. This is key to gaining the continuous support of executives who don't yet understand the power of good developer relations. Let's remember that the developer relations strategy with APIs needs to be aligned with both the company and organization's business model and with the developer community.

APIs and developer relations are intimately linked to the success of your organization in the programmable economy, to transform your product into platforms, and your platforms into ecosystems. From API to IPO!

Chapter 17 | How to Win Developers Hearts: Don't Break Their Software. Ever.

Brian McManus: Senior Director Product Management - Visa

As you engage external developers who work with your APIs, it is often early in their product lifecycle that they discover, evaluate and integrate your services. The good times, if you will. As with many other aspects of life, developers will make a longer term, and more sustainable, judgement of your company and its offering based on how you interact with them throughout the lifecycle of your relationship. This period can often include some not-so-good times when you need to communicate bad news about the status of your system, upcoming changes in your APIs and eventual deprecation of APIs. In this chapter, I'll talk about the best way to ensure that developers dependent on your services are kept informed, content and stick with you through the good times, and the bad times.

The separate disciplines of Developer Relations and Developer Marketing were defined and differentiated up front in the book's introduction and while this book clearly focuses on Developer Marketing, this subject of this chapter probably overlaps with Developer Relations more than any other. What we have learned at Visa is that there is no better way to build credibility with developers than to be there when they need help. Not just help with documentation or domain expertise or evaluating your service. But also help when they are in the midst of a crisis, a crisis that your software may or may not have been responsible for. If you can be just as forthcoming with responses, explanations, tools, at these times, when they need you, as you are with emails, blog posts, beta programs when you need them, then you will have something that all platforms, all businesses, crave; a customer for life.

Introduction

Throughout this book we have talked about developers' fundamental issue with marketing and the fact that it is all too often a one-way conversation. The scenarios described in this chapter can represent embarrassing or mission critical situations for your company, but they also present opportunities to have substantial and meaningful two-way conversations with your developer community.

I will reinforce the key point to remember when building and managing any commercially available API; your customers rely on this API to run their business. As a global payment platform provider, at Visa we are more acutely aware of this fact than many API providers. In this chapter I hope to pass on Visa's experience and learning, to help ensure your communication with developers is great in the good times and really great in the bad times.

I have broken up the narrative of the full lifecycle of any service or API and identify areas where we can always do better if we think about the situation from the developer's perspective. I cover key touch points where the Developer Marketing team can lend a hand throughout a service lifecycle: when it is introduced, when it is generally available in production and when it is retired. The common theme is that each of these touch points must be a two-way conversation, otherwise other developer marketing efforts could be futile. If you do a good job in these areas, it will help generate authenticity and goodwill that no marketing budget in the world can buy.

Visa's Developer Ecosystem

Visa is a world leader in digital payments. Our mission is to connect the world through the most innovative, reliable and secure payment network - enabling individuals, businesses and economies to thrive. The Visa developer ecosystem is a broad and diverse community of developers working on applications and solutions for issuing banks, acquirers, merchants and technology partners. Visa developer platforms and brands enable use cases as simple as charging a credit card, with the CyberSource API or as complex as building a global peer-to-peer payment application with the Visa Direct API.

I have been with Visa for eight years, spending about half of that time as a Java and .NET developer on the Authorize.Net and CyberSource platforms. As the rapidly changing payments landscape moved from primarily a retail e-commerce feature to a core component of almost every application and service, it became clear that APIs and Developer Experience needed to be managed as a first-class product portfolio. I moved into product management to help lead this effort for Authorize.Net and then CyberSource. Our teams pioneered many efforts within Visa, which today are taken for granted in most developer programs, such as open source SDKs on GitHub, API status pages and community forum post mortems.

To help developers build easier, faster, more secure ways to power commerce, Visa Developer offers direct access to a growing number of APIs, tools and support resources, which had previously only been available to select financial institutions. Through these efforts and through acquisitions such as CyberSource and Cardinal Commerce, a Visa developer can be a small business merchant, a global enterprise ecommerce company, an issuing bank or a disruptive fintech startup.

While other developer marketing efforts covered in this book may be segmented and targeted for different segments and personas, most all of the content in this chapter is, uniquely, universal to all Visa developers, and, indeed, to most developers, period. Introducing new APIs, retiring old APIs, dealing with availability or performance issues, these are fundamental challenges that all platforms face, regardless of their business domain.

Communicating Future Changes

New services and features are exciting to introduce, launch and promote. However, developer products, unlike end-user products, cannot be adopted without development effort on the customer's side. With end-user products, a human being can interpret the changes, intuitively adapt to the new behavior and even choose whether to adopt a new feature or not. As much as software is taking over the world, a computer can still not do any of these simple things. When new developer/programmatic features are introduced, you are responsible for documenting every minute detail of the change, providing steps and guides to adapt to the change from older versions. Most fundamentally, you need to convince developers that the change is worth integrating.

New Features

Contrary to what many marketers think, developers are not always falling over themselves to try new features. When a new API or new feature is introduced, developers want very clear communication as to why this new API/feature is easier to integrate, more performant and why it is worth their time and effort to adopt. Certain developer communities embrace rapid change because it's already part of their technology stack, e.g. JavaScript. In contrast, developers on crucial mission-critical Enterprise stacks can be much slower to adopt anything new. Beta programs, early access opportunities and limited feature releases should clearly communicate the expectations for both sides of the agreement. What is supported, what changes can be expected, what the upgrade path will be, and so forth.

In addition to backward compatibility, one thing that cannot be overlooked is parity with legacy APIs. That is, what is NOT in the new API. Regardless of your justification for removing an existing feature, somewhere out there, that feature could be the cornerstone of someone's business.

At CyberSource, Visa's global merchant services platform, new REST APIs have been introduced with a completely new Developer Center which explicitly defines the APIs available. An additional design feature of the Developer Center was to route all legacy gaps, questions about features, and comparison with older versions through a single Upgrade Guide, which reiterates the evolutionary path of the integration technology before linking the developer back to the legacy docs. In this way developers can educate themselves about future roadmap plans rather than being forced down those paths prematurely. I'll discuss this guide later.

What about the old version?

One of the biggest mistakes that API providers make is expecting/believing that people will move off old technologies simply because you have released a fantastic new version. The world doesn't work like that; many people still have desktop computers, listen to CDs and use Internet Explorer, after all!

New features should be consumed on the developer's terms not yours. Even without a hard migration, such as a forced upgrade, if developers/customers have to spend the time and money to upgrade, you should make sure that it's for a very good reason. The onus is on you to demonstrate the business value of any new API or integration method. Developers may be motivated to move to REST APIs because of a more efficient JSON message format or broader tool support but when a new REST API is introduced you should also highlight additional business benefits, such as new API methods or enhanced data access.

There are times when a forced upgrade is unavoidable. Developers understand why these scenarios occur and they judge your service based on how the process is managed with respect to THEIR software and THEIR business. We saw this most recently when the payments industry made the decision to disable older, insecure communications protocols and force customers to upgrade to the latest version of TLS. The value of doing this was clear and uncontested, however merchants still had to spend significant resources to ensure their own software and all their dependent systems were compatible.

Effective communications cannot stop at emails and marketing campaigns but rather should include tools and platforms: sandbox systems, version checkers, sample code and practical advice, even beyond the realms of your own services (e.g. compatibility of base platforms such as .NET, Java, etc). Clear timelines are vital and timeline extensions are often necessary; they may be undesirable but are often unavoidable if large clients are impacted. Well managed brown-outs are also an effective way for developers to be included in testing efforts and to alert customers should other communications prove ineffective. CyberSource recently removed some old IP addresses through carefully planned, well communicated, short periods of downtime before the final decommissioning, allowing us to minimize the impact to our developer customers.

Any forced migration, such as the TLS upgrade mentioned above, is clearly a last resort. However, even when the benefits of newer APIs are obvious and you have provided tools to simplify migration, developers still need to be shepherded to the new and away from the old. While it is never a good idea to remove documentation or completely cut off support, simple low-impact methods are often overlooked. For example, older integration methods should be deemphasized in all forms of marketing and support material, those methods should be unavailable for new customers to use, with advance notice, new features should not be added to the older APIs, and so on. Sunsetting a developer feature is an order of magnitude more effective when the entire business is coordinated around that objective and follows a consistent strategy.

Operational Changes

Shorter term, smaller, future activities can also be key touchpoints for you to interact with your developers and provide an opportunity to build trust, or lose it. Planned downtime should be an oxymoron in today's Platform-as-a-Service environment, however there may be situations where it is unavoidable. In addition to sensible scheduling based on analysis, developers should always be included in any communications or alerting of these occurrences. For example, announcements should be made in advance through developer dashboards, forums and email distributions in addition to customer and business channels, such as account managers, application alerting or notifications.

Even when downtime is not part of scheduled maintenance, any planned or known activity where a change in behavior may result, should be communicated through developer channels. Something as simple as a tweet like: "As part of ongoing efforts to enhance our sandbox, test transactions will now return error code 234 for transactions which fail AVS checks" will help build trust and goodwill.

An additional note on sandbox systems. A common bugbear for developers is when changes hit production systems (or are even announced for production systems) without being implemented on the pre-production (sandbox) systems ahead of time. It is always worth restating that sandbox communications should be just as important to your developer marketing team as production communications. A good rule of thumb is to make sandbox changes available for the entire "reasonable advance warning" period, otherwise the advance notification is essentially useless to developers, as they cannot act on the call to action. We recently had to extend the production date for a change due to the fact that we had been delayed getting the change to sandbox. Business pressure to maintain the production date, albeit with a compressed sandbox period, must be balanced against adequate testing time for developers.

Experimental Features

At CyberSource we have seen one area of future communications become more important as we innovate rapidly, with an ever-stronger focus on developer experience. A critical step we have incorporated into the product life cycle is a validation stage, shortly after ideation and before we ramp up the creation stage of building the product. For our developer products this validation stage may involve API specification reviews, usability studies and sometimes alpha/limited release sandbox builds.

Candidates to help with future product validation could be "MVP" developers, developers from partner companies as well as "blind test" developers who can often be recruited through usability test agencies. These developers are often key influencers in their technology community and can be clear advocates for your platform. Transparency is critical and objectives must be clearly defined internally across the broadest range of stakeholders to ensure these relationships grow and thrive. Commonly, companies ignore feedback, expect technical reviewers to provide quality assurance and miscommunicate the production readiness of their software.

The Future should be a Two-Way Conversation

At Authorize.Net, one successful way we have found to make sure developers feel invested in enhancements to the product is to make sure they are part of the process. When we launched the Ideas forum on our developer community we were committed to including at least 2 or 3 of these requested features every quarter of our product lifecycle. We let the community know when features were in the final stages of consideration and worked with the ideas of supporters (up voters) directly while the feature was in development, to ensure we delivered the correct functionality as they understood it. By demonstrating that submitted ideas were under consideration, in development and eventually released, we encouraged developers to engage, submit ideas and make the program (and ultimately the product) successful.

Communicating Current Events

Other chapters have talked about developer events, developer programs and communicating with developers in the context of the present. The focus for developer marketing is almost always on the good messages; the great APIs, the interactive documentation, the comprehensive sample code. That's the proactive, planned, predictable version of the current state of play.

This section deals with the burning questions that developers may have on a day to day basis, over and above general developer support, which I will not cover here. How and when these reactive events are handled is a key factor in their overall developer experience.

API Status

Communicate effectively about status. That is, the status of your APIs, the status of their issues, the status of any feature requests. These can be some of the most difficult conversations to resource, to manage and to make successful. At Authorize.Net we implemented a status page so that customers could check on the status of our service and be updated on the progress of ongoing issues. Some lessons we learned early on were:

- Try to update the status page as soon as you are alerted on an issue. We have found it's much better to be over communicative than have developers determine there is an issue and make alarmist posts on social media before your site is updated.
- Use automated alerting of API slowdown/downtime where possible. There can be understandable reluctance from marketing and corporate relations to alert without manual intervention. However with careful consideration of event type, alert threshold and status message,

automated alerting can save your developers hours of troubleshooting analysis.

- Regular updates reassure your customers and developers that you are prioritizing the issue. We have found that sentiment can quickly degrade when developers are called in the middle of the night to manage and mitigate issues, which turn out to be your service, but see no evidence that you are addressing those issues.

API Status via API

A common requirement from large-scale API consumers is to provide a "ping" request, or a status API method which will return the status of your API. What seems like a simple and reasonable feature can turn out to be much more difficult, particularly if there are multiple downstream parties. So while you can easily determine and return that your system is up and taking requests, your customers may find the API is effectively down because a third-party backend is returning a system error. So my advice here would be to determine what is practically possible and feasible, then clearly communicate limitations. Remember, that while your developer audience may understand the nuance here, the business they work with may not. There will always be times when the only way to determine if an API is up and working correctly is to call the API itself.

Sandbox Status

When we initially thought about improving service status and transparency, our operations team came up with a plan for 24/7 production support and week day, US business hours, sandbox support. Everyone thought this was a fantastic plan until we got the very loud and clear feedback that, for developers, comprehensive 24/7 monitoring and alerting of the sandbox environment was often more important than production. This makes total sense when you consider that the bulk of developers' time is spent interacting with your pre-production systems, not production systems. Developers will often be working evenings and weekends coming up to a release, even during a normal development period engineers' work schedules can vary significantly, not to mention software developers are working all across the globe. Your sandbox should be fully operational, monitored and supported 24/7.

API Performance

More and more companies are pushing the boundaries of transparency with real-time performance metrics. Benefits of this include increasing customer trust, winning prospective customers, and deflecting possible inbound support requests if customers can self-diagnose issues. A simple graphing of API response times allows developers and customers to see any spikes at a glance and correlate their own monitoring and alerting systems.

API Issues

Similar to real time API response times and performance metrics, developers will evaluate your commitment to them by considering how issues are solicited, gathered, tracked and resolved. In the past this may have been through a proprietary ticketing system but with so many companies providing source code, SDKs and samples on GitHub, handling of issues is available for all to see. While there can certainly be a management overhead in adding an additional issue-tracking system to your process, it is critical that dedicated resources are committed to every repository you host. A well-maintained project is a valuable asset to your developer program and community, cultivating relationships which can benefit recruitment, evangelism and industry recognition.

API Changes

An API Change Log can be thought of as release notes for your API. It should be updated when API changes are deployed to production and as with everything else in this section it should also be updated when sandbox changes are released. In the context of past events, this simple log of changes, organized by date and API version, means that developers can reconcile any changes in features or responses with observed impacts or side-effects on their own system.

It's worth noting that the Change Log is not the place to publicize a breaking change for the first time (see Communicating Future Changes and also note the title of this chapter!). For substantial changes, links to new documentation, blog posts or tutorials should be included. If properly maintained and organized, this current event communication mechanism develops into a trusted record for communicating historic changes, which is the focus of my next topic.

Communicating Past Issues

While supporting a business critical service such as payments, one important thing we have learned about developers is that they understand and accept that issues will arise, latent bugs will surface, cables will get severed, human error can occur. After all, these same developers are responsible for a system of their own, which may be more mission critical to their customers than our payments component. What developers cannot accept is a lack of transparency or a proliferation of excuses when these things happen. They want the cold hard facts, the root cause analysis, the mitigation steps put in place, etc. and they want it in a timely manner. In addition, when technology is superseded, deprecated or retired, developers want to know if, where and for how long, they can get support for that technology.

Historical Incident & Performance Logs

When something does interrupt or delay your service, details of the duration and impact should be clear, concise and simple to find on your Developer Center or status page. Similar to the Change Log, this feature could save a developer hours of troubleshooting on their own system if they can satisfy themselves that the incident was monitored, logged and addressed. Services like StatusPage can be used to offer industry experience and best practices, effectively becoming a de facto standard for incident communication. A log entry for an hour-long performance degradation generally includes an initial entry to confirm the issue, a further update to describe progress and estimated duration with a final update to confirm resolution. For significant material outages, for example a hard down situation, the standard incident logs may not be enough and that's when a more detailed post mortem may be required.

Post Mortems

The level of integrity and transparency with which service outages are handled can often be the difference between a developer leaving your platform or staying. While the appetite for full transparency can vary widely between organizations, often for valid reasons, developer marketing and developer experience groups should always be advocating for the highest possible level of detail, in both the root cause analysis and future mitigation plan. A comprehensive post mortem should have an issue summary, a detailed description of the impact, a root cause analysis and a remediation plan. While contractual obligations (Service Level Agreements) and discretionary compensation (for example, service/support credits) vary across business segments, a sincere apology is universal and always appreciated by developers. Regardless of the level of disclosure, recognition of the incident and its impact on your customers is non-negotiable.

Legacy Documentation & Support

An API is like a puppy; it's for life, not just for Christmas. As soon as an API is in the public domain and customers, even just one customer, builds on top of that API, you are obliged to document and support it, until the end of its natural life. We generally draw a distinction between alternative/older APIs, deemphasized APIs, deprecated APIs and sunset APIs. For each of these groupings there is a different level of support and documentation that any developer can justifiably expect. While we cannot claim to get that level right all of the time here's how we generally break it down:

Alternative/Older APIs

This classification can often be as subtle as the message format or the transport mechanism. If you do have alternative APIs then they should have parity with newer versions and features should be delivered via both at the same time. These "flavors" should always have the same level of support and documentation. The only exception may be where certain styles of documentation simply may not be available or make sense for a particular flavor.

Deemphasized APIs

Often this grouping may not seem necessary, but we have seen the usability benefits of streamlining the pathways to newer APIs, meaning that less used/more legacy APIs may inevitably become deemphasized. The level of support and documentation should not be significantly less than the first grouping, but when your ultimate goal is to deprecate and sunset an API, this phase of making it less accessible can be effective in reducing uptake by new customers, which therefore starts reducing support costs.

Of course, as I mentioned earlier, you need the support of the entire business to exclude anything you deemphasize from marketing and sales materials.

Deprecated APIs

This is generally the first point where you will make public announcements that an API is on its way out. At this point there may be decisions to change support levels, move documentation, mark up legacy pages, and so on. Critically there is no public, definitive timeline or sunset plan at this stage, since customers must feel assured that the API is not going away yet (usually not any time in the coming three years).

One important thing to note here is that the term "Deprecated" is one that is almost always understood by developers but hardly ever understood by anyone else. The term was introduced widely to software developers with early versions of Java and has been co-opted as part of software versioning nomenclature. But you cannot rely on the designation alone being sufficient. Support teams must be ready to answer calls and questions on what it means, the timelines for sun-setting, how developer customers should plan their move to a replacement API, and more.

Another point that is commonly left dangling is non-developer marketing material that still references deprecated APIs as if they were current. Deprecating any API or service must be part of a broader, thoughtful, planned campaign.

Sunset APIs

When an API is sunset it is officially on a path to End-Of-Life, which ultimately means at some date in the future, software using that API will cease to function correctly. This is a significant and material decision for a company to make and can often require executive approval along with corporate relations and legal advice.

While that statement was meant to be impactful it should not mean that product management or marketing shirk from making the decision when the time has naturally come to move customers off an older API. By the same token product management should never be coerced into sun-setting an API simply because engineering or operations are tired of supporting it. Remember that cute puppy, everyone said they would feed and walk and pick up after, right?

Establish guidelines and, when the time does come to say goodbye to an API, the most important thing is to decide upon the timeline, and in particular, to communicate and stick to it. The timeline must be annotated with clear goals and objectives from all stakeholders; regular metrics on declining usage, results of marketing campaigns to move customers, direct contact with any large client users, and so on.

Taking a product to end-of-life is a discipline that should be owned by product management. However, developer marketing and developer relations have a critical role to play. Like everything in this chapter, sun-setting an API becomes an opportunity to differentiate your developer experience and to add authenticity and legitimacy to everything else you do.

Evolution/Upgrade Guide

An Upgrade Guide, or as we've begun to call it at CyberSource, an Evolution Guide, becomes an essential resource for both internal and external teams to understand how they can begin to take advantage of the fantastic new developer features while plotting a clear and considered path from their current integration. We have found that rather than sprinkle FAQs or advice or migration tips around your developer documentation, you should funnel developers to a single resource where they can feel like they're being briefed on the what and the why (while also being expertly advised on the how). Of course, options should be available but it's important to have a strong point of view on a sensible path for upgrade, on timelines and on cut offs/hard deadlines if you have them. You think about this resource as closing the loop, referring back to the beginning of this chapter when we talked about communicating future changes, this page will lay the groundwork with your developer audience, for how, when and why those future changes are being delivered.

In Conclusion

Our biggest lessons on this journey with the Visa developer community have been:

- Think about migration first rather than last - It's simply too easy to get caught up in beta release, MVP, pilot program and before you know it those things have rolled into General Availability, a full rollout and no easy upgrade path for your existing developers. From day one write down your Developer Marketing KPIs and make the first one "#users left on legacy = 0". That way you focus on ease of migration from the first ideation, architecture and design.

- Transparency trumps everything – Many times throughout this book we have highlighted developer's natural aversion to marketing. This distaste is rooted in developers' instinct to understand, look under the hood, get to the bottom of everything. The effectiveness of your Developer Marketing will be directly proportional to your capacity to have an honest, authentic and transparent, two-way conversation with your developer and partner community.

- Tools, tools, tools – While clearly overlapping into the discipline of Developer Product Engineering, I have called it out here for that precise reason; the messaging/marketing scenarios in this chapter can almost always be made more effective, authentic and acceptable, with simple web-based tools to aid and inform developers. Tools such as response code lookups, compatibility checkers, migration wizards, etc.

Most importantly, remember the number one rule:

Don't break their software, ever.

What's Next

Despite the lessons learned and the collective experience of over half a million developers, we are still striving to improve in all the areas described in this chapter. One of our brands may do a fantastic job of real time issue response while still needing to improve on post mortems. Another platform may have expertly managed beta programs but an immature end-of-life capability. One of our biggest goals over the next few years is to drive towards consistency in Developer Marketing and Developer Experience across every platform, making the Visa Developer program a consistent experience for our developers regardless of which they are using.

Chapter 18 | The Foundations of Working With a Creative Agency

Mike Pegg: Head of Developer Marketing 2010-2018, Developer Relations Lead Google Maps Platform 2018-Present – Google

Over the last twelve years, I have led teams at Google that have worked closely with external agencies to produce work for a developer audience. I have learned a huge amount about finding and trusting a partner company, which is critical to reaching your goals. I'm going to share the foundations for working with an agency team to develop a deep understanding of your developer audience.

Introduction

There's a point in time when you need to extend your developer marketing surface area to reach more developers. You have a product, service or event that you want developers to adopt, take up or attend, and you have limited resources to produce or adapt content, market your event or extend your brand to reach more developers.

Maybe you have a marketing team who are already over extended or they may simply not be the best adapted to market directly to developers. Perhaps they come from traditional

277

consumer or business-to-business marketing backgrounds so don't have much experience running developer marketing programs.

Conversely, for those who can relate to, and already are, developers – your own developers and engineers – you likely don't want them to spend their time getting your developer marketing efforts off the ground, but instead to weigh in on developer perspective along the way. If all this is happening and you can find the marketing budget, it's time to choose an external agency to help you reach your goals as a developer product or service provider. And, for this kind of work, it's important to choose the right partner. Someone who has sound creative, media, and brand chops but who also knows each of these marketing disciplines when it comes to the developer audience. Someone who understands the developer profile you're trying to reach.

Finding an agency that has experience with developer-facing projects is tough. Very few specialize in this field given the amount of business that exists, and the work falls somewhere between consumer and business-to-business marketing, depending on the project.

Three Steps to get started

There are 3 key steps involved in the creative process with an agency:

1. Write your creative brief
2. Choose your agency partner
3. Receive creative content.

1. Write your creative brief

A good creative brief will telegraph to the agencies you are evaluating what the project entails, and will ensure they have everything they need to attempt to win your business. The word "brief" refers to something just that – brief. Keep your document simple, don't be wordy and avoid jargon that people outside your company won't understand. Make sure the brief is something your team has had the chance to collaborate on, and that it's representative of not just you as the lead, but the entire team.

Here is a simple checklist of things to include (and not to include).

The following is a simple set of 10 questions you'll want to answer in your creative brief. Ideally you should write no more than 1 paragraph for each of these to ensure brevity:

- What is your project title?

- What is the purpose of your project? (Explain why are you doing this and your business rationale)

- How is this good for your brand?

- Who is your target user or audience and what is your one key insight about them?

- What is the product/program benefit to your user? – (Remember to be inspiring here!)

- What do you want your target user or audience to do differently?

- What are the creative deliverables?

- What is your target launch date and where will it launch?

- How large is your budget? (This is optional as to whether to include in the brief. I would suggest talking through instead)

- Who are the project owners? (our name, the name of co-leads who will interface with the agency and how to contact them).

2. Choose your agency partner

In any agency engagement, it's important that you choose the right partner. I would venture to say that when you're performing outreach to any developer ecosystem, choosing how and with whom you're extending your marketing team is even more important.

During the selection phase there are some key factors to choosing a great partner.

Are they developers and designers too?

Try to learn more about the developers and designers that will be contributing to the deliverables. Are these individuals internal to the agency, or are they subcontracting the technical aspects of the project to contractors outside their company?

When we selected an agency partner for the 2011 Google I/O website, it was important to us that we selected a partner who could build something that would impress the developer community at large. We wanted to get developers excited, to view the source and pull that code down and create things with it. We needed to find someone who fully understood the technology we were using, and would get as excited about building with it as we were about the possibilities for our ecosystem. That same digital agency (Instrument) would go on to produce numerous digital aspects of Google I/O from 2011 to 2019.

The odds are good that your in-house developers and designers will be working closely with one another, so get them involved in the process of vetting samples of work and design portfolios. Your internal team are likely to be great at researching the projects the agency have worked on, even digging deeper into things like Github and other public repositories where their work resides. Really, what you're trying to confirm is that this collection of minds understands the developer landscape and the nuances between different types of developers. For example, back-end developers working with cloud technologies differ from front-end mobile developers building Android apps. Does this team understand these differences and can they bring this to bear in their work?

The result of not vetting properly will lead to additional time and work spent by your highly skilled and precious engineering resources. This happened once when we didn't loop in our engineering or developer relations teams to look carefully at what skills a new agency possessed before bringing them on to a project with us. We didn't make it clear what role the agency had (in this case reviewing highly technical API mashup integrations) in the statement of work and what resulted was our own internal technical teams picking up this part of the work.

Beyond this group of in-house developers on the agency side, who do the agency project leads work with to get opinions on certain directions or to explore new paths to go down for parts of a project? In our experience, knowing these in house developers also have a network outside the walls of their company or agency was refreshing because they had an honest and straightforward focus group to bounce things off.

What is their technical knowledge and skill set?

Now that you know that the team you're working with has an in-house team, let's go a level deeper and learn more about their specific technical skills. For example, are you expecting a native app, while the agency you've chosen has developers more familiar with web development technology?

As you get deeper into the specific skills they have, are you getting the impression that they're *excited* to be working on helping to market your platform or product? Do they use it in any of their professional or personal development projects? Are they fangirls and fanboys of your technology? The best case scenario is that they appear to already be users of your API (and competing platforms) for example, or have implemented your SDKs and already have a list of suggestions or perhaps even a wishlist of new features (that can be quite rare! Don't get your hopes up!).

When we were building out the 2014 Google I/O website, our agency partner had a lot of feedback around App Engine (a service from Google to develop and host web applications); it was a requirement for us to build the site on AppEngine, the only such service from Google at the time to do so. The technical lead at the agency we were working with had a lot of feedback on why it was great, and what could make it better. We knew the agency were able to offer a good point of view on whether we could do everything we wanted and host it on AppEngine. This gave us a great feeling that we had chosen the right partner. Even in the early scoping phase it created this sense that they were a part of our team.

I am personally turned off by those agencies that try to fake this and exude a level of confidence that aims to fill in a pothole in their knowledge levels. I've seen this in the past. They don't ask you questions and instead try to promote something they have done, which is highly irrelevant to the project at hand.

Digging in a little further on their discipline as a development team, how do they test and triage bugs? Are they familiar with handing off code? Have they checked-in projects on Github before? These things will prove that they're living breathing developers with their finger on the pulse of your project.

What is their content and copy writing ability?

An important element of working closely with the developer agency you're choosing to work with is their ability to talk in developer speak. Their voice and tone needs to match that of the developer audience for your product. At Google this depends on the product or platform in question. If your target market are front-end mobile developers, your content will need to be different than, say, an advertising or cloud product that is targeting an enterprise developer.

The dream scenario here is that the team helping to deliver your content are active developers with great writing skills. There have even been times in the past where our own marketing team have asked individual developers at our partner agency to review copy and provide alts, we've even asked them to help us tone down the marketing-speak of our copy! This can't always be the case, though, so ideally your agency has skilled writers with a pool of developers they can work with to review the copy and marketing communications.

Get it in writing

This section will obviously need to carefully follow your company's legal processes for engaging with outside vendors, but it is worth suggesting that a simple statement or scope of work document be crafted for the project. This ensures that both parties are completely clear on the expectations surrounding what services and creative deliverables you are planning to purchase from the agency, when those services will be due and what you will pay for those services. This chapter isn't intended to get into the legal specifics of your engagement, but you should carefully consider and include this in your process since even the most friendly of partnerships can sour.

3. Receive Creative Content

Building the Relationship

Like any relationship between groups or individuals there are 3 key aspects to making your newfound agency relationship a success.

Trust

I really can't stress this enough, but the true foundation of a great relationship with your agency is trust. You likely know this already, and it may seem completely obvious, but really take this idea to heart. Start with trust, keep giving it freely and never look back. Be realistic, don't set the bar too high for your partner to earn trust either. You chose them to work on your project and creating an environment for them to deliver their best work will give them the best chance to show you that you made the right decision. This was the cornerstone of how we worked with our agency partner, Instrument, on Google I/O over the years.We always had this feeling of trust between our two teams, without it, you'll second guess everything, waste time, and end up questioning everything. It also won't give them the oxygen to give you their best work. "Trust" me, it works.

An extension of your team

To quote my friend, Amie Pascal at Instrument: "This relationship in particular has developed to model the best kind of professional relationship; it's respectful and it's appropriate, it's human, real, and lasting." The agency you've selected has instantly become an extension of your own team and you should think of them in that way, in everything you do.

Communication

Frequent and open lines of communication were the cornerstone for how we worked with agency partners on the digital aspects of Google I/O. Direct, open, honest. In some cases choosing to communicate in person with either your agency partners visiting you, or your team going to their offices are important if distance and travel budgets allow. In some cases this also means choosing to volume down the communications channels as your agency works on their deliverables.

Ensure high quality

When marketing to developers it's important to show that your final, live project deliverables (your web and mobile apps and any creatives powered with code) have to be something of high quality, and something that developers will respect. This is a critical moment where you can build goodwill, respect your developer audience and earn respect from them in turn.

When we initially set out to build our Google I/O website experiment in 2011 (and each year thereafter) we aimed to push the limits of web technology. We knew that whatever we put live for the developer community, it would be heavily scrutinized by the public. It needed to be flawless in terms of its clean code and execution, while the visuals and copy needed to be appealing.

Once I/O concludes we encourage our agency partner to post the code to their own GitHub repositories, talk about the development on their blog and use their work to attract business beyond our engagement. This shows 2 things. 1) That we care deeply about the final deliverable and 2) That we're invested in the success and credibility of our partner, as much as they are in our own success.

Reviewing the work

Careful and thoughtful review and consensus is a necessary part of any project. It requires that you understand your leadership's necessity to review (or not review) work. Communicating this and helping the agency you engage with understand these timelines is very important. This involves being very clear on what the timelines are and giving your agency partner enough time to make these deadlines. Be open with the nuances of how your leadership works. What makes them happy? What do they *not* like? This could be as simple as the format in which they prefer to see work, to specific language, to color and branding. What can be expected as you present work to them? Help your agency partner get a good sense for this so you're all going into the leadership review process together.

In one example our move of Google I/O from Moscone Center in San Francisco to Shoreline Amphitheatre in Mountain View involved a major shift in direction, deviating from things that were in place in our previous venue. This meant that we needed to be lock step with our agency to navigate a tighter timeline and a higher volume of approvals. This meant we had to hold daily standups with our partners and be acting as one to meet the increase in reviews and keep the project moving.

Another example came when we introduced the Material Design visual design language. These guidelines were being incorporated into the design of the event's website and because the design guidelines were so new, it required multiple reviews to get everyone comfortable with the design direction.

During all phases - from the initial pitch to various rounds of deliverables - submerge yourself in the work that's being presented to you. Look over the proposals in detail, take notes and be clear and concise on what the agency can do differently to help the work reach a more authentic place for your audience.

I would however discourage being overly prescriptive about how to get to that place. You've contracted this agency because you trust their creative principles, so let them reach that place without detailed and specific things they need to do to follow through on your feedback. Give your feedback, what emotion you have, what you're feeling after looking at the work. A good agency partner will take that in and build toward the next revision for you.

Be timely about your feedback. In my experience, it's good to take part in the agency's review while taking enough initial notes to fit on a few post-it notes. Go around the room and have everyone share their feedback. If it's possible to reach consensus in that meeting on what you and your team's feedback is, great! The agency can then proceed from there toward the next phase. If this isn't possible, aligning with your team and delivering feedback within the day is critical to keep the project on track. If you know the review is happening with the agency on a given day, I recommend pre-scheduling time on your internal reviewers' calendars. The helps prevent the crush of the day from surfacing as the excuse to not spend the time to think deeply about the work that's been shared.

What is certain is that not everything will go smoothly with the creative agency you select. Even the best working relationship can expose some wrinkles as timelines get tight or mistakes and mishaps take place. It's best in these moments to be transparent and open with your agency contacts about the situation. Spend dedicated time reviewing where things are and tactfully negotiating exactly what you need from them to get over the finish line.

During this negotiation remember that there will be sufficient time to debrief on the highs and lows of the project, what went well and what could have been better, after things have launched. Doing so after-launch when things are more calm and rational will ensure an optimal outcome for your key learnings, and if you intend on continuing the relationship with this company, it will serve to strengthen both of your teams for your second engagement.

Share in the celebration

You've worked hard to find the right creative partner, you've established a relationship built upon trust, and upon clear and honest communication throughout your engagement. Hopefully by now, your developer community is thrilled to interact with and take part in your campaign. Share the success of the program with your agency partner and make them feel like they're a part of your team - because they are! Everyone wants to bask in the glory of things that go well, so don't do this without including them! Thanks doesn't always have to come in the form of payment! I even recall taking part in a champagne toast and celebration over video conference between us in San Francisco and an agency team we had worked with in New York.

...Cheers!

Chapter 19 | Developing The Right Mindset To Create Great Content

Matthew Pruitt: Head of Global Community & Social Media - Unity

This chapter will take you through real-life examples and best practices, as well as help you create the best possible content. Throughout, you will learn the importance of process and how critical it is to clearly convey it to everyone you work with. Building great content requires buy-in from an entire team, big or small, and you'll walk away from this chapter outfitted with some helpful tips and data to make that happen.

Introduction

To bring attention to your project, you need highly engaging content. People only remember 20% of what they've read online if there is no accompanying visual (sdata.me/UsSKAT). With all of the content that is on the internet at any given moment, yours needs to stand out.

You might think this means that there's a lot of hard work in your future, but that's not true. Engaging content doesn't need to be insanely complicated, luxurious, or expensive to create. Remember what you were told as a kid: keep it simple, stupid.

287

Stop for a second and think about the content you see when scrolling through Facebook. Those videos with a ton of shares and likes are likely cats doing funny things. I'm not telling you to put cats in your content (or am I?), but you get the point. Highly engaging content is something that quickly and effectively catches your viewers' eyes and draws them in.

I am the Head of Global Community & Social Media at Unity Technologies. My team and I oversee all social media marketing and community campaigns across the company. Before joining Unity Technologies, I spent time in multiple marketing and product roles at IGN Entertainment, Machinima, Electronic Arts, and Quicken Loans. In my previous roles I worked across multiple business disciplines including product management, product marketing, and online marketing. Having operated in both the product and marketing ecosystems, I've been able to draw valuable insights that have helped me bridge gaps in organizational communication.

When I started at Unity two years ago, content was like gold: it was sparse, but when you found it, it was priceless. To try and create awesome social media posts that are engaging and interesting to our audience without compelling content is tough, to say the least. My team and I had two choices: accept it for what it was and keep trudging on, or do something to change it. We chose the latter. And if you're in a similar scenario, you should too.

The path to great content is earned

Unity is not a small company, it employs over 1,500 people. Those 1,500 plus people are working on making amazing demos, editorial improvements, tutorials, educational articles, and so much more. And by the way, they are also pumping out a lot of content as part of their day jobs. Content is good. Engaging content is great. There's a very big difference there that is extremely important to understand. If you're developing as part of a team or on your own, you owe it to yourself and/or your team to create GREAT content. Why would you want anything less? Only the best should be representing your project or product.

So my team and I took a "road trip" of sorts. We started to meet with every team within Unity that touches content and go through best-in-class examples of great, engaging content. But we didn't just show them great content and say "do this," we built a meaningful relationship and educated them on the WHY. Explaining the process is more critical than the outcome. In general, I think it's safe to say that employees, and people in general, don't want to be told what to do. Rather, they want to be empowered with valuable information to make informed decisions.

For example, we met with our Evangelism team, who create amazing Unity video tutorials for the developer community. They were uploading tutorial videos weekly on our YouTube channel and, while they performed well, my team knew they could perform better with one major tweak - duration - to make the transformation from good content to great content.

Data shows that users consume content, especially video content, in short chunks. A 60-minute video tutorial would not be classified as a "short chunk." We suggested to the Evangelism team that they break down their 60 minute tutorial videos into shorter, bite-sized chunks of about three to five minutes. The team pushed back against this change in methodology as it would take them a little more time to cut up the segments and just weren't sold that it would be worth their time.

You will experience push-backs when trying to create change, but remember that this is a good thing! This opens the door for you to educate through data and build a stronger relationship. This is a natural occurrence at any company, big or small, so keep cool and carry on.

Our response to the Evangelism team was that we totally understood their hesitation, but let's test it. They agreed that the next few tutorial videos they published would be broken into smaller chunks and we would measure performance against the long-form videos. This is exactly the outcome that we wanted. They were joining us on the journey and we would discover the answer together.

The results spoke for themselves. During the test, we saw a 49% increase in total views and a 239% increase in average percent viewed - meaning that people were watching more. Smaller, bite-sized segments allow users to find what they're looking for much more quickly and allow them to easily pick back up where they left off.

Sure, it would have saved time and been easier if they would have just listened to us in the first place, but that likely would have led to more conversations down the road and required even more time because people tend to fall back into what is familiar if they don't experience the learning process first-hand. That's exactly why I said that the process is more critical than the outcome. They are now empowered with the knowledge to create engaging content. And they know why they're doing it!

Now that I've walked you through one example of how to turn good content in to great content, I want to dive deeper into the content itself, best practices, and where and how to deploy it.

Mindset makes great content

We've already discussed that it's important to build relationships and educate on your thought process to deliver great content. But the mindset needed to create great content isn't just communication and education, it is also needed if you are working individually. You don't need to work in a large organization or have multiple teams to support you. I've seen great, successful content produced by solo indie developers and that's because they put themselves in the right mindset.

Let's explore what I mean by developing the right mindset. Before you start creating content, you should be asking yourself two very important questions: "What is the one takeaway I want someone to have after viewing my content?" And: "Why should they care?"

Think back to the beginning of this chapter when I said "keep it simple, stupid." Ask yourself those two very questions and you're already miles ahead of your competitors.

Everything you do should be viewed through the lens of your end users. Sometimes we get too close to our project and we forget why our end user should or would care. By asking yourself those two questions, it forces you to take a step back and look at your project objectively and then allows for your content to reflect that. That doesn't mean that we don't want users to connect to the material - we absolutely do. But you want them to be able to form their own opinion through a clearly communicated message.

A great example of this is posting on social media for the sake of posting on social media. Sometimes my team gets requests to post that someone from Unity will be speaking at an event. Don't get me wrong, that's important and exciting, but why would our end user care? Unless they're attending the event, there is no relevance to the greater audience. This doesn't mean we don't post about it at all, it just means that we need to work harder to make it more engaging by asking questions such as "Is it being live streamed?", "What are the topics they're talking about?", "Are there any new announcements?" These questions are allowing us the opportunity to potentially build an exciting piece of engaging content.

If you take one thing away from this, remember the fact that we don't know what we don't know. You don't want a potential user to make assumptions about your project. They don't know what you know - they didn't work on the project. Like any good story, you want to take them on a journey that paints the full picture of what your project is and for them to walk away wanting a sequel. In this case, the sequel is playing your game, watching your movie, using your product, or whatever it may be.

Video is THE MOST engaging piece of content that you can create for your project. It's no coincidence that Facebook's algorithms place a higher value on video than static graphics or text. They know that videos generate more views, more engagement, and lead to higher conversion, whether it's a purchase or simply a click to a website to learn more. And did you know that YouTube is the second largest search engine behind Google? Video is key. That said, video is also the most complicated asset (in terms of time and effort) to create. While I can't stress enough how important video is, don't think that it's the be all end all of ways to market your project. If you're in a larger organization, high-quality video is probably more possible to obtain than if you're a one-person team. And that's OK, because now that you're in the right mindset to develop great content, your possibilities are limitless.

Sometimes all you have to work with are static images. Static images are the least ideal asset to have because they don't stand out. That doesn't mean that static images can't be valuable, but they're more of a complimentary piece. Once you get your user into the consumer journey funnel, static assets are a good way to give them more information and keep them wanting more. But as I've said before, there's good content and great content.

However, here's one solution. Let's say you're in a room of 15 statues. You're staring at all of them and all of the sudden one of them moves. Your eyes will immediately focus on that and everything else gets blurred out. It's human nature. Static assets work the exact same way. There's a great app called "Lumyer" that I absolutely love. It gives you the ability to add elements of motion to still images. All of the elements are pre-created so the time and effort spent by you is minimal. There are all kinds of different apps and programs that do this, but this is a simple example of how to transform your static image from good to great and ensure that it stands out above the rest.

I was recently at a social media conference where an agency used Lumyer to turn a client's static image into a motion graphic. The company created candles and were posting still images of their candles on their Facebook page. The agency came in, added a flicker motion to the flame of the candles and their purchase conversion increased by 250%. Five minutes of effort for a massive increase.

Make your content work harder for you. I've been a part of many conversations over the years where I hear "Oh, we don't have any content." 95% of the time, that has not been the case. Sometimes it takes getting creative with what you do have. Get scrappy and start digging through all of the raw assets available to you. I promise that there will be something that you can transform into engaging content.

As long as you're developing the right mindset along the way, content will come more easily. Much like the education process that was discussed earlier, focus more on the journey than the end result. If you're setting yourself up correctly from the beginning, the end result will usually take care of itself.

In terms of asset importance, remember that video reigns supreme, followed by motion graphics and still graphics in that order. They all have their place in the marketing food chain to communicate different messages. So now that we've established what great content looks like, the next section will dive into where, why, and how to deploy those assets so that you're maximizing their value.

Deploying content in social media: best practices

The Internet is a big place full of many people and many places. Now that you've created some awesome assets, you need to get the attention of the right people in the right places. Like any good salesperson, you need to go to them where they live, not the other way around. Luckily there is something called social media that makes this task a whole lot easier.

For the sake of this section, we're going to focus on three main social media channels: Facebook, Twitter, and YouTube. If you have to pick three to market your project, it should be them. Facebook is an awesome tool for shareability, Twitter allows you to be a part of multiple conversations through hashtags and tagging, and YouTube is the second largest search engine behind Google.

This is not a deep dive into every social media tool, this is meant to lightly touch on the best practices for each and to point you in the right direction. There are a ton of social media books in the marketplace and I highly suggest reading some of them. Just like the assets you created, you want to ensure that these tools are working the hardest for you.

Facebook

As we find at Unity, and as you'll probably find for your project, Facebook is not generally where your core audience lives, and that's OK! Facebook tends to be comprised of a more vast, general audience that loves great content, but it may not translate to an end user. This doesn't mean that it's any less valuable, in fact, it makes it more valuable to the realm of brand awareness, which is Facebook's strength. Play to the strengths of each social media tool and you'll have all of your bases covered.

Be sure to create your Facebook page as a business page. While Facebook posts don't populate in search engines, it's one of the best ways for your content to get shared. Populate your page with all of the relevant information and assets before pushing it live. Once live, this is when you need to start being a marketer.

If you're a one-person or small team, be sure to have all of your friends like your page and share your content. Sharing on Facebook is the fastest way to bring attention to your content and grow your page. Your friends are an easy access point into jump starting that process, so ask them to help out. If you're part of a larger organization, use your company's employees! This is so important and something that I can't stress enough. If you receive any push back from employees who are wary of using their own personal social media, be sure to highlight examples of positive reactions from the community to previous social media posts and explain the importance of shareability and spreading the word. It might take some time, but they'll see the light.

Employees are the best evangelists for your project or product. At Unity, I send out weekly "Social Shareable" emails to the entire company, including our C-Suite. In that email, I highlight the best performing social content that we've posted and use easy one-click share buttons that allows them to share it on their personal Facebook pages. Not only does this give great visibility to the entire company on how social media is performing, but it also includes them as part of the process.

This is the next stage of developing the right mindset. You've used the process to create great content, now you need to evolve it to evangelize your team or organization to act on your behalf. Inclusion is one of the best ways to do that. Be sure to explain to them why it's important they help support your social initiatives. Again, it's about the journey more than the end result.

As we discussed previously, Facebook's algorithms favor video assets. So if you have video, this is the place to use it. Be sure that you're uploading it natively versus linking to YouTube or somewhere else. Native video is prioritized the highest by Facebook, so ensure that you're taking advantage of every extra inch you can.

If you're part of a larger organization or have a little bit of money to spare, you can boost some of your posts. Facebook has a massive, in-depth segmentation library for you to choose from. You can ensure that your money works the hardest for you by choosing locations, audiences, and/or interests that most pertain to your content. This is also a great way to help build your Facebook audience. By delivering them relatable content, you're now able to reach an entirely new set of people that you likely wouldn't be able to reach with organic social media.

Twitter

As much as Facebook is about brand awareness and reach, Twitter is about connecting with your users on a more 1:1 basis. At Unity, we find that the majority of our most leaned-in, core users live on Twitter. This provides us an excellent opportunity to ensure that the content and messaging we put out on Twitter is most relevant to those users.

The ability for a user to directly tweet you and engage in a 1:1 conversation is invaluable. It allows you to build interest and engagement on a micro level, while at the same time covering the macro as well. Use Twitter as a tool to push out content, but also ensure that you're maximizing its capability to connect with users. As an example, while our Unity Twitter is not a customer support account, we do have direct messages come to us from users who may be experiencing issues with billing or their account. We're always happy to connect them with a customer support representative directly via email rather than letting their message sit there unreplied to.

At Unity, our best performing tweets (measured by engagement - shares, likes, retweets, replies) are those that are generally technical in nature, such as a new editor feature release. These posts always enjoy the most engagement, but it doesn't mean that we don't support them with engaging assets. GIFs are very popular on Twitter and get shared widely. Sometimes if we have a video that has a really cool, engaging sequence within it, we'll pull it out and create a GIF that we'll then share separately on Twitter. This is a quick and easy way to expand the life of an asset and create a format that is more likely to be shared wider.

There are many tools out there that allow you to do this, including YouTube's own integrated tool. It's yet another simple tip that allows you to take good content and make it great for the vehicle in which it's living. You may have heard the saying "The right message in the right place at that right time." This is an example of that. Recognize who your user is, where they're living, and how they like to consume content.

Another fantastic feature of Twitter is the use of hashtags. You may see some people that create a tweet and have about 30 hashtags after it - don't be that person. Hashtags are actually very important and allow you to enter wider conversations without having to already have an established audience. For example, at Unity, our most popular hashtags are #unity3d, #gamedev, and #indiedev.

These hashtags pool together all of the conversations that are using them across Twitter. So, obviously, you want to ensure that you're using relevant hashtags. Find hashtags that are relevant to your project and include them in your tweet. Be sure to limit them to two or three per tweet, otherwise it just looks like spam. And there's no faster way to kill your content than people thinking it's spam. Stay brief and to the point in all of your social media postings - less is always more. Remember that, in most instances, your social media post's goal is to drive someone to do something (click, watch, learn more, etc.).

So now that you're ready to create your tweet, I'll leave you with a few final thoughts. As with anything, make sure you have a great, engaging asset. Make sure that you're using hashtags. And most importantly, make sure you're creating a "what's next." Meaning, be sure that you're directing them somewhere, whether it's to your website, blog, or another page. You want to keep your users in the consumer journey funnel so that they can learn more. Twitter is the top of the funnel, be sure that you're helping them stay and get to the bottom.

YouTube

The last social media property I'll touch on is YouTube. Did I already tell you it's the second largest search engine behind Google? That's a rhetorical question, but I say it again because it's just so important. Even if you only have one or two videos currently, create a YouTube page for your project and upload them!

If you're running a website or blog for your project and you want to place videos on those pages, be sure you're using the YouTube video embed. Embedding the video with YouTube versus other websites allows you to gain their SEO advantage and also keep your users within one ecosystem.

As previously mentioned in relation to the Unity training tutorial videos, video length is very important. Try to keep your videos to two to three minutes and make sure you're jumping into the "what" as soon as possible. Most people only watch three to five seconds of a video before they decide whether they're staying or leaving. You must grab their attention in this timespan if you want your content to be successful.

Video titles are almost as important as the video content itself. Make sure that you're putting a lot of thought into your title before publishing. Try to include your company name, project name, and a brief description of what the video is. If your video is a trailer, make sure you're actually saying "trailer" in the title. Trailers are hugely popular and a frequent search term on YouTube, so you want to ensure that you're part of that search criteria if someone searches it.

YouTube video descriptions are also very important. This is a text based field that allows you to write a quick description of what the video is and why they should care. It also allows you the opportunity to insert links to your other social media properties and websites. Use this space because if someone really loves your content, they're going to want to learn more. And if you don't make that readily available to them, they're not going to try and hunt it down.

The final aspect of YouTube I'll touch on is the use of an end screen. An end screen is a native feature of YouTube that allows you to include interactive elements at the end of your video such as a link to another video, link to your website, or a subscribe button. These are all meant to help keep the viewer in the funnel, so take advantage of them!

Next steps

We covered a lot in this chapter and I want to take the opportunity to pause and reflect. This chapter started with the idea of developing a mindset for both a team and yourself. If everyone is on the same page, it makes it a lot easier to execute great content. If you really take this seriously and make it an objective, you will find success.

If there's one thing you do right now after reading this chapter, go talk to your teams and build relationships. If you're a small team, start looking at the assets you already have and start thinking about how they can work harder for you. Great content, much like a great plan, is built over time. Don't rush it. Build it organically and ensure that everyone is following along the way.

Remember to have fun. Your content and your assets should reflect the joy that goes into your project. You want to make sure that's visible to your users. Stop and think about the message you want to convey and, with that in mind, look objectively at the assets available to you and how you can convert them from good to great.

I also highly suggest reading literature on overall marketing, content and social media. There are a ton of books out there, so I won't list them, but continue to educate yourself. As much as I talked about educating others on the process, you should be doing the same for yourself. Never stop learning.

Also, when you're surfing the Internet and a great piece of content catches your eye, stop and note the thing that made you care about it. Why did you stop scrolling to watch? Did you click for more info? Why? Ask yourself these questions and apply what your answer is to your own project strategy.

Creating engaging content isn't hard if you set yourself up for success from the very beginning. Good luck and start creating!

ABOUT THE AUTHORS

Authors are in alphabetical order by first name and their bios were current at the time their chapters were first published in September 2018 (First Edition) 2019 (Second Ed.) or September 2020 (Third Ed.).

Adam FitzGerald is responsible for Developer Marketing at Amazon Web Services. He oversees global technology evangelism, developer engagement programs, community building and startup marketing. His technical interests include fault-tolerant composable service architectures, infrastructure automation, and data science. Prior to joining Amazon, Adam ran Developer Relations for Pivotal, VMware, SpringSource, and BEA Systems. He is a recovering mathematician, aging gamer, occasional swimmer and proud geek parent.

Ana Schafer is director of Product Marketing for Qualcomm Technologies, Inc. where she oversees channel programs in support of the company's smartphone, compute, connectivity, and IoT businesses. Under her leadership the company introduced the Qualcomm® Advantage Network, a program designed to support business collaboration between Qualcomm and the companies selling, recommending and building solutions based on Qualcomm technologies. She is also responsible for the long-standing Qualcomm Developer Network, which has expanded over time to support not only mobile app developers targeting Qualcomm Snapdragon™ based smartphones, but also the burgeoning ecosystem of hardware and software engineers working in areas that range from XR, AI, robotics and IoT. Ana brings a breadth of experience to channel marketing at Qualcomm, having led developer-focused outreaches for over 10 years, and she was part of the pioneering effort with BREW that introduced one of the world's first app stores. She also led the marketing initiative for Qualcomm Technologies' reference design program for smartphones, working to provide ecosystem benefits across the device manufacturer, software provider and hardware component provider communities engaged with our reference designs.

Andreas Constantinou is Founder and CEO at SlashData. Andreas has been working at the crossroads of the mobile and software industries since 2000, helping take the very first smartphones to market. Since then he's worked with the top brand names in the software industry including Microsoft, Apple,

Google, Facebook and Amazon. Over the past twelve years, Andreas has grown SlashData into the leading analyst firm in the developer economy, with a client base and reputation that out-rivals companies many times the size. In his academic life, Andreas is an Adjunct Professor at Lund University, Sweden, where he teaches Digital Business Models. He also founded the Athens chapter of EO Accelerator, the largest founder accelerator program globally. Andreas holds a Ph.D. from the University of Bristol, UK. Andreas has been diagnosed with acute self-improvement syndrome. He has a passion for book reading, training for triathlon and has a goal of visiting 48 new countries in the next 9 years!

Arabella David is a Senior Director, Global Developer Marketing at Salesforce. She has formed and executed strategy for more than 15 years at companies including Google, Microsoft, and Nokia. When not helping developers become more successful, she gives back by mentoring those entering the workforce through programs like YearUp, and is active in her local community's emergency response programs, focusing on earthquake and fire preparation.

Brian McManus has been at Visa for 8 years, working as a developer on both the CyberSource and Authorize.Net platforms before moving into product management, working on API & Developer Experience. He led the product development of the Authorize.Net Accept suite and now oversees Developer, Digital Acceptance & Commerce Services across Authorize.Net & CyberSource. Brian is passionate about bringing startup values to large corporations, before joining Visa he helped found a fintech startup in Seattle and prior to that he worked for HBOS bank in the UK. Brian is a native of the Emerald Isle although he now calls the Emerald City home and enjoys all the outdoor life that the Pacific Northwest has to offer.

Christine Jorgensen, Director of Product Marketing for Qualcomm Technologies, Inc., is helping to grow Qualcomm's developer community in areas such as Internet of Things (IoT), embedded computing, AI, and XR. As part of the Qualcomm Developer Network team, she creates compelling showcases of Qualcomm's compute and connectivity technologies to inspire next generation IoT and embedded solutions, and drive purchase intent of Qualcomm technologies. She also creates motivational projects which developers can leverage to accelerate their efforts from prototype to production devices.

Christine has been with Qualcomm since 1997, in a variety of roles, including managing design and development of some of the first CDMA handsets, satellite phones, transportation and logistics products, and personal location tracking products and companion iOS and Android apps. Christine received a Bachelor of Science in Computer Science from the University of California, Santa Barbara, and an MBA from the University of San Diego.

Cliff Simpkins heads up Developer Audience Marketing for Microsoft Azure, helping bring the Microsoft cloud to life for developers around the world. He has been at Microsoft for the last 12 years, working in a variety of roles to help improve the lives of developers, including Developer Evangelism, Product Planning, Product Management, and Developer Marketing. His approach combines customer obsession with sound storytelling, working to land those stories with as little spin as possible. Prior to joining Microsoft, Cliff worked in governmental consulting and a couple of startups as a programmer.

Desiree Motamedi has almost two decades of experience building and executing successful go-to-market strategies. As Head of Developer Product Marketing at Facebook, she manages marketing to the developer ecosystem - through superior inbound, outbound, strategy and content. Her efforts are focused on getting developers excited about Facebook's global reach and innovation, with measurable results. She leads a growing team that drives the conversation around emerging technologies such as augmented reality, virtual reality, artificial intelligence, Building 8, and open source initiatives, on a global scale. Prior to joining Facebook, Desiree was Product Marketing Lead for Mobile Apps at Google. There she was responsible for rolling thunder marketing strategy for mobile app developers and built a vibrant developer ecosystem around the Mobile App Ads Platform, which includes AdMob, AdWords, and Google Analytics. She formed the cross-functional team comprised of various stakeholders touching mobile apps, and created a cohesive narrative for mobile apps across Google. A graduate of the University of California, Santa Cruz, Desiree started her career in Silicon Valley with Adobe, where she spent over 7 years as Group Product Marketing Manager. She oversaw several product launches including the Adobe Flash Media Server family of products and repackaging of Creative Suite. Desiree's strength lies in her ability to orchestrate the efforts of multiple groups and coordinate with counterparts across teams from product marketing to PR to finance. She brings her technical knowledge, communication skills, and boundless energy into all her endeavors.

Dirk Primbs is European Developer Ecosystem lead at Google and has been in the industry for over 15 years, contributing to the ecosystem in companies like Google and Microsoft but also developing a passion for teaching and community work. He is a web technologist, accomplished startup mentor, author and speaker with a passion for connected systems, the web and technology at large and led globally distributed international teams of senior professionals. As a student of computer science, business and psychology he focused his academic work on Developer Relations as a strategic function and the role of volunteers in the creation of community ecosystems which complements a decade of experience in the creation of highly scalable global programs.

Jacob Lehrbaum is Vice President of Developer and Admin Relations at Salesforce where he helps developers and admins discover new career-paths and skill up via tools, videos and content on developer.salesforce.com and admin.salesforce.com. Jacob has held leadership roles in engineering, marketing, product marketing and developer relations over a 20-year career in the software industry, and is passionate about helping customers and developers transform their business and succeed with technology. Throughout his career, he has taken numerous products from vision to launch and has built and marketed disruptive open-source and cloud-based developer products at companies such as Sun Microsystems, Oracle, and Engine Yard.

Joe Silvagi is a Director of Customer Success for the HCI group at VMware and is VCDX #175. He has been in IT for over 20 years, in roles ranging from administration, engineering, design, and management. Over the last 5 years at VMware he has worked in pre-sales along with various consulting roles. During his time with VMware he previously worked in the Hands-on Labs, helping to develop content and new ways of using technology, making building better content for the labs easier. He now works in Customer Success, leading a group of top architects to help ensure VMware's customers are successful with their products.

Katherine Miller currently leads the events program for the Google Cloud Developer Relations team. She has been at

Google for nearly 13 years, and has worn many hats during her tenure - including scalable communications and marketing for agency products and programs, content strategy for large-scale developer events, and more recently, creating and leading global developer programs. She is driven by the desire to inform, educate, empower and drive success by bringing the right content to the right users. Prior to Google, she managed the pre-doctoral admissions process at Tufts University School of Dental Medicine - focusing on improving program diversity, served as a legislative fellow for the American Dental Education Association, and worked as a success coach for InsideTrack. She holds an MA from Stanford's Graduate School of Education (Policy, Organization and Leadership Studies), and graduated summa cum laude with a BA in History from Hamilton College. Outside of work, Katherine runs for the all-women's Impala Racing Team, as well as after her husband Jason, 2 kids, and a cat.

Larry McDonough is the Director of Product Management for R&D Operations and Central Services at VMware. He oversees the VMware {code} Dev Portal and associated Developer Services, as well as the VMware Cloud Marketplace. Larry has spoken at conferences on his work in Developer Relations & Developer Evangelism, DevOps, Mobile App Development and Home Automation/IoT. Larry serves on the board of advisors for the University of California Riverside Bourns College of Engineering, and a few Silicon Valley startups including Weavr, an innovative technology company focusing on new ways to engage developers and grow developer ecosystems. Previously, Larry led Developer Evangelism at BlackBerry, Java ME Product Management and JavaFX Engineering at Sun Microsystems, and managed the OpenGL APIs at Silicon Graphics. Larry has written code for NASA JPL, in the Pentagon for the US Department of Defense Joint Chiefs of Staff, at Walt Disney Studios, and was pictured in National Geographic Magazine demonstrating early full-body motion capture technology. Larry has a BSCS from UCR's Bourns College of Engineering and an MBA from UCLA's Anderson Graduate School of Management.

Leandro Margulis is the VP of Developer Relations at UnifyID. He is an entrepreneurial leader with strong Business Development experience, effective sales and marketing skills used to launch new products and businesses. Leandro sits at the intersection between business and product, thinking creatively about product and partnerships to fulfill the customer's use case.

Leandro is the customer's advocate internally and the company's advocate externally. He is an emphatic and creative leader. He is a Yale MBA and a former Big 4 management consultant. Prior to joining Unify ID, Leandro led Developer Relations at TomTom. In this role, Leandro led a global, multidisciplinary team including Sales, Marketing, Product Marketing and Developer Portal engineers with the mandate to build the developer community around TomTom Maps APIs.

Lori Fraleigh is the Senior Director of Developer Relations at Samsung Electronics. She is an established industry thought leader in developer relations, software tools, development environments, and platforms. Lori is passionate about delivering an awesome developer experience and excels at breaking things. Prior to Samsung, Lori held similar roles at Intuit, Amazon/Lab126, HP/Palm and Motorola Mobility. Earlier, she led RTI's developer tools business to a successful acquisition by Wind River. Lori started her career working on mission control software at NASA/Loral and is a Virgin Galactic Future Astronaut. Lori holds a Bachelor's of Science in Computer and Electrical Engineering from Purdue University and a Master's of Science in Electrical Engineering from Stanford University.

Luke Kilpatrick started as a Website Developer in 1996, transitioning to managing technology communities in 2007. In 2010 Luke moved to marketing program management as his full time role on VMware's social media marketing team. 2012 saw Luke at Sencha working in developer relations programs as well as focused social media, speaking at events around the world. In 2014, as Senior Developer Programs Manager, Luke managed Atlassian's ecosystem developer events and programs, bringing hundreds of new apps to their marketplace. Recently he joined Nutanix as Senior Manager, Developer Marketing to bring an engaging experience to developers using their new PaaS products.

Matthew Pruitt is the Head of Global Community & Social Media at Unity Technologies, creator of the world's leading real-time 3D development platform. From indie developers to large enterprise development teams and gaming to architecture, the audience is diverse and the content distributed needs to speak to them all. He and his team oversee all social media marketing and community campaigns across the company. Prior to Unity Technologies, Matthew spent time in multiple marketing and product roles at IGN Entertainment, Machinima, Electronic Arts, and Quicken Loans.

Mehdi Medjaoui is the founder of the worldwide apidays conferences series he started in 2012 in Paris. Mehdi is highly involved in the API community and API Industry, as author, lecturer, consultant and investor in the API tooling space. His industry research involves publishing and maintaining the API Industry Landscape and the yearly State of Banking APIs. In 2019, Mehdi become H2020 European Commission expert to lead the APIS4Dgov study on public sector and government APIs. As entrepreneur, Mehdi co-founded in 2014 OAuth.io that was acquired in 2017. Mehdi's new venture GDPR.dev develops a Personal data API framework and protocol to democratize data regulations usage for mass users and compliance for applications developers, making GDPR programmable.

Mike Pegg leads Google Maps Platform Developer Relations. His team helps developers add Google Maps to their web and mobile apps through guides, samples and outreach programs. He has been involved with Google Maps from the beginning. He started the Maps Mania blog as a hobby in 2005 (weeks after Google Maps was launched) and was hired by Google a year later after guest speaking at the company's first ever developer event, the Geo Developer Day, 2006. He would go on to incubate developer marketing efforts for several developer products at Google including the Maps APIs, Android, Chrome, Firebase and Flutter, and led the Google I/O developer conference from 2011-18. He is a self-proclaimed "maphead" and enjoys playing, coaching and watching ice hockey with his family in California.

Neil Mansilla is the Head of Developer Experience (DevX) at Atlassian. His team provides support for, and advocates on behalf of all developers in the ecosystem - from vendors building apps sold in the Atlassian Marketplace, to customer developers building private apps and integrations for their own use. The DevX team also supports Atlassian's developer events, from helping to organize content and tracks to providing onsite developer support. Neil's career has been primarily focused on developer ecosystems and platforms. Prior to joining Atlassian, Neil served as Head of Apps Ecosystem & Marketplace at Poynt, Vice President of Developer Relations at Runscope, Director of Developer Platform and Partnerships at Intel Services

(Mashery), and founded a few tech companies across several verticals, including search, e-commerce, and healthcare.

Nicolas Sauvage is Senior Director of Ecosystem and Corporate Development at TDK-InvenSense, responsible for all strategic ecosystem relationships, including Google and Qualcomm, and other HW/SW/System companies. Nicolas was previously part of NXP's Software management team, responsible for worldwide sales, and later P&L and product management of the OEM Business Line. Nicolas is an alumnus of Institut supérieur d'électronique et du numérique, London Business School, INSEAD and Stanford. Nicolas believes life is full of special moments and is deeply passionate about products that enhance these special moments. He moved to the Bay Area in 2017 after 12 years living in Asia.

Pablo Fraile is Director of Developer Ecosystems, for the Client line of Business at Arm. In his role, he works with the mobile software developer community to increase the quality and performance levels of applications such as gaming, and drive the adoption of APIs and standards across new ones like machine learning and virtual reality. Before joining Arm, Pablo worked at Frontier Smart in Cambridge. There, he fulfilled a number of technical and commercial roles before heading the product management team, where he directed their solution strategy and built partnerships with global players in content distribution, web and semiconductor industries. Previous to Frontier, he was part of the video and graphics team at Imagination Technologies.

Siddhartha Agarwal is Group Vice President of Product Management and Strategy at Oracle, responsible for division strategy and revenue growth (organic and inorganic) for Oracle Cloud Platform (PaaS) and Oracle Fusion Middleware across all product lines globally, a more than $4.5B business. Siddhartha is also responsible for driving Oracle's global developer initiative to ensure developers are building next generation cloud applications using Oracle's Cloud Platform, and seeing it as a modern, open, easy, and intelligent platform. Known as a hands-on technical business leader developing and driving company strategy with "start-up" mentality, Siddhartha brings effective leadership qualities and market development skills to Oracle's lines of business. To this, add a deep technical background and experience in cloud-native application development, mobile/chatbots, and integration, blockchain, and security. He has a proven track record in general business management, product management and strategy, and enterprise/cloud software sales experience. Before rejoining Oracle in 2014 (he had previously worked at Oracle from 1994 through 1999), Siddhartha served as Vice President of Worldwide Field Operations for Zend Technologies Inc. He has an MS in Computer Science/Economics from Stanford University, a Bachelor of Engineering from Caltech, and a BA in Computer Science from Grinnell College.

Thomas Grassl is Global Head of Developer and Community Relations at SAP. With over 388 thousand customers, the SAP Community and Developer ecosystem is a leading program in the enterprise space. As an experienced marketer and a developer at heart, he works closely with developers, community members, companies and startups around the world helping them learn and apply new technology innovations to solve complex business problems.

ACKNOWLEDGMENTS

The momentum for the three editions of these books has been astonishing, and we'd like to thank everyone who has given us insight and inspiration throughout our journey.

We particularly like to thank our third edition editors, Caroline Lewko and Dana Fujikawa, whose light touch upon each chapter has brought consistency throughout and made the book more just than the sum of its *not* inconsiderable parts.

We are very excited to be able to share a foreword from Adam FitzGerald, the head of worldwide developer marketing at Amazon Web Services.

This book would not have been possible without the generosity of all who contributed their experience and insight to it. We would like to extend our appreciation to the authors and their teams for sharing their wisdom:

Ana Schafer Muroff: Senior Marketing Manager, Ecosystems Relations, Qualcomm

Arabella David: Senior Director, Global Developer Marketing - Salesforce

Brian McManus: Senior Director Product Management - Visa

Christine Jorgensen: Director, Product Management - Qualcomm

Cliff Simpkins: Director, Azure Dev Marketing - Microsoft

Desiree Motamedi: Head of Developer Product Marketing - Facebook

Dirk Primbs: Developer Relations Lead - Google

Jacob Lehrbaum: Vice President of Developer and Admin Relations - Salesforce

Joe Silvagi: Director of Customer Success for the HCI group - VMware

Katherine Miller: Developer Relations Program Manager - Google Cloud

Larry McDonough: Director of Product Management for R&D Operations and Central Services - VMware

Leandro Margulis: Vice President & General Manager, Developer Relations - TomTom

Lori Fraleigh: Senior Director, Developer Relations - Samsung Electronics

Luke Kilpatrick: Senior Manager, Developer Marketing - Nutanix

Matthew Pruitt: Head of Global Community & Social Media - Unity Technologies

Mehdi Medjaoui: Founder - apidays Global, Oauth and GDPR.dev

Mike Pegg: Head of Developer Marketing 2010-2018, Developer Relations Lead Google Maps Platform 2018-Present

Neil Mansilla: Head of Developer Experience (DevX) - Atlassian

Pablo Fraile: Director of Developer Ecosystems, for the Client line of Business - Arm

Siddhartha Agarwal: Group Vice President of Product Management and Strategy - Oracle

Thomas Grassl: Global Head of Developer and Community Relations – SAP

We are also incredibly grateful to the whole team at SlashData, and in particular, Moschoula Kramvousanou, Sofia Aliferi, and Stathis Georgakopoulos, to name just a few of those involved in layout, marketing and web presence. Steve Vranas designed the book cover with an obsession with typography no less deserving than today's state of the art in developer-focused design. Christina Voskoglou and Richard Muir from the analyst team supported the book and provided the latest data on developer influence metrics. And finally the proofreader, Joanne Rushton, whose dedication and attention to detail brought consistency to this text.

Finally, we'd like to acknowledge the thousands of developers that take part in our Developer Economics surveys every six months. They help us take the pulse of the software trends, from mobile to machine learning and from edge computing to cloud, which are continually evolving and shaping the future of computing innovation. Working in this industry is a constant learning experience and we wouldn't have it any other way.

Andreas Constantinou adds:

I tend to dislike acknowledgements written by multiple authors, as they fail to show the real people and minds behind the book. And so I would hate to see this acknowledgement missing its most important entry: Nicolas Sauvage. He was the single person without whom this book would have never been possible. Nicolas hatched the idea, devised the master plan for the book and saw it through to completion; he met every single author in person to share the passion, vision and establish commitment from over 20 thought leaders who are contributing to this book. This is an amazing accomplishment given the hectic schedules of everyone involved. Nicolas engineered his way out of challenges - whether it was authors dropping out or changing - through caring support, perseverance, ingenuity and perhaps a touch of stubbornness too! When I initiated this project on behalf of SlashData I hadn't the slightest notion of how complex a project it would turn out to be, including getting authors from commitment to delivery, getting legal sign-off from the top platform companies that employ the authors, to guiding and steering each author to help readers get the most out of each chapter. Thank you Nicolas: in you I found a new friend and collaborator who is a source of inspiration.

Nicolas Sauvage adds:

While I have said many times that the best part of writing this book is to raise the bar of a nascent industry in such an important discipline, the best part really has been to work with my dear friend Andreas on a project we both care so much about. We have co-written blogs in the past, but this was nothing compared to working on this book project, since Andreas imposed on us the tall order of creating *THE* Essential Guide to Developer Marketing and Developer Relations. Strategy is in many ways a language few speak well, but not only is Andreas fluent in strategy, but he masters its grammar and structure in a way that uncover logics and value creation models visible to very few. This Essential Guide brings countless insights because Andreas is intentional and laser-focused about making sure everything he and his team touches brings value and insights to the next level.

Andreas Constantinou: CEO – SlashData

Nicolas Sauvage: Sr. Director Ecosystem - TDK-InvenSense

Caroline Lewko and Dana Fujikawa, Editors of the third edition, WIP

September 2020

Printed in Great Britain
by Amazon